Lecture Notes in Computer Science   8718

Commenced Publication in 1973
Founding and Former Series Editors:
Gerhard Goos, Juris Hartmanis, and Jan van Leeuwen

Frédéric Lang   Francesco Flammini (Eds.)

Formal Methods for Industrial Critical Systems

19th International Conference, FMICS 2014
Florence, Italy, September 11-12, 2014
Proceedings

 Springer

Volume Editors

Frédéric Lang
Inria, 38330 Montbonnot, France
E-mail: frederic.lang@inria.fr

Francesco Flammini
Ansaldo STS, 80147 Naples, Italy
E-mail: francesco.flammini@ansaldo-sts.com

ISSN 0302-9743   e-ISSN 1611-3349
ISBN 978-3-319-10701-1   e-ISBN 978-3-319-10702-8
DOI 10.1007/978-3-319-10702-8
Springer Cham Heidelberg New York Dordrecht London

Library of Congress Control Number: 2014946586

LNCS Sublibrary: SL 2 – Programming and Software Engineering

Typesetting: Camera-ready by author, data conversion by Scientific Publishing Services, Chennai, India

Printed on acid-free paper

Springer is part of Springer Science+Business Media (www.springer.com)

Preface

This volume contains the papers presented at FMICS 2014, the 19th International Workshop on Formal Methods for Industrial Critical Systems, which took place on September 11–12, 2014, in Florence, Italy.

The FMICS 2014 workshop took place during the one-week scientific event FLORENCE 2014, which also hosted the 12th International Conference on Formal Modeling and Analysis of Timed Systems (FORMATS 2014), the 11th International Conference on Quantitative Evaluation of SysTems (QEST 2014), the 33rd International Conference on Computer Safety, Reliability and Security (SAFECOMP 2014), and the 10th European Workshop on Performance Engineering (EPEW 2014).

The aim of the FMICS workshop series is to provide a forum for researchers who are interested in the development and application of formal methods in industry. In particular, FMICS brings together scientists and engineers who are active in the area of formal methods and interested in exchanging their experiences in the industrial usage of these methods. The FMICS workshop series also strives to promote research and development for the improvement of formal methods and tools for industrial applications.

The topics of interest include, but are not limited to:

- Design, specification, code generation, and testing based on formal methods
- Methods, techniques, and tools to support automated analysis, certification, debugging, learning, optimization, and transformation of complex, distributed, dependable, real-time systems, and embedded systems
- Verification and validation methods that address shortcomings of existing methods with respect to their industrial applicability, e.g., scalability and usability issues
- Tools for the development of formal design descriptions
- Case studies and experience reports on industrial applications of formal methods, focusing on lessons learned or identification of new research directions
- Impact of the adoption of formal methods on the development process and associated costs
- Application of formal methods in standardization and industrial forums

This year we received 26 submissions. Papers had to pass a rigorous review process in which each paper received three reports. The international Program Committee of FMICS 2014 decided to select 13 papers for presentation during the workshop and inclusion in these proceedings. The contributions focused on the following main topics:

- Cyber-physical systems

- Computer networks
- Railway control systems
- Verification methods
- Hardware and software testing

The workshop program was therefore organized in sessions according to these topics.

The workshop also featured invited talks by Pietro Marmo (Ansaldo STS, Italy), and by David Parker (University of Birmingham, UK).

Following a tradition established over the past few years, the European Association for Software Science and Technology (EASST) offered an award to the best FMICS paper. This year, the reviewers selected two contributions ex aequo:

- "Assertion-Based Monitoring in Practice — Checking Correctness of an Automotive DSI3 Sensor Interface," by Thang Nguyen and Dejan Nickovic
- "Improving Static Analyses of C Programs with Conditional Predicates," by Sandrine Blazy, David Bühler and Boris Yakobowski

We would like to thank the FLORENCE 2014 general chair Enrico Vicario (University of Florence) for taking care of all the local arrangements in Florence and the FMICS 2014 local organization chair Alessandro Fantechi (University of Florence) for liaising between FMICS and FLORENCE 2014 organizations. We also thank the FMICS 2014 publicity chair Wendelin Serwe (Inria and LIG, France) and the webmasters Marco Paolieri and Simone Mattolini (University of Florence) for contributing to the international visibility of the workshop. Finally, we thank the ERCIM FMICS working group coordinator Radu Mateescu (Inria Grenoble and LIG) for his help, EasyChair for supporting the review process, Springer for the publication, all Program Committee members and external reviewers for their substantial reviews and discussions, all authors for their submissions, and all attendees of the workshop. Thanks to all for your contribution to the success of FMICS 2014.

September 2014   Frédéric Lang
                                              Francesco Flammini

Organization

Program Committee

Maria Alpuente	Universitat Politècnica de Valencia, Spain
Alvaro Arenas	IE University, Spain
Jiri Barnat	Masaryk University, Czech Republic
Cinzia Bernardeschi	University of Pisa, Italy
Simona Bernardi	Centro Universitario de la Defensa, AGM, Zaragoza, Spain
Jean-Paul Blanquart	Astrium Satellites, France
Eckard Böde	Offis, Germany
Rocco De Nicola	IMT Lucca, Italy
Michael Dierkes	Rockwell Collins, France
Susanna Donatelli	University of Turin, Italy
Cindy Eisner	IBM Research - Haifa, Israel
Alessandro Fantechi	Università di Firenze, Italy
Jérôme Feret	CNRS and ENS and Inria, France
Francesco Flammini	Ansaldo, Italy
Wan Fokkink	Vrije Universiteit Amsterdam and CWI, The Netherlands
Andrew Gacek	Rockwell Collins, USA
Stefania Gnesi	ISTI-CNR, Italy
Matthias Güdemann	Systerel, France
Keijo Heljanko	Aalto University, Finland
Jan Jurjens	TU Dortmund and Fraunhofer ISST
Frederic Lang	Inria and LIG, France
Tiziana Margaria	University of Potsdam, Germany
Pedro Merino	University of Málaga, Spain
Benjamin Monate	TrustInSoft, France
Gethin Norman	University of Glasgow, UK
David Parker	University of Birmingham, UK
Charles Pecheur	Université catholique de Louvain, Belgium
Ralf Pinger	Siemens AG, Germany
Wendelin Serwe	Inria and LIG, France
Hans Svensson	Quviq, Sweden
Jaco van de Pol	University of Twente, The Netherlands
Valeria Vittorini	University of Naples Federico II, Italy
Angela Vozella	CIRA, Italy

Additional Reviewers

Ballis, Demis
Bauch, Petr
Ferrari, Alessio
Houtmann, Clément
Isberner, Malte

James, Phillip
Kuismin, Tuomas
Margheri, Andrea
Romero, Daniel
Tinacci, Marco

Abstracts of Invited Talks

20 Years Past and (Hopefully) 20 Years to Come: My Experience in Ansaldo STS with Formal Methods and Railways

Pietro Marmo[*]

Ansaldo STS, Italy

Mailsa

Abstract. On next November, 20 years will have passed since the first time I used a "formal method" for a real job in my company. Actually it was a Petri Net model used to evaluate the safety of a two out of three system. Since then, I have experimented a whole set of formal methods (formal languages, model-checking, Theorem Proving, stochastic nets, etc.), either for ad hoc studies with universities and research centers, or for European research projects. Many of them aimed at providing a fully automatic environment with the power of mathematics and the ease of use of a toy but few have found real applications with valuable results. All those years have brought many improvements and more and more utilizations of formal methods are now possible in industry. In this talk we present the challenges that are required to formal methods in railways, where they have won and where they have lost in the past, together with a glance at what will be required and with what possible results in the next twenty years (or so).

Keywords: Formal Method, Petri Net, Railway, AnsaldoSTS.

---

[*] Contact Author

Quantitative Verification:
Formal Guarantees for Timeliness,
Reliability and Performance

David Parker

School of Computer Science,
University of Birmingham, UK

Abstract. Quantitative verification is a technique for analysing quantitative aspects of a system's design, such as timing, probabilistic behaviour or resource usage. It provides a means of automatically deriving formal guarantees on a wide range of system properties, such as timeliness, reliability or performance, for example, "the airbag will always deploy within 20 milliseconds after a crash" or "the probability of both sensors failing simultaneously is less than 0.001". Recent years have seen significant advances in the underlying theory, verification techniques and tool support in this area, and these methods have been applied to an impressive array of systems, from wireless networking protocols to robotic systems to cardiac pacemakers.

This talk will give an overview of the state-of-the-art in quantitative verification, focusing in particular on probabilistic model checking, a quantitative verification technique for the analysis of systems with stochastic behaviour. The talk will explain the key ideas behind the approach, highlight some of the application areas where it has been successful, with particular emphasis on case studies with industrial involvement, describe a few of the current research directions in the area and discuss some of the challenges which remain.

Table of Contents

Formal Verification of Steady-State Errors in Unity-Feedback Control Systems

Muhammad Ahmad and Osman Hasan

School of Electrical Engineering and Computer Science (SEECS),
National University of Sciences and Technology (NUST),
Islamabad, Pakistan
{muhammad.ahmad,osman.hasan}@seecs.nust.edu.pk

Abstract. The meticulousness of steady-state error analysis of unity-feedback control systems has always been of vital significance as even a trifling glitch in this analysis may result in grievous penalties. To ensure a rigorous steady-state error analysis, this paper presents the formal verification of a generic relationship that is applicable to all kinds of inputs and types of unity-feedback control systems. This formalization builds upon the multivariate calculus theories of HOL-Light and our prior work on developing formal models of feedback control systems. To illustrate the usefulness of this result, the paper presents the formal steady-state error analysis of a Pulse Width Modulation (PWM) push-pull DC-DC converter, which is an extensively used component in various power-electronics and aerospace applications.

1 Introduction

Control systems [18] form an integral part of all automated systems used in a wide range of safety-critical applications, including industrial automation, surgical robots, automobiles and aerospace systems. These control systems work along with the given systems (plants) and are designed in such a way that they ensure the desired behavior of their corresponding systems while adhering to the stability constraints and allowable error margins.

Control systems can be configured in an open or a closed loop topology [18]. In open-loop systems, the controller generates the control signals based on a reference or input signal $R(s)$, as shown in Fig. 1.a . A disadvantage of this kind of configuration is that the controller has no information about the output of the plant (with open-loop transfer function $G(s)$) and thus cannot cater for unexpected disturbances. To overcome this limitation, control systems are often configured in a feedback or closed loop pattern where the output of the plant $C(s)$ is measured and compared with a reference or an input signal $R(s)$, as shown in Fig. 1.b. This error signal $E(s)$ is then used for decision making in the controller to compensate for disturbances. A unity-feedback is a frequently used closed-loop system where the output of the system is compared with the reference input signal as is, i.e., without any gain or loss in the feedback path.

F. Lang and F. Flammini (Eds.): FMICS 2014, LNCS 8718, pp. 1–15, 2014.

The quality of the control system is judged based on its steady-state response [19], i.e., the response of the system when a large number of iterations in the closed-loop have taken place and the steady-state conditions have been attained. Steady-state error gives a parametric measure for the controllability of system and how well the system will respond to certain disturbances.

The steady-state analysis of unity-feedback control systems is performed in the Laplace domain because this choice allows us to model the main system in terms of the transfer functions of its sub-systems, as a block diagram. The overall transfer function of the plant $G(s)$ is then expressed as follows by manipulating the transfer functions of its subsystems using a set of predefined rules[18]:

$$G(s) = \frac{1}{s^b} \frac{Y(s)}{Z(s)} \tag{1}$$

where the integer variable $b : 0, 1, 2 \cdots$ categorizes the system type or the number of integrators in the forward path[18], and $Y(s)$ and $Z(s)$ represent the zeros and poles of $G(s)$ apart from $\frac{1}{s^b}$. Now, the net transfer function for unity-feedback error model is mathematically expressed as[18]:

$$E(s) = \frac{R(s)}{1 + G(s)} \tag{2}$$

where $R(s)$ models the input to our system, which in the case of steady-state error analysis is traditionally taken to be as the *unit step* $(\frac{1}{s})$, *ramp* $(\frac{1}{s^2})$ and *parabola* $(\frac{1}{s^3})$ functions. The steady-state error is measured at a very large time, i.e., when the time t tends to infinity. Thus, it can be defined in the Laplace domain by applying the Final Value Theorem to the error model:

$$e_\infty = \lim_{s \to 0} sE(s) \tag{3}$$

Traditional methods, like paper-and-pencil proof methods and computer simulations and numerical methods, cannot guarantee the accuracy of the above-mentioned steady-state error analysis. The paper-and-pencil based analysis methods are error prone due to the human involvement. Moreover, it is quite often the case that many key assumptions of the results obtained of sub-system using

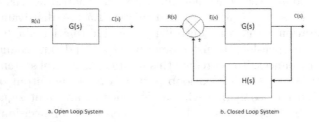

Fig. 1. Control System Configurations

paper-and-pencil proof methods are not documented, which may lead to to erroneous systems. Computer simulations and numerical methods, such as MathWorks Simulink [17], cannot guarantee accurate results while dealing with feedback-control systems mainly due to their inherent non-exhaustive nature coupled with the imprecision of computer arithmetics. The mathematical models of control systems can also be analyzed in computer algebra systems (CAS), such as Mathematica [15]. CAS are very efficient for computing mathematical solutions symbolically, but are also not completely reliable due to the presence of unverified huge symbolic manipulation algorithms.

In order to overcome the above-mentioned limitations, the usage of formal methods in the safety-critical domain of control system analysis is increasingly being investigated [20,3]. However due to the continuous nature of the steady-state error analysis, automated theorem provers and model checking tools cannot ascertain absolute precision of analysis. Higher-order logic theorems provers have shown some promising results and a detailed review of the literature will be presented in the next section. One of the most interesting contributions, related to the formal steady-state analysis of control systems, is the higher-order-logic formalization of the basic building blocks[12], like forward transfer functions, summing junctions, feedback loops and pickoff points, of control systems using the multivariate analysis theories available in the HOL-Light theorem prover. These foundations can be built upon to formally specify a wide range of control systems in higher-order logic and reason about their steady-state errors within the sound core of a theorem prover. The process involves the verification of the error function for the given system based on its structure and the behavior its sub-blocks. This is followed by the verification of the limit of the error function of the given system, according to Equation (3), using the multivariate analysis libraries of HOL-Light. The approach was illustrated by verifying the steady-state error of a solar tracking control system. However, the reasoning process about the steady-state error model with closed loop transfer function T(s), shown in Fig. 2, is very cumbersome, the reason being the extensive user interaction requirement in verifying the limiting behavior, expressed in Equation (3), for the net expression for the error model of the given system. Moreover, this reasoning process has to be repeated all over again if the steady-state for a different type of input (unit step, ramp or parabola) is required for the same system, which is a very common occurrence in steady-state error analysis.

The main scope of this paper is to overcome the above mentioned issues. We build upon the formalization of the control system blocks of [12] to formalize the error model for the unity-feedback control systems. Moreover, we formally

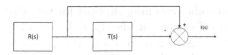

Fig. 2. Steady-State Error Model

verify a generic expression for the steady-state error of unity-feedback control systems using the multivariate analysis theories of HOL-Light. The unique feature of this expression is that it can be used to reason about the steady-state error of any system type and input. Moreover, it facilitates reusability when reasoning about the state-state error of the same system while considering different inputs. The quest for minimizing the user interaction in the higher-order-logic theorem-proving based analysis for steady-state errors led us to develop this useful relationship, which to the best of our knowledge has not been reported in the control systems literature before. In order to illustrate the utilization and practical effectiveness of our formalization for verifying real-world control systems, we use it to conduct the steady-state error analysis of the Pulse Width Modulation (PWM) push-pull DC-DC converters[8], which is a widely used component in power electronics and many safety-critical aerospace applications. In order to evaluate the usefulness of our work for control system engineers, we engaged a domain expert; trained her with basic theorem proving abilities in a couple of weeks and assigned her the task to use our formalization for analyzing the PWM push-pull DC-DC converter and her experiences are also shared in this paper.

2   Related Work

ClawZ [4] allows us to translate models of control systems developed in MathWorks Simulink into Z language specifications, which are then verified by proving the equivalence of the controller implementation using Ada in ProofProver. Another similar approach is presented in [1] in which the author translates the discrete-time Simulink model to Circus notations, which combines Z language and refinement calculus and then compares a parallel Ada implementation. An interesting methodology adopted in [7] calls for using the Timed Interval Calculus (TIC) library to capture the behavior of Simulink blocks, which could be verified in a theorem prover. A similar approach was adapted by Mahony, and modeling and analysis of feedback control systems was introduced using the DOVE environment [16]. Model checking has also been successfully used to analyze dynamic systems by abstracting the behavior of the system to a state-space model [22]. Herencia-Zapana [13] proposed to formally analyze control software properties by first expressing the stability proofs as C code annotations and then translating them to PVS proof obligations and automatically verifying them. All these pioneering frameworks are based on automatic formal verification tools and thus require some sort of abstraction mechanism to model the exact behavior of real-world control systems and their environments, which are always continuous in nature.

In order to formally model and analyze continuous models of control systems, Boulton et al. provided some reasoning support for verifying frequency response of continuous-time control systems using Hoare logic using the HOL98 theorem prover [6]. The main idea is to reason about the gain and phase relationships of a control system using the gain and phase relationships of its subsystems in the block diagram. This framework does not provide generic functions to model arbitrary block diagrams for control systems and also lacks reasoning support for complex number analysis principles, such as limits and summation, which are essential to reason about many control system design related parameters, such as steady-state errors and stability. In order to overcome these shortcomings, Boulton et al [5] proposed to use automated symbolic methods to replace the classical graphical charts, such as Nichole and Bode plots along with their formal models. Based on this principle, the authors developed a prototype tool using Maple and the PVS system. Maple is used to compute the verification conditions for the given control system and PVS is used to discharge these conditions using theorem proving principles. Due to the usage of Maple, the accuracy of the analysis is again somewhat compromised as has been mentioned above.

The foremost foundation of analyzing the steady-state error of control systems is the formalization of complex number analysis theories. The multivariate calculus theories of HOL-Light theorem prover [11] fulfill this requirement. These theories have been recently used to formalize the basic building blocks of control systems [12] and the Laplace theory [21], which are the most relevant contributions to our work. We build upon and enhance the results reported in [12] to analyze steady-state errors of unity-feedback control systems and facilitate the formal reasoning process by verifying a generic expression for steady-state error in this paper. The recent formalization of Laplace theory[21] opens up many interesting research directions in the context of our work since now we can link our formalization to the time-domain as well.

3   Preliminaries

In this section, we give a brief introduction to the multivariate analysis theories in the HOL-Light theorem prover and the block diagram formalization of [12]. The intent is to provide some preliminaries to make the paper self contained and thus facilitate its understanding for a wider audience, including both formal methods and control communities.

3.1   Multivariate Calculus Theories in HOL-Light

A n-dimensional vector is represented as a $\mathbb{R}^n$ column matrix of real numbers in HOL-Light. All of the vector operations are then handled as matrix manipulations. This way, complex numbers can be represented by the data-type $\mathbb{R}^2$, i.e, a column matrix having two elements [9]. In this formalization of complex numbers, the first real number represents the real part and the second real number represents the imaginary part of the given complex number[10]. The main advantage of this choice is that all the topological and analytic formalization developed for vectors is inherited by the complex numbers.

Definition 1: *Complex Number*
⊢ ∀ x y. complex (x,y) = vector [x; y]

The following mappings allow us to obtain the real and imaginary components of a complex number:

Definition 2: *Real and Imaginary Components of a Complex Number*
⊢ ∀ z. Re z = z$1
⊢ ∀ z. Im z = z$2

Here the notation z$n represents the nth component of a vector z. A real number a can be converted to an equivalent complex number as follows:

Definition 3: *Cx*
⊢ ∀ z. Cx(a) = complex(a,&0)

The normalization of a complex number is also a widely used phenomena and has been formalized in HOL-Light [10] as follows:

Definition 4: *Normalization of a Complex Number*
⊢ ∀ z. norm z = sqrt (Re z pow 2 + Im z pow 2)

where sqrt represents the HOL-Light square root function for real numbers.

The concept of limit of a function is used in our formalization to model the steady-state error and is formalized in HOL-Light as follows:

Definition 5: *Limit of a function*
⊢ ∀ f net. lim net f = (@l. (f → l) net)

The function lim is defined using the Hilbert choice operator @ in the functional form. It accepts a *net* with elements of arbitrary data-type A and a function f, of data-type $A \rightarrow \mathbb{R}^m$, and returns l:$\mathbb{R}^m$, i.e., the value to which the function f converges to at the given net.

Similarly, we also use the following theorem in our development:

Theorem 1: *Sum of a geometric Progression*
⊢ ∀ z. norm z < &1 ⇒
((λk.z pow k) sums z pow n / (Cx(&1) - z)) (from n)

Where the function f sums k (from n) ensures that the infinite summation of a multivariate sequence f is equal to k with n as the starting point.

3.2   Formalization of Block Diagrams in Control Systems

This section provides a set of formal definitions [12] of the basic building blocks of control systems, given in Fig. 3. These definitions can in turn be used to formalize a wide range of control systems in higher-order logic. The net transfer function of n subsystems connected in *cascade* is the product of their individual laplace transfer functions (Fig. 3.a).

Definition 6: *Cascaded Subsystems*
⊢ series [] = Cx (&1) ∧ (∀ h t. series (CONS h t) h * series t)

The function series accepts a list of complex numbers, corresponding to the transfer functions of all the given subsystems, and recursively returns their product. Here two type injections & and Cx are used to transform a positive integer to its corresponding real and complex number, respectively.

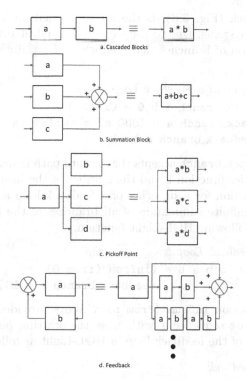

Fig. 3. Basic Building Blocks of a Control System

Fig. 3.b depicts a *summation junction* of transfer functions where the net transfer functions of a set of incoming branches is formed by adding their individual transfer functions. The formalization of this behavior accepts a list of complex numbers and returns their sum.

Definition 7: *Formalization of Summation Junction*
⊢ sum_junction [] = Cx (&0) ∧
  (∀ h t. sum_junction(CONS h t) h + sum_junction t)

The *pickoff point* represents a subsystem connected to a network of parallel branches of subsystems (Fig. 3.c):

Definition 8: *Formalization of Pickoff point*
⊢ ∀ A h t. pickoff A [] = [] ∧
           pickoff A (CONS h t) = CONS (h * A) (pickoff A t)

The function pickoff, accepts a complex number a, corresponding to the transfer function of the first subsystem, and a list of complex numbers, corresponding to the transfer functions of the subsystems in the branches, and returns a list of complex numbers corresponding to the equivalent block diagram.

The *feedback* block (Fig. 3.d), is the foremost element required to model closed-loop control systems. Due to the feedback signal, it primarily represents an infinite summation of branches that comprises of serially connected subsystems.

Definition 9: *Branch of a Feedback Loop*
⊢ ∀ a b n. feedback_branch a b 0 = Cx (&1) ∧
            feedback_branch a b (SUC n) = series [a; b] *
                (feedback_branch a b n)

The function feedback_branch accepts the forward path transfer function a, the feedback path transfer function b and the number of the branches n. It returns the net transfer function for n branches of a feedback loop as a single complex number. Now, the infinite summation of all branches of the feedback loop can be modeled as the following HOL-Light function:

Definition 10: *Feedback Loop*
⊢ ∀ a b. feedback_loop a b = (infsum (from 0)
                        (λk. feedback_branch a b k))

The HOL-Light function infsum (from n) f above provides the infinite summation a multivariate sequence f with n as the starting point. Now, we can model the behavior of the feedback loop in HOL-Light as follows:

Definition 11: *Feedback*
⊢ ∀ a b. feedback a b = series [a; (feedback_loop a b)]

The function feedback accepts the forward path transfer function a and the feedback path transfer function b and returns the net transfer function by forming the series network of the summation of all the possible infinite branches and the final forward path transfer function, since the output is taken after the forward path a.

A couple of simplification theorems used in this paper, are as follows:

Theorem 2: *Feedback loop simplification*
⊢ ∀ a b. norm (a * b) < &1 ⇒ feedback a b = a / (Cx(&1) - a * b)

The proof of Theorem 2 is primarily based on the infinite summation of a geometric series [10], given in Theorem 1.

Similarly, the equivalence relationship between the block diagrams, shown in Fig. 4, has been formally verified as follows:

Theorem 3: *Feedback loop simplification*
∀ a b c. (norm (a*b) + norm (a*c)) < &1⇒
    feedback a (sum_junction (pickoff Cx(&1) [b;c])) =
                feedback (feedback a b) c

The proof of Theorem 3 utilizes Theorem 2 along with some complex arithmetic reasoning. We use this theorem to convert any non-unity-feedback control system into a unity-feedback control system required for steady-state error analysis.

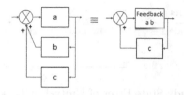

Fig. 4. Multiple Feedback Simplification Rule

4 Steady-State Error Analysis

We now present the formal verification of a generic expression that can be used to reason about the steady-state error of any unity-feedback system (Fig. 5), irrespective of its type and input. We proceed in this direction by first formalizing a generalized representation of the transfer function according to Equation (1).

Definition 12: *General Transfer function*
⊢ ∀ Y Z a. general_tf Y Z b = (λs. Y s / (s pow b * Z s))

The function **general_tf** accepts two complex functions Y and Z of data type $\mathbb{R}^2 \rightarrow \mathbb{R}^2$ along with a complex number b and returns the transfer function using the lambda abstraction format.

Now, the error model of unity-feedback systems in terms of the generalized representation of $G(s)$, according to Equation (2), is as follows:

Definition 13: *Steady-state-error-model*
⊢ ∀ G a. uf_error_model G a =
(λs. series [Cx (&1) /s pow a; feedback_loop (G s) (--Cx(&1))])

The function **uf_error_model** accepts a variable $G : \mathbb{R}^2 \rightarrow \mathbb{R}^2$, which represents the general transfer function, and a complex number $a : \mathbb{R}^2$, which generalizes the input type, i.e., if the input is a unit step then $a = 1$ and similarly $a = 2$ and $a = 3$ for the ramp and parabola inputs, respectively. The function uses the functions **series** and **feedback** to capture the structure of the error model of the unity-feedback system, depicted in Fig. 5, and returns its net transfer function with data type $\mathbb{R}^2 \rightarrow \mathbb{R}^2$.

Now, the steady-state error can be formally defined as the limit of the net transfer function of the error model, as given in Equation (3),

Definition 14: *steady-state-error*
⊢ ∀ E. steady_state_error E = lim (at (Cx(&0))) (λs. s (E s))

where the function lim(at(vec i))(λx.f x), represents the limit of a function f at point i, i.e., $\lim_{x \rightarrow i} f(x)$ in HOL-Light. The function **steady_state_error** accepts a variable $E : \mathbb{R}^2 \rightarrow \mathbb{R}^2$, which represents the net transfer function of the error, and returns its corresponding steady-state error as a complex value.

Now, based on the above definitions, we verified our generic expression as the following theorem

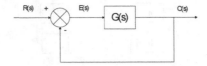

Fig. 5. Steady-State Error of Unity-Feedback Systems

Theorem 4: *Unity-feedback steady-state error*

⊢ ∀ Y Z a b l m.   (∀ s. Z continuous at s) ∧ ¬(l = Cx(&0)) ∧
  ¬(m + 1 = Cx(&0)) ∧ 0 ≤ b ∧ 1 ≤ a ∧ a ≤ b+1 ∧ (Y → l)
  (at Cx(&0)) ∧ (Z → m) (at Cx(&0)) ∧ ¬(Z (Cx(&0)) = Cx(&0)) ∧
  (?k. &0<k ∧ (∀s. norm s<k ⇒ norm (Y s /(s pow b * Z s)) < &1))
  ⇒ steady_state_error (uf_error_model (general_tf Y Z b) a) =
    (if b = 0 then m / (m+1) else if a = b+1 then m / l
       else Cx(&0))

The first three assumptions are used to avoid singularities. The next two assumptions declare the allowable ranges of the system type and input characterization variables, respectively. The next assumption (a ≤ b+1) defines the upper bound of the input type based on the type of the system. The next two assumptions ensure that the variables, l and m, represent the limiting values of the functions Y and Z at point 0, respectively. The last assumption is required for the feedback simplification. To the best of our knowledge, this relationship between the type of the system and its allowable input, given in Theorem 4, is not mentioned in most of the control systems literature. To ascertain our finding, we consulted some control systems experts and they confirmed our results. Missing such corner cases is a common problem in paper-and-pencil based mathematical analysis and simulation and is one of the major causes for faulty system designs. The proof of Theorem 4 is based on various properties of limit of a complex function and complex arithmetic reasoning.

The formalization presented so far in this section consumed about 300 manhours, which are mainly spent in the user guided verification due to the undecidable nature of the higher-order logic. Our proof script is available at [2]. The main benefit of this development, however, is that it greatly facilitates the formal reasoning about unity-feedback control system properties by reducing the human interaction in such proofs, as will be illustrated in the next section.

It is important to note that the universal quantification over the variables Y, Z, a and b in Theorem 4 allows us to use this result for reasoning about steady-state error of any unity-feedback control system irrespective of its type, input and behavior. To the best of our knowledge, such a generic relationship for the steady-state error for unity-feedback systems has not been reported in the control systems literature.

Now, we outline the step-wise process for reasoning about the steady-state error of unity-feedback systems using Theorem 4. The first step is to use the formal definitions, given in Section 3, to develop a formal model of the given system using its structural description. Next, we verify the equivalence of this model and the expression `general_tf Y Z b`, by choosing appropriate assignments of the functions Y and Z and the variable b. Next, we express the theorem for the steady-state error of the given unity-feedback system: `steady_state_error (uf_error_model (<transfer function of the given system>) a) = <steady state error>`. Now, using Theorem 4 along with the fact that all of its assumptions hold for the given values of Y, Z, a and b, we can conclude the proof of steady-state error of the given unity-feedback system. In order to illustrate the effectiveness and practical utilization of Theorem 4 and the above mentioned process, we analyze a real-world control system in the next section.

5   Application: Pulse Width Modulation (PWM) push-pull dc-dc Converter

The Pulse Width Modulation(PWM) push-pull dc-dc converters are widely used to step down dc voltages and thus have many applications in areas, like aerospace applications, where dc voltage is produced and consumed. The steady-state response of this electronic device is of utmost importance and thus has been extensively studied [14,8]. A commonly used model [8] for steady-state error analysis of the PWM push-pull dc-dc converter is given in Fig. 6.

In this section, we share the experiences of a control system specialist in verifying the steady-state error relationship for the PWM push-pull dc-dc converter using our formalization. This person is a graduate student of Electrical Engineering and her research interests are in the area of mathematical analysis of control systems. The person had taken academic courses on discrete mathematics, programming languages and calculus but had no background about formal methods. We provided a two week HOL-Light extensive training to the person with major focus on formal reasoning about complex arithmetic and limits. During the course of the training as well as the case study, the person struggled in understanding the syntactical and type checking errors of HOL-Light and thus was significantly assisted in this regard.

The person initiated the exercise by developing the following higher-order-logic model for the block diagram, given in Fig. 6. Initially, she got confused in defining multiple feedback paths while using the function `pickoff` and mistakenly used the transfer function of `1/s` instead of 1 in the pre-fan-out block. She caught this mistake herself during the second step of our proposed approach, where the equivalence of the formal model is verified with the one obtained via the `general_tf` function and the correct definition is given below:

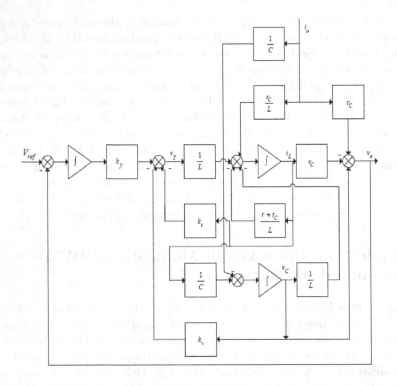

Fig. 6. Steady-State Error Model of PWM push-pull dc-dc converters

Definition 15: *PWM push pull dc-dc converter*
∀ L C r rc Ky Kv Ki s.
  dc_dc_converter L C r rc Ky Kv Ki s =
    series [Cx(&1)/s ; Ky ; feedback (series [Cx(&1)/L;
    feedback (Cx(&1)/s) (--sum_junction (pickoff (Cx(&1))
    [(r+rc)/L; series [Cx(&1)/s; Cx(&1)/C; Cx(&1)/L]]))]
    (--sum_junction (pickoff (Cx(&1)) [Ki;
    series [Kv; Cx(&1)/s; Cx(&1)/C]])); sum_junction [rc;
    series [Cx(&1)/s; Cx(&1)/C]]]

Where the -- symbol represents the minus operator in HOL-Light. The variables L, C, r and rc donate inductor, capacitor, the equivalent resistance in series with an inductor and the equivalent resistance in series with a capacitor, respectively. While kv, ki and ky are the voltage, current and feedback loop gains, respectively. None of these variables can be zero for the correct operation of the dc-dc converter. A subgoal of the equivalence theorem is given below, where the structure of the PWN push pull dc-dc converter is simplified to obtain its corresponding characteristic equation given in [8]:

Theorem 5: *dc-dc converter Transfer function simplification*
⊢ ∀ L C s r rc Ky Kv Ki.
   ¬(C * L * r * rc * Ki * Kv * Ky = Cx (&0)) ∧ ¬(s = Cx (&0)) ∧
   ¬(s pow 2 *C *L + s*C*(r + rc) +Cx(&1) = Cx(&0)) ∧
   norm (inv s * --((r+rc) * inv L + inv (s*C*L))) < &1 ∧
   norm ((s * C) / (s pow 2 * C * L + s * C * (r + rc) +
   Cx(&1)) * --(Ki + Kv * inv (s *C))) < &1
   ⇒ dc_dc_converter L C r rc Ky K Ki s =
      (Ky * (s*C*rc +Cx(&1))) / (s pow 3 * C* L + s pow 2 *
      C * (r+rc+Ki) + s (Cx(&1)+Kv))

Note that none of the physical values in the model can be zero and this is ensured by the first assumption. The next two assumptions are used to avoid singularities and the last two assumptions are required for solving the feedback paths. Our control engineer was not able to guess the right set of assumptions upfront and thus added the missing assumptions during the reasoning process based on the feedback she got from the generated subgoals. Thus, it was clearly observed in this exercise that interactive theorem provers do guide their users to find the right set of assumptions.

Since our given model is a Type 1 system, therefore its steady-state-error for the unit step input should be zero[14]. The result is verified as:

Theorem 6: *Steady-State Error for step input*
⊢ ∀ L C r rc Ky Kv Ki.
   ¬(C * L * r * rc * Ki * Kv * Ky = Cx (&0)) ∧
   ¬(Cx (&1) + Kv = --Ky) ∧
   ¬(Cx (&1) + Kv = Cx (&0)) ∧
   (?k. &0 < k ∧
   (∀s. norm s < k
   ⇒ norm ((Ky * (s * C * rc + Cx (&1))) /
   (s pow 1 * (C * L * s pow 2 + s * C * (r + rc + Ki) +
   Cx (&1) + Kv))) < &1))
   ⇒ steady_state_error (uf_error_model (general_tf
      (λs.Ky * (s*C*rc + Cx(&1))) (λs.C*L* s pow 2 +
      s*C*(r+rc+Ki) + Cx(&1) + Kv) 1) 1) = Cx(&0)

The first assumption ensures that none of the component in the dc-dc converter has a zero value and the next three assumptions are uesd to avoid singularities. The last assumption is for the feedback simplification.

The verification of the above theorem involves the equivalence theorem, as described in the previous section, along with Theorem 4. Besides the above theorem, the control engineer also verified the relationship of the steady-state error for ramp input. The theorem is described below:

Theorem 7: *Steady-State Error for ramp input*
⊢ ∀ L C r rc Ky Kv Ki.
   ¬(C * L * r * rc * Ki * Kv * Ky = Cx (&0)) ∧

```
¬(Cx (&1) + Kv = --Ky) ∧
¬(Cx (&1) + Kv = Cx (&0)) ∧
(?k. &0 < k ∧
(∀s. norm s < k
⇒ norm ((Ky * (s * C * rc + Cx (&1))) /
(s pow 1 * (C * L * s pow 2 + s * C * (r + rc + Ki) +
Cx (&1) + Kv))) < &1))
⇒ steady_state_error (uf_error_model (general_tf
    (λs. Ky * (s*C*rc + Cx(&1))) (λs. C*L* s pow 2 +
    s*C*(r+rc+Ki) + Cx(&1) + Kv ) 1) 2) = (Cx(&1) + Kv) / Ky
```

The reasoning process was very similar to the one used for Theorem 6 since the same values for the functions Y and Z are used in these theorems. Further details about its verification can be found in our proof script[2].

The exercise of involving a control systems engineer for conducting these proofs was quite a learning experience for us as well. Some of the feedback that we got is shared here. The user faced many issues in interpreting the type checking and syntactical error messages generated by HOL-Light and this was the most frustrating issue for him. Thus, this is an area that can be improved. Moreover, the person was not too comfortable with the text-based interface of the theorem prover and suggested to bring in a more user-friendly graphical interface, specially for control system analysis. On the other hand, the user was quite amazed at the feedback she got from the theorem prover in understanding the behavior of the control system model and the requirement of an exhaustive set of assumptions to verify any theorem. She felt that this sort of rigorous analysis is a dire need in the case of safety-critical control system design. It was quite encouraging for us that the engineer was able to verify the goals with the basic understanding of limits and complex numbers in HOL-Light. This fact also demonstrates the effectiveness of our generic theorem.

6   Conclusions

This paper presents a formal framework to reason about the net transfer functions and steady-state errors of unity-feedback control systems within the sound core of a theorem prover HOL-Light. The main contribution of the paper is the formal verification of a generic theorem that facilitates in the formal reasoning about any kind of unity-feedback system. For illustration purposes, we presented a formal analysis of a PWM push pull dc-dc converter. Some of the interesting future directions of our work are to formally analyze the stability of control systems and establishing a link between the formalized Laplace transform theory[21] to be able to link time and Laplace domain models of a control system.

References

1. Clayton, P., Cavalcanti, A., O'Halloran, C.: From Control Law Diagrams to Ada via Circus. Formal Aspects of Computing 23(4), 465–512 (2011)

2. Ahmad, M.: Formal Verification of Steady State Errors in Unity-Feedback Control Systems (2014), http://save.seecs.nust.edu.pk/students/ahmad/sseufcs.html
3. Alur, R.: Formal Verification of Hybrid Systems. In: Embedded Software, pp. 273–278 (2011)
4. Arthan, R., Caseley, P., O'Halloran, C., Smith, A.: ClawZ: Control Laws in Z. In: Formal Engineering Methods, pp. 169–176 (2000)
5. Boulton, R.J., Gottliebsen, H., Hardy, R., Kelsey, T., Martin, U.: Design Verification for Control Engineering. In: Boiten, E.A., Derrick, J., Smith, G.P. (eds.) IFM 2004. LNCS, vol. 2999, pp. 21–35. Springer, Heidelberg (2004)
6. Boulton, R.J., Hardy, R., Martin, U.: A Hoare Logic for Single-Input Single-Output Continuous-Time Control Systems. In: Maler, O., Pnueli, A. (eds.) HSCC 2003. LNCS, vol. 2623, pp. 113–125. Springer, Heidelberg (2003)
7. Dong, J.S., Chen, C., Sun, J.: A Formal framework for Modeling and Validating Simulink diagrams. Formal Aspects of Computing 21(5), 451–483 (2009)
8. Czarkowski, D., Pujara, L.R., Kazimierczuk, M.K.: Robust Stability of State-Feedback Control of PWM DC-DC push-pull Converter. IEEE Transaction on Industrial Electronics 42(1), 108–111 (1995)
9. Harrison, J.: A HOL Theory of Euclidean Space. In: Hurd, J., Melham, T. (eds.) TPHOLs 2005. LNCS, vol. 3603, pp. 114–129. Springer, Heidelberg (2005)
10. Harrison, J.: Formalizing Basic Complex Analysis. Studies in Logic, Grammar and Rhetoric 10, 151–165 (2007)
11. Harrison, J.: The HOL Light Theory of Euclidean Space. Journal of Automated Reasoning 50(2), 173–190 (2013)
12. Hasan, O., Ahmad, M.: Formal analysis of steady state errors in feedback control systems using HOL-light. In: Proceedings of the Conference on Design, Automation and Test in Europe, DATE 2013, pp. 1423–1426 (2013)
13. Herencia-Zapana, H., Jobredeaux, R., Owre, S., Garoche, P.-L., Feron, E., Perez, G., Ascariz, P.: PVS Linear Algebra Libraries for Verification of Control Software Algorithms in C/ACSL. In: Goodloe, A.E., Person, S. (eds.) NFM 2012. LNCS, vol. 7226, pp. 147–161. Springer, Heidelberg (2012)
14. Hote, Y.: A New Approach to Time Domain Analysis of Perturbed PWM push-pull DC-DC Converter. Journal of Control Theory and Applications 10(4), 465–469 (2012)
15. Lutovac, M.D., Tošic, D.V.: Symbolic Analysis and Design of Control Systems using Mathematica. International Journal of Control 79(11), 1368–1381 (2006)
16. Mahony, B.: The DOVE approach to the Design of Complex Dynamic Processes. In: Workshop on Formalising Continuous Mathematics, pp. 167–187. NASA Conference Publication (2002)
17. MathWorks Simulink (2012), http://www.mathworks.com/products/simulink
18. Nise, N.S.: Control System Engineering. Wiley and Sons (2003)
19. Ogata, K.: Modern Control Engineering. Prentice-Hall (1997)
20. Pike, L.: Pervasive Formal Verification in Control System. In: Formal Methods in Computer-Aided Design. Panel Discussion (2011)
21. Taqdees, S.H., Hasan, O.: Formalization of Laplace Transform Using the Multivariable Calculus Theory of HOL-Light. In: McMillan, K., Middeldorp, A., Voronkov, A. (eds.) LPAR-19. LNCS, vol. 8312, pp. 744–758. Springer, Heidelberg (2013)
22. Tiwari, A., Khanna, G.: Series of Abstractions for Hybrid Automata. In: Tomlin, C.J., Greenstreet, M.R. (eds.) HSCC 2002. LNCS, vol. 2289, pp. 465–478. Springer, Heidelberg (2002)

Assertion-Based Monitoring in Practice –
Checking Correctness
of an Automotive Sensor Interface

Thang Nguyen[1,*] and Dejan Ničković[2]

[1] Infineon Technologies AG, Austria
Thang.Nguyen@infineon.com
[2] AIT Austrian Institute of Technology GmbH, Vienna, Austria
dejan.nickovic@ait.ac.at

Abstract. In this paper, we evaluate the assertion-based monitoring technology for mixed-signal systems by applying it to real-world case study from the automotive domain.

We first motivate the case study by presenting the state-of-the-practice verification and validation work-flow typically used in the automotive industry. We identify the shortcomings of this work-flow, and propose a more rigorous and automated methodology based on monitoring correctness of simulated mixed signal designs with respect to assertions, which formalize in Signal Temporal Logic (STL) the requirements from the design specification.

We apply the assertion-based monitoring framework for mixed signal designs to check the correctness of Distributed System Interface (DSI3) in a modern airbag system-on-chip application. We present all the relevant steps in our proposed work-flow, evaluate the results and discuss the framework's benefits as well as its identified missing features.

1 Introduction

A modern car is a system-of-systems (SoS) that merges a number of embedded elements that are often developed independently. The systems in a car are heterogeneous, combining digital controllers with analog sensors and actuators. They interact with their physical environment and are interconnected through the vehicle physics, as well as communication protocols. This results in complex interactions generating emergent behaviors that are not predictable in advance. Many components in a car, such as the airbag systems, are *safety critical*. Hence, correct system integration in the automotive domain is crucial to achieve high standards with respect to safety.

Due to the heterogeneity and the complexity of components and sub-systems in modern cars, verification and validation (V&V) poses a major challenge in the

* The research leading to these results has received funding from the ARTEMIS Joint Undertaking under grant agreement Nr. 295311 and the Austrian Research Promotion Agency FFG under the program "Forschung, Innovation und Technologie fr Informationstechnologien (FIT-IT).

F. Lang and F. Flammini (Eds.): FMICS 2014, LNCS 8718, pp. 16–32, 2014.
© Springer International Publishing Switzerland 2014

automotive domain and represents the main bottleneck in the design process. Verification by simulation and manual testing are the dominant methods used in the V&V practice of the automotive industry. However, these techniques have the weakness of being ad-hoc, inefficient and prone to human errors.

The research community has investigated a number of approaches that address V&V issues for mixed-signal systems. Formal verification of systems combining continuous and discrete dynamics has been mainly studied by the *hybrid systems* [18,2] community. It consists in computing over-approximations of reachable sets of states of the circuit, modeled as a hybrid automaton (differential equations with mode switching). Despite the important progress achieved in this research field in recent years [13], such technique [6,14,17,24,1] still cannot scale up to the size and complexity of transistor-level circuit models. In addition to hybrid system verification, there are other orthogonal analytical approaches to study similar systems. For instance, static analysis and abstract interpretation were used to develop a framework for inferring continuous time properties of systems consisting of synchronous components that interact by quasi-synchronous composition [5].

Assertion-based monitoring is a promising technology for verification of analog and mixed-signal (AMS) designs, i.e. designs that consist of interacting digital and analog components. It successfully exports some well-established ingredients from digital verification to the AMS domain, while retaining the relative simplicity and scalability of the simulation-based verification. In essence, assertion-based monitoring frameworks consist of an assertion language used to formalize the requirements that describe the correct interaction between analog and digital components, including timing constraints due to the communication delays. The formal assertions are then automatically translated into *monitors*, programs that read simulation traces of the design-under-test and check for the assertion satisfaction/violation.

Signal Temporal Logic (STL) [19,20] is an assertion language extending Linear Temporal logic (LTL) [22]. LTL enables declarative, formal and compact specification of reactive system requirements. Its original use was for evaluating sequences of states and events in digital systems. A typical property stated in temporal logic is `always (req -> eventually! ack)`. This property says that it is always the case that a request `req` eventually triggers an acknowledgment `ack`. STL extends LTL to specification of properties involving both digital and real-valued variables defined over dense time. Offline monitoring of STL was implemented in the tool AMT [21]. The monitoring flow based on using STL for formalizing assertions and monitoring them with AMT is depicted in Figure 1. This specification language has been successfully used in the past for monitoring in various application domains, such as analog circuits [16], biochemical reactions [7], synthetic biological circuits [4] and music [11]. STL has also been extended in several other directions. In [11], the authors developed a first attempt of time-frequency logic-based (TFL) specification, and successfully applied it to detect music patterns. TFL expresses frequencies as atomic predicates (using sliding FFT to evaluate the intensity of the signal around a frequency) and time using intervals and the classic temporal operators. The classic qualitative semantics of STL was recently extended with more powerful and precise notions of quantitative semantics [12,10,9] (or robustness degree), providing a real value measuring the level of satisfaction or violation for a trajectory of the property of interest. Several tools, such as BIOCHAM [23], S-TaLiRo [3] and Breach [8], are available to perform robustness analysis on the time series collected in wet-lab experiments or produced by simulation-based techniques.

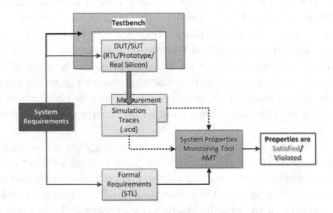

Fig. 1. Assertion-based monitoring flow with STL assertion language and AMT tool

In this work, we apply the assertion-based monitoring framework from Figure 1 to check the correctness of a sophisticated automotive sensor interface integration in a modern system-on-chip (SoC) airbag system, developed by Infineon Austria AG. The correct integration of the SoC with its sensor interface is specified in the Distributed System Interface (DSI3) protocol standard [15]. We present the work-flow of the case study in which we use STL to formalize DSI3 requirements and AMT tool to monitor the simulation traces. We evaluate the case study results and discuss the lessons that we learned regarding the applicability of this approach in industry.

2   Verification Flow in the Automotive Domain – State-of-the-Practice

Figure 2 illustrates the state-of-the-practice verification work-flow by Power Train and Safety department at Infineon Technology Austria AG. The work-flow describes as well collaboration between Tier-1 (system developer and integrator) and Tier-2+ (HW - Hardware and SW Software element developers) teams. The work-flow starts with the requirements and specifications phase at the Tier-1 level. In this step system functionalities and related HW/SW components are defined. The HW requirements are provided to Tier-2 supplier, e.g.

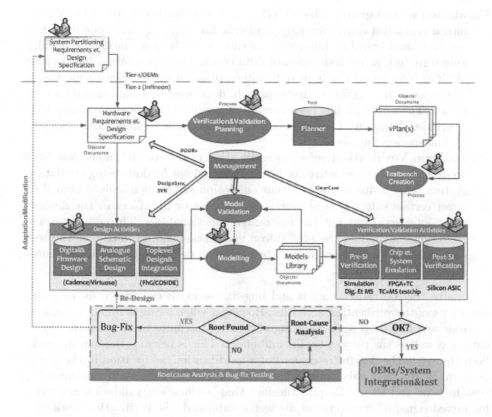

Fig. 2. Verification workflow for complex mixed signal IC development

Infineon so that HW concept and design specification can be further defined. Right after this phase, the design and verification/validation activities will be launched (almost in parallel). The design activities covers conceptual and design work, which including digital and firmware design, analog schematic design and top-level integration. Most of the tasks defined during design phase are mainly done under the Cadence Virtuoso/AMS-Designer tooling environment, whereas for the proof-of-concept, the COSIDE (Complex System Integrated Development Environment) from Fraunhofer IIS is used. Nearly at the same time, verification engineering team also based on the hardware requirements and design specification starts their verification and validation planning process. This process (with the support from some planning tools, e.g.: in-house tool) results in a verification plan which then used by verification/validation engineer for test bench creation. The verification plan is categorized with different verification approaches including:

Pre-silicon verification covers all type of simulation at different design level (block, module and chip top-level) using different techniques from mixed-signal to mixed-abstraction simulation.

Emulation at integrated circuit (IC) and system level uses FPGA with mixed-signal test chip as an early prototype for verifying many scenarios that are very impractical or impossible to simulate. These scenarios are usually long term test, stress test or sensor data transmission test over a long period of time (e.g.: could result in data interception of million sensor message). This approach is an innovative approach, developed by Infineon and its customer. The approach has been recently accepted as publication in the SAE Journal of Passenger Car - Electrical and Electronic System (SAE Society of Automotive Engineer).

Post-silicon Verification refers to verification of the real IC in the lab. It is an extension of those test scenarios which could not be done using emulation system. This is due to the fact that emulation system is mainly designed to cover certain safety critical functions (e.g.: sensor interfaces or the deployment interfaces) but not the full design functionalities. Through extensive tests done in the lab, the post-silicon verification should maximize the test coverage at HW component level before being delivered to the system integrator Tier-1 supplier.

Finally, the rootcause analysis and bug-fix testing is considered as an undesired part of the verification activities. However, when a bug is found, rootcause analysis and bug-fix testing could significantly contribute to increase the verification as well as the project timing and effort. This is because the bug-fix could be a change in the design (re-design) of a modification/adaptation in the specification. In any case, this would trigger the verification regression run, meaning cost in time and effort. Despite the fact that verification/validation activities for mixed-signal IC development are well established, the verification work-flow above still involves simulation and manual testing methods used in the practice of the automotive industry. These methods consist in verification engineers creating input stimuli, executing simulation models and observing the waveforms for correctness. They are known for the following weaknesses: ad-hoc, inefficient and prone to human errors. In addition, it is widely accepted that for complex mixed-signal multi-cores System-on-Chip (SoC) IC products, verification accounts for around 60%-70% of the total development. This is especially true for automotive safety critical SoC product with a high number of analogue interfaces to the physical components, e.g.: an airbag SoC chipset in an automotive airbag system application. As such, any approaches which could help to reduce design and verification effort, improve time-to-market and product quality, e.g.: formal verification, boost up verification runs using hardware acceleration platform and verification automation are of extreme interest.

3   Signal Temporal Logic

In this section, we give a brief overview of the Signal Temporal Logic (STL) that we use to formalize the case study requirements. For the full details regarding the assertion language and the monitoring algorithms for STL, we refer the reader to [20].

We consider the STL logic with both *future* and *past* operators, interpreted over a finite multi-dimensional signal w. A signal w is a partial function $w : \mathcal{T} \to \mathbb{B}^m \times \mathbb{R}^n$, where $\mathcal{T}$ is the interval $[0, d)$ denoting a time domain of duration d. Let $X = \{x_1, \ldots, x_m\}$ be the set of real valued variables and $P = \{p_1, \ldots, p_n\}$ the set of STL propositions. We denote by $w|_x$ and $w|_p$ the projection of the signal w to a real-valued or propositional variable $x \in X$ or $p \in P$. A *Boolean constraint* over X is a predicate of the form $x \circ c$, where $x \in X$, $\circ \in \{<, <=, =, >=, >\}$ and $c \in \mathbb{Q}$. The syntax of an STL formula φ over X and P is defined by the grammar

$$\alpha := p \mid x \circ c$$
$$\varphi := \alpha \mid \textsf{not } \varphi \mid \varphi_1 \textsf{ or } \varphi_2 \mid \varphi_1 \textsf{ until!}_I \ \varphi_2 \mid \varphi \textsf{ since!}_I \ \varphi_2$$

where $p \in P$, $x \in X$, $c \in \mathbb{Q}$ is a constant and I is an interval of the form $[a, b]$, $[a, b)$, $(a, b]$, (a, b), $[a, \infty)$ or (a, ∞) where $0 \le a \le b$ are rational numbers. As in LTL, basic STL operators can be used to derive other standard Boolean and temporal operators, in particular the time-constrained `eventually!`, `once!`, `always`, and `historically` operators:

`eventually!`$_I \ \varphi = true \ $`until!`$_I \ \varphi$ `once!`$_I \ \varphi = true \ $`since`$_I \ \varphi$

`always`$_I \ \varphi = $`not eventually!`$_I \ $`not `$\varphi$ `historically`$_I \ \varphi = $`not once`$_I \ $`not `$\varphi$

The semantics of an STL formula φ with respect to an n-dimensional signal w is described via the satisfiability relation $(w, t) \models \varphi$, indicating that the signal w satisfies φ at time t, according to the following recursive definition, where $\mathcal{T}$ is the time domain.

$$
\begin{aligned}
(w, t) &\models x \circ c & &\leftrightarrow w|_x[t] \circ c \\
(w, t) &\models p & &\leftrightarrow p[t] = 1 \\
(w, t) &\models \textsf{not } \varphi & &\leftrightarrow (w, t) \not\models \varphi \\
(w, t) &\models \varphi_1 \textsf{ or } \varphi_2 & &\leftrightarrow (w, t) \models \varphi_1 \textsf{ or } (w, t) \models \varphi_2 \\
(w, t) &\models \varphi_1 \textsf{ until!}_I \ \varphi_2 & &\leftrightarrow \exists \, t' \in (t \oplus I) \cap \mathcal{T} \ (w, t') \models \varphi_2 \textsf{ and} \\
& & &\quad \forall \, t'' \in (t, t') \ (w, t'') \models \varphi_1 \\
(w, t) &\models \varphi_1 \textsf{ since!}_I \ \varphi_2 & &\leftrightarrow \exists \, t' \in (t \ominus I) \cap \mathcal{T} \ (w, t') \models \varphi_2 \textsf{ and} \\
& & &\quad \forall \, t'' \in (t', t) \ (w, t'') \models \varphi_1
\end{aligned}
\tag{1}
$$

A formula φ is satisfied by w if $(w, 0) \models \varphi$.

Example 1. An example of a property that can be expressed in STL is a mixed signal stabilization property that has the following requirements:

- The absolute value of a continuous signal x is always less than 5;
- When the (Boolean) trigger rises, within 600 time units `abs(x)` has to drop below 1 and stay like that for at least 300 time units.

This property is illustrated in Figure 3 and expressed in STL as:

```
always (abs(x) < 6 and
        (rise(trigger) -> eventually!_[0,600] always_[0,300] (abs(x) < 1)))
```

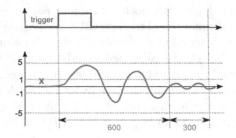

Fig. 3. Example: stabilization property

4   Case Study

4.1   Case Study Description

The increasing number of airbags in a vehicle, the requirement to comply with stricter safety requirements, while costs must be reduced has brought automotive airbag system application to a new approach with SoC design, shown in Figure 1. Consequently, verification has dramatically increasingly challenges the design of complex mixed-signal System-on-Chip (SoC) products. This is especially true for automotive safety critical SoC products with a high number of analogue interfaces to the physical components, e.g.: an airbag SoC chipset in an automotive airbag system application.

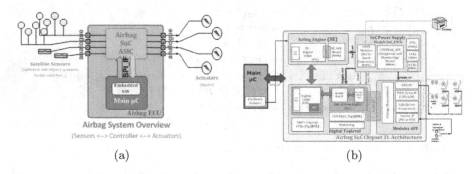

(a)   (b)

Fig. 4. A typical airbag system: (a) overview; (b) airbag SoC chipset top-level implementation architecture

During the operation, the sensors (buckle switches, accelerometers, pressure sensors, etc.) mounted in key locations of the vehicle, continuously measure the positions of impact, the severity of the collision and other variables. This information is provided to the airbag SoC chipset in form of analog signals. The airbag SoC chipset translates the analog sensor signals into digital words. The translated digital sensor data is reported to the main uC via the SPI (Serial Peripheral Interface) communication. Based on this information the airbag main uC decides if, where (location) and when the airbags (e.g.: actuators) is deployed. Accordingly, this makes the verification (computer-based simulation) and validation (lab evaluation) of the airbag SoC product, especially the sensor interfaces become a challenging task, mainly because of:

- Verification for the airbag SoC and its sensor interfaces has to cover real-time embedded mixed signal domains.
- Failure during the reception, decoding and processing of sensor data in the airbag controller system can originate unexpected or false deployment events of the airbag system putting human safety in danger.
- Most of the functionalities of sensor interfaces can only be verified at the system level of the chip and at the system application level. Only using classical mixed-signal simulation approach becomes a bottle neck.
- Many verification scenarios of the sensor interfaces such as long-term verification run with checking of millions sensor data frames are not suitable using computer-based simulation.

In addition, reducing time-to-market and first time right design in automotive electronics industry, which are key requirements in project to win customer and market share, has posed a great challenge to the design and verification team. With this case study, we are evaluating the assertion-based monitoring methodology on the modern airbag system application with the focus on the new airbag sensor interface using the new DSI3 standard, promoted by the DSI consortium[1]. DSI3 goals are to improve performance, reduce cost and promote open standard but still remains at the lowest cost possible compare to the current widely used PSI5 standard. Higher performance is achieved among others, by increased communication speed from the slave sensor to the master.

4.2   Formalization of DSI3 Discovery Mode Requirements

In this section, we formalize DSI3 *discovery mode* requirements, illustrated in the highlighted section of Figure 5. In the DSI3 discovery mode, μC interacts with the sensor interfaces via the voltage (v) and current (i) lines. It is the initial phase of the DSI3 standard protocol and it works as follows. First, the power apply is turned on, resulting in the voltage ramp from $0V$ to V_high (phase (1) in Figure 5). Then, μC issues commands for probing the presence or absence of sensors. These commands are converted by the SoC to analog pulses carried over the voltage lines. In Figure 5, (2) shows a discovery pulse command. A sensor that is connected to the sensor interface responds by an inverted analog pulse carried over the current line (shown in (3) of Figure 5). Finally, if a sensor is not connected to the sensor interface, the discovery pulse command is not followed by any response on the current line, as illustrated in (4) of Figure 5.

In addition to the correct ordering of events, described in the previous paragraph, the DSI3 Bus Standard also defines a number of timing requirements that must be met by any correct implementation of the protocol:

---

[1] http://www.dsiconsortium.org

1. The minimal time between the moment that the power is applied and the first discovery pulse command is sent, as shown by (a) in Figure 5;
2. The maximal total duration of the discovery mode, measured between the moment that the power is applied and the end of the sensor probing by the μC, as illustrated by (b) in Figure 5;
3. The expected time between any two consecutive discovery pulse commands ((c) in Figure 5); and
4. The expected time between a discovery pulse command and the response by the sensor (or its lack of response if the sensor is not connected), as shown by (d) in Figure 5.

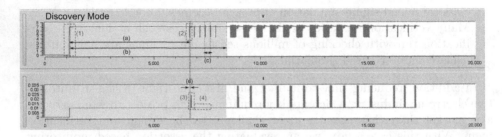

Fig. 5. DSI3 Discovery Mode requirements - overview

Specification of Events of Interest. In order to be able to formalize these timing properties defined by the DSI3 Bus Standard, we first must be able to accurately characterize and recognize the "events" corresponding to power application, discovery pulse commands, the sensor response and its lack of response. The graphical specification of these patterns is shown in Figure 6.

We first consider applying power to the SoC, illustrated in Figure 6 (a), which is characterized by a ramp that goes from $0V$ to V_{high}. We consider that the power is on, characterized by the event pw_app, when the voltage signal goes above V_{high}.

```
% Regions of interest
1:  define b:v_zero := a:v == 0;
2:  define b:v_above_high := a:v >= Vhigh;
3:  define b:v_between_high_zero := a:v > 0 and a:v <= Vhigh;

% Power applied
4:  define b:pw_app :=
5:     rise(b:v_above_high) and
6:     (b:v_between_high_zero since! fall(b:v_zero));
```

A *discovery pulse command* is carried on the voltage line and is characterized by its *shape* and *duration*, as shown in Figure 6 (b). The DSI3 standard requires

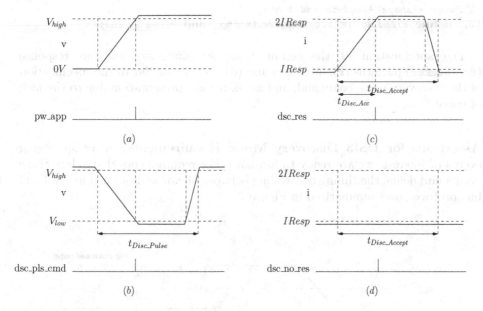

Fig. 6. Graphical specification of events of interest: (a) power applied; (b) discoverly pulse command; (c) sensor response; and (d) sensor no response

that the distance between two consecutive discovery pulse commands is t_{Disc_Per} ($\pm$ tolerance). In order to formalize this requirement in STL (shown in the next paragraph), we first define the regions of interest that are needed to capture a discovery pulse command (lines $1-3$). We then characterize the correct shape of the pulse (lines $4-7$) and its duration (lines $8-11$), resulting in the specification of the discovery pulse command (line 12).

```
% Regions of interest
1:   define b:v_above_high := a:v >= Vhigh;
2:   define b:v_below_low  := a:v <= Vlow;
3:   define b:v_between_high_low := a:v >= Vlow and a:v <= Vhigh;

% Pulse shape
4:   define b:cmd_dp_shape :=
5:     fall(b:v_above_high) and
6:     (b:v_between_high_low until! b:v_below_low until!
7:     b:v_between_high_low until! b:v_above_high);

% Pulse end-to-end timing
8:   define b:cmd_dp_e2e_timing :=
9:     fall(b:v_above_high) and
10:    ((not rise(b:v_above_high)) until![tDisc_Pulse-tol:tDisc_Pulse+tol]
11:    rise(b:v_above_high));
```

```
% Pulse = shape + end-to-end timing
12:  define b:cmd_dp := b:cmd_dp_e2e_timing  and b:cmd_dp_shape;
```

The specification of the sensor response (dsc_res) and no response (dsc_no_res) patterns (Figures 6 (c) and (d)) is very similar to the specification of the discovery pulse command, and we skip their presentation due to the lack of space.

Assertions for DSI3 Discovery Mode Requirements. After specifying events of interest, we are ready to formalize the requirements that relate these events and define the timing constraints between them, as described in the DSI3 bus protocol, and summarized in Figure 7.

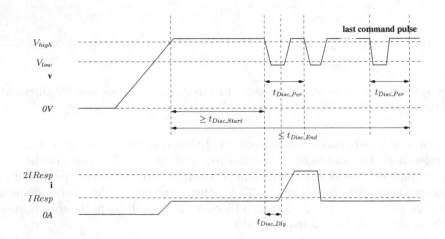

Fig. 7. Graphical specification of DSI3 discovery mode requirements

We start with the requirement saying that between the power applied event and the first discovery pulse command, there must be at least t_{Disc_Start} time elapsed. We formalize this requirement with the following assertion.

```
% Timing between power applied and first discovery pulse commands
1:  first_disc_cmd_dly  assert:
2:     always (b:pw_app -> (((not b:cmd_dp ) until![tDisc_Start:inf]
3:     b:cmd_dp);
```

The second requirement says that the discovery mode has a maximum duration of t_{Disc_End}. We consider that the discovery starts when the power is applied, and that it ends t_{Disc_Per} time after the last discovery command is issued. We first define the auxiliary property **end_disc** to characterize the end of the discovery mode, and then formalize the assertion as follows.

```
% Discovery end
1:  define b:end_disc :=
2:    ( notb:cmd_dp since![=t_Disc_Pulse] b:cmd_dp )  and
3:    always not b:cmd_dp ;

% Discovery mode maximum duration
4:  disc_duration assert:
5:    always (b:pw_app -> (eventually![0:t_Disc_End] b:end_disc);
```

The third requirement defines the correct timing between a discovery pulse command, and the associated sensor response when the sensor is connected (and its lack of response when it is not connected). This requirement is dependent on the actual configuration of the system, and we formalize the property in which only the first sensor is connected. In order to specify this requirement, we also need to characterize the first discovery pulse command.

```
% First discovery pulse command
1:  define b:first_cmd_dp :=
2:    (b:cmd_dp and historically notb:cmd_dp ;

% Discovery pulse command - response delay
3:  cmd_resp_delay assert:
4:    always ((b:cmd_dp and b:first_cmd_dp ->
5:    (eventually![t_Disc_Dly-tol:t_Disc_Dly+tol] b:dsc_res);

% Discovery pulse command - no response delay
6:  cmd_resp_delay assert:
7:    always ((b:cmd_dp and not b:first_cmd_dp ->
8:    (eventually![t_Disc_Dly-tol:t_Disc_Dly+tol] b:dsc_no_res );
```

Finally, the last requirement says that every two consecutive discovery pulse commands must be separated by $t_{Disc\_Pulse} \pm$ some tolerance, which is formalized with the following STL assertion.

```
% Timing between consecutive discovery pulse commands
1:  cmd_disc_pulse_period assert:
2:    always (b:cmd_dp -> (((not b:cmd_dp ) until![tDisc_Per-tol:tDisc_Per+tol]
3:    b:cmd_dp) or (always not b:cmd_dp )));
```

4.3   Case Study Evaluation

The design-under-test used in the case study was implemented by Infineon Technologies in VHDL (RTL) and VHDL with real number behavior. The design-under-test represents a mixed-abstraction of RTL and behavior model, consists of 23 different functional modules which are connected together via a complex logic core. The simulation time for this design takes approximately between 2 and 3 hours per simulation.

The formalization of the DSI3 requirements was lead by AIT, and was done in several iterations, involving feedback from the Infineon's designers and engineers. The tool used for monitoring the simulation traces against the formalized requirements was AMT [21]. The monitoring was done on a computer with Intel Core i7 processor, 8GB of RAM and the 64-bit Ubuntu 12.04 LTS running on a virtual machine from 64-bit Windows 7 operating system. The simulated traces files had approximately $210MB$ per simulation. The assertions were checked against the simulation traces one by one, and all the monitoring times were lower than $20s$ per assertion. It follows that the monitoring presented a negligible overhead compared to the simulation time.

The monitoring results provided several interesting insights regarding the formalization of requirement documents. The formalization for discovery pulse commands and the event when the voltage is applied proved to be sufficient to catch these events. However, in our first iteration, we were not able to catch the sensor response. In fact, the DSI3 standard does not specify the minimal duration of the pulse falling (see Figure 6 (c)), but our intuition was that due to the physical constraints the duration must be strictly positive. We thus imposed this constraint in our original formulation of the dsc_res property. However, after clarification from Infineon's designers, we found out that at this given stage of development, the design is approximated by a simpler model that allows instantaneous ramps between values, as we can see in Figure 8.

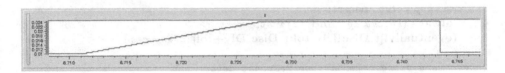

Fig. 8. Zoom in on the simulated sensor response on the current line

The monitoring tool reported a violation of the cmd_disc_pulse_period assertion. In the formal assertion, we used the value of $125\mu s$ for t_{Disc_Per}, while the actual distance between consecutive discovery pulse commands in the simulated trace was close to $250\mu s$, as shown in Figure 9. The value $125\mu s$ for t_{Disc_Per} was taken from Table 6-2 in the standard [15]. After discussions with the Infineon's engineers, it turned out that the standard gives only an average value for t_{Disc_Per}, while allowing the designer to choose any other value for t_{Disc_Per} as long as all the other hard timing constraints are met. After reformulating the assertion with the new value for t_{Disc_Per} provided by Infineon's engineers, the simulation traces satisfied the assertion.

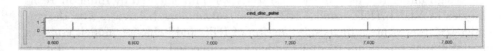

Fig. 9. Zoom in on the detected discovery command pulses extracted from the simulations by the monitoring tool

We conclude that generally requirement documents are not always fully precise regarding parts of the specification, which makes the formalization of requirements a non-trivial task. For some of the properties, interpretation freedom is left, and one must take extreme care to make assumption which match the intended meaning.

5 Lessons Learned and Future Directions

Requirements document often give interpretation freedom to the designer which can result in ambiguous understanding of the desired property. Using STL to monitor the compliance of the airbag SoC to the DSI3 standard protocol, it helps to remove these kinds of ambiguity. In addition, when the STL is implemented as an assertion, it strengthens the communication between different disciplinary teams, ensuring a clear and common understanding between teams on the system properties and requirements. We found that the monitoring itself represents a negligible overhead to the design simulation, while automatically providing useful debugging information to the designer as well as reducing time and error prone due to manual inspection of the simulation results.

We identified a number of features that are still missing in the STL-based monitoring framework and that we will investigate in the near future:

Template Specification Languages for STL: while STL is a rigorous, unambiguous and powerful specification language, it is often not very intuitive to the engineers, and especially to analog designers. Inspired by the graphical specification of properties, as described in the DSI3 bus standard, we will develop a graphical language for specifying common STL patterns, while hiding away low-level STL details from the future.

STL Assertion Libraries: we identified that building libraries of common STL properties for specific applications would greatly facilitate application of this technology and would enhance the reuse of assertions across different phases of design, various actors in the automotive value chain and different project. For instance, an assertion library specifying the full DSI3 bus standard would be reused in every project that requires using this communication protocol. The assertion skeletons would remain the same across the project, and only instantiations of project-specific parameters would need to change. In order to facilitate this goal, we need a more flexible syntax for STL that allows declaration of variables and constants outside of the assertions. We are currently working on adding this feature to the STL language.

Diagnostics for Assertion Violations: when an assertion is violated, it is extremely important to be able to easily extract the reasons of the violation. The AMT tool already provides extensive information about the assertion violation, by computing and making visible to the user the information about the satisfaction/violation in time of all sub-formulas in the violated assertion. However, the causality analysis still needs to be done manually by the engineer in order to gain insight into reasons for assertion violation. We are planing to further automate this process, by generating reports explaining in human readable language the reasons of assertion violations.

Assertion Language Extensions: in this paper, we focused on the discovery mode of the DSI3 protocol, in which STL can be directly used to accurately specify needed requirements. The expressive power of STL might not be sufficient for later phases of the protocol, when actual data is exchanged between the sensors and the μC over the voltage and current lines. This protocol uses multi-level source and Manchester coding for transferring data. We will look in the future for additional features that STL may need in order to support accurate specification of the full DSI3 bus standard and study the necessary extensions.

Algorithms for Hardware FPGA Monitors for STL: we used in this paper the offline STL monitoring tool AMT for case study evaluation. The offline monitoring has the advantage of being indifferent about the source (simulation, emulation or measurement) of the trace files – their provenance does not affect the monitoring results. However, the trend of implementing mixed-signal designs on FPGA hardware enables much longer design emulations of the design, generating huge amount of data to be processed. It follows that online hardware FPGA implementation of STL monitors, running in parallel with the design emulation, would be beneficial as they would limit the amount of data that needs to be stored at any time and would enable aborting emulation upon assertion violation detection.

6 Conclusions

We have evaluated the mixed-signal assertion-based monitoring methodology by applying it to check correctness of DSI3 sensor interfaces in a modern airbag system-on-chip application. We have demonstrated the usefulness and the potential of the approach, highlighting its benefits but also identifying the features that need to be added to the framework in order to make it mature for industrial use. AIT and Infineon will continue working together to strengthen the assertion-based monitoring technology and tailor it for its effective application in the V&V of automotive applications.

References

1. Althoff, M., Rajhans, A., Krogh, B.H., Yaldiz, S., Li, X., Pileggi, L.: Formal verification of phase-locked loops using reachability analysis and continuization. In: Proceedings of the International Conference on Computer-Aided Design, pp. 659–666. IEEE Press (2010)
2. Alur, R., Courcoubetis, C., Halbwachs, N., Henzinger, T.A., Ho, P.-H., Nicollin, X., Olivero, A., Sifakis, J., Yovine, S.: The algorithmic analysis of hybrid systems. Theoretical Computer Science 138(1), 3–34 (1995)
3. Annpureddy, Y., Liu, C., Fainekos, G., Sankaranarayanan, S.: S-TaLiRo: A tool for temporal logic falsification for hybrid systems. In: Abdulla, P.A., Leino, K.R.M. (eds.) TACAS 2011. LNCS, vol. 6605, pp. 254–257. Springer, Heidelberg (2011)

4. Bartocci, E., Bortolussi, L., Nenzi, L.: A temporal logic approach to modular design of synthetic biological circuits. In: Gupta, A., Henzinger, T.A. (eds.) CMSB 2013. LNCS, vol. 8130, pp. 164–177. Springer, Heidelberg (2013)
5. Bertrane, J.: Static analysis by abstract interpretation of the quasi-synchronous composition of synchronous programs. In: Cousot, R. (ed.) VMCAI 2005. LNCS, vol. 3385, pp. 97–112. Springer, Heidelberg (2005)
6. Dang, T., Donzé, A., Maler, O.: Verification of analog and mixed-signal circuits using hybrid system techniques. In: Hu, A.J., Martin, A.K. (eds.) FMCAD 2004. LNCS, vol. 3312, pp. 21–36. Springer, Heidelberg (2004)
7. Donzé, A., Fanchon, E., Gattepaille, L.M., Maler, O., Tracqui, P.: Robustness analysis and behavior discrimination in enzymatic reaction networks. PLoS ONE 6(9), e24246 (2011)
8. Donzé, A.: Breach, A toolbox for verification and parameter synthesis of hybrid systems. In: Touili, T., Cook, B., Jackson, P. (eds.) CAV 2010. LNCS, vol. 6174, pp. 167–170. Springer, Heidelberg (2010)
9. Donzé, A., Ferrère, T., Maler, O.: Efficient robust monitoring for STL. In: Sharygina, N., Veith, H. (eds.) CAV 2013. LNCS, vol. 8044, pp. 264–279. Springer, Heidelberg (2013)
10. Donzé, A., Maler, O.: Robust satisfaction of temporal logic over real-valued signals. In: Chatterjee, K., Henzinger, T.A. (eds.) FORMATS 2010. LNCS, vol. 6246, pp. 92–106. Springer, Heidelberg (2010)
11. Donzé, A., Maler, O., Bartocci, E., Nickovic, D., Grosu, R., Smolka, S.: On temporal logic and signal processing. In: Chakraborty, S., Mukund, M. (eds.) ATVA 2012. LNCS, vol. 7561, pp. 92–106. Springer, Heidelberg (2012)
12. Fainekos, G.E., Pappas, G.J.: Robustness of temporal logic specifications for continuous-time signals. Theor. Comput. Sci. 410(42), 4262–4291 (2009)
13. Frehse, G., Le Guernic, C., Donzé, A., Cotton, S., Ray, R., Lebeltel, O., Ripado, R., Girard, A., Dang, T., Maler, O.: SpaceEx: Scalable verification of hybrid systems. In: Gopalakrishnan, G., Qadeer, S. (eds.) CAV 2011. LNCS, vol. 6806, pp. 379–395. Springer, Heidelberg (2011)
14. Frehse, G., Krogh, B.H., Rutenbar, R.A.: Verifying analog oscillator circuits using forward/backward abstraction refinement. In: DATE, pp. 257–262. European Design and Automation Association (2006)
15. Distributed System Interface. DSI3 Bus Standard. DSI Consortium
16. Jones, K.D., Konrad, V., Nickovic, D.: Analog property checkers: a ddr2 case study. Formal Methods in System Design 36(2), 114–130 (2010)
17. Little, S., Walter, D., Jones, K., Myers, C.: Analog/Mixed-signal circuit verification using models generated from simulation traces. In: Namjoshi, K.S., Yoneda, T., Higashino, T., Okamura, Y. (eds.) ATVA 2007. LNCS, vol. 4762, pp. 114–128. Springer, Heidelberg (2007)
18. Maler, O., Manna, Z., Pnueli, A.: From timed to hybrid systems. In: Huizing, C., de Bakker, J.W., Rozenberg, G., de Roever, W.-P. (eds.) REX 1991. LNCS, vol. 600, pp. 447–484. Springer, Heidelberg (1992)
19. Maler, O., Nickovic, D.: Monitoring temporal properties of continuous signals. In: Lakhnech, Y., Yovine, S. (eds.) FORMATS/FTRTFT 2004. LNCS, vol. 3253, pp. 152–166. Springer, Heidelberg (2004)
20. Maler, O., Nickovic, D.: Monitoring properties of analog and mixed-signal circuits. STTT 15(3), 247–268 (2013)

21. Nickovic, D., Maler, O.: AMT: A property-based monitoring tool for analog systems. In: Raskin, J.-F., Thiagarajan, P.S. (eds.) FORMATS 2007. LNCS, vol. 4763, pp. 304–319. Springer, Heidelberg (2007)
22. Pnueli, A.: The temporal logic of programs. In: FOCS, pp. 46–57 (1977)
23. Rizk, A., Batt, G., Fages, F., Soliman, S.: On a continuous degree of satisfaction of temporal logic formulae with applications to systems biology. In: Heiner, M., Uhrmacher, A.M. (eds.) CMSB 2008. LNCS (LNBI), vol. 5307, pp. 251–268. Springer, Heidelberg (2008)
24. Steinhorst, S., Hedrich, L.: Model checking of analog systems using an analog specification language. In: DATE, pp. 324–329. ACM (2008)

Analysis of Real-Time Properties of a Digital Hydraulic Power Management System*

Pontus Boström[1], Petr Alexeev[1], Mikko Heikkilä[2], Mikko Huova[2],
Marina Waldén[1], and Matti Linjama[2]

[1] Åbo Akademi University, Finland
firstname.lastname@abo.fi
[2] Tampere University of Technology, Finland
firstname.lastname@tut.fi

Abstract The paper presents a case study involving a Digital Hydraulics Power Management System (DHPMS). The system is a cyber-physical system, where actions need to be taken with high precision in order to ensure that the system works safely and energy efficiently. Here high precision actions demand very low latency of the control software. The contribution of this paper is an approach to analyse real-time properties of a common type of cyber-physical system. The paper also highlights the need to carefully analyse the effects of timing errors on performance and safety. The timing analysis is based on timed automata models and model-checking in the TIMES tool. Some lessons learned from the case study are also discussed.

1 Introduction

This paper reports on a case study involving a Digital Hydraulic Power Management System (DHPMS), which is a universal flow source for hydraulic systems [12]. Such systems are based on a digital pump-motor technology, where the flow can be shared between several outlets with arbitrary pressure levels. The pumping pistons of the DHPMS are controlled actively by on/off valves. This system represents a common type of cyber-physical systems, where actions need to be taken with high accuracy with respect to a rotation angle of an axle. Other examples of such systems include e.g. fuel injection systems, robots powered by (electric) motors and computer hard drives.

The software of the DHPMS is used to trigger opening and closing of valves at the right moments in time corresponding to the selected flow direction (mode) and position of the rotating shaft (axle). Incorrect valve timing may cause problems such as:

- Dangerous pressure peaks;
- Low efficiency of the system or cavitation;
- Premature wear-out of hydraulic components.

* The work has been partially funded by the EDiHy project (no. 139540 and no. 140003) funded by the Academy of Finland.

F. Lang and F. Flammini (Eds.): FMICS 2014, LNCS 8718, pp. 33–47, 2014.

An initial version of the control software of the DHPMS developed earlier by the authors from IHA, Tampere University of Technology is based on polling, i.e., the occurrence of the moments for triggering of valve is checked periodically. The computational platform used in the system is an embedded single-core CPU. The length of the polling period should be short enough to achieve good precision for triggering of valves. Unfortunately reduction of the length of the polling period is limited by the OS and usually cannot be less than 50-100 μs. Further reduction of the period causes unacceptable high CPU load even for controlling of a single valve. This can lead to deadline misses in valve triggering, which is unsafe for the hydraulics. Hence, there is a need for a better solution. In this paper we propose an alternative architecture for the software of the DHPMS that solves the highlighted limitations. A FPGA or multi-core solution could be utilized to increase computational power of the platform, but due to cost factors and development complexity, a single-core solution is preferable.

The new software architecture presented in the paper is based on interrupts and use of hardware timers for time-triggered tasks. Using this architecture we were able to reduce critical latencies significantly and reduce CPU load by about 5-10 times comparing to the existing architecture. We show that the system works in experiments and verify that it satisfies desired real-time properties. This allows further improvements of the DHPMS, e.g., increasing the number of pumping pistons and independent outlets or adding fault-tolerance mechanisms.

The contribution of this paper is an approach to analyse real-time properties of cyber-physical systems. The paper highlights the need to carefully analyse the effects of timing errors on performance and safety. It describes a method to analyse worst-case response times based on properties of the environment, which also takes into account the constraints found by analysing the impact of latencies on the system. The method is based on using timed automata to model the almost periodic (sporadic) rotation of the electric motor driving the pump. We believe that our approach is useful for other similar systems, where events are triggered based on certain desired positions of a rotating axle.

The rest of the paper is organized as follows. In the next section we present the case study and the proposed software architecture. Section 3 contains a description of tools used for timing analysis, while the following section describes the models used in the analysis of timing. Section 5 contains the results of the analysis. Lessons learned and topics for further research are then discussed in Section 6. In Section 7 we conclude.

2   Case Study

For simplicity, only one pressure outlet of the DHPMS is considered, i.e, a digital pump-motor is studied. The overall hydraulic architecture of the digital pump motor is presented in Fig. 1. Let N_v be the total number of on/off valves in the DHPMS. Each valve should be opened and closed exactly once in one turn of the rotating shaft. Therefore the software of the DHPMS needs to initiate $2N_v$ triggering events within one period. Let e_j denote an event of opening or closing

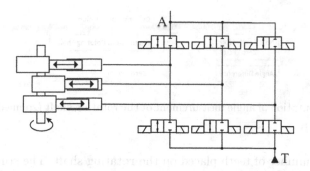

Fig. 1. The hydraulic architecture of a digital pump-motor. The figure shows three pistons connected to a rotating shaft to the left. Each piston is connected via valves to a high pressure line A and a tank line T.

of a valve $j \in [0, 2N_v - 1]$, t_e^j and θ_e^j denote the desired time and angle of the rotating shaft for the event e^j respectively. The angle θ_e^j and all other angles are given relative to a fixed position on the axle. The calculation of θ_e^j depends on factors such as desired hydraulic fluid flow direction (mode), the angular velocity of the shaft ω, the size of the hydraulic chamber and compressibility of the fluid. The details of the calculation of θ_e^j can be found elsewhere [11]. Only ω and t_e^j need to be calculated by the DHPMS, all other parameters can be considered as input data arriving from the rest of the hydraulic system. The angular velocity ω is defined as $\omega = \frac{d\theta}{dt}$, where θ denotes the current angle of the rotating shaft. If ω is constant, the time delay before triggering of the valve t_e^j can be estimated as $t_e^j = \frac{\theta_e^j - \theta}{\omega}$. Hence, estimation of both ω and t_e^j requires measurement of the actual angle of the rotating shaft. This task is solved with an *incremental rotary encoder* presented in Fig. 2, which is commonly used for angular velocity measurement. The measurement requires the following two sensors:

- Zero sensor that produces an impulse when $\theta = 0°$.
- Tooth sensor that outputs an impulse when it meets with one of teeth placed at fixed positions on the rotating shaft.

There is some angle difference between starting point of angle measurement and teeth as shown in Fig. 2. In practice this difference cannot be eliminated due to technological reasons. Therefore impulses from zero sensor and tooth sensor never arrive simultaneously. In the system the shaft is attached to an electric motor, which runs unloaded with $\omega_{max} = 25\pi s^{-1}$ (12.5Hz or 750rpm).

We assume that all teeth are placed absolutely uniformly at the shaft. The discrete character of sensor signals implies that θ can be known precisely only at the moment of arrival of a signal from either zero or tooth sensor. During the rest of the time, θ can be estimated with an existing kinematic models, e.g., model of a rotating shaft with constant angle velocity. We used the following definitions for discretisation:

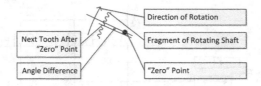

Fig. 2. Implementation of angle measurement of the rotating shaft (zoomed and rotated from Fig. 1)

- N – total number of teeth placed on the rotating shaft. The studied system has 144 teeth;
- i – index of the current tooth met by the tooth sensor, $i \in [0..N-1]$;
- θ_0 – angle difference between positions of the zero sensor and the first tooth presented in Fig. 2;
- t_i – time of arrival of impulse from the tooth sensor at position i.

This allows estimation of θ_i and ω_i at the moment of t_i with (1) and (2).

$$\theta_i = \theta_0 + \frac{2\pi i}{N} \tag{1}$$

$$\hat{\omega}_i = \frac{\theta_i - \theta_{i-1}}{t_i - t_{i-1}} \tag{2}$$

Here θ_i gives the angle at the time t_i, while $\hat{\omega}_i$ gives an estimate of the angular velocity at the same moment. Calculations according to formulas (1) and (2) are used in the proposed software architecture. This requires measuring a time of arrival of impulses from sensors. This time can be acquired from the CPU clock in handlers of interrupts raised by the impulses. Note that we could use more precise estimation of $\hat{\omega}_i$, but as discussed in Section 2.2, time delays caused by the real-time schedule are more important for the resulting precision of the system.

The DHPMS in the case study of the paper has three cylinders and each cylinder has two valves, one for the pressure line and one for the tank line as shown in Fig. 1. Let $\theta_{b,k}$ denote the angle position of the shaft that corresponds to the position with maximum extraction (bottom-dead-centre) of piston of cylinder k. The angle of the shaft is counted from the bottom position of piston of the first cylinder, so that $\theta_{b,1} = \theta_0 = 0°$. Positions of pistons of other cylinders are shifted by 120° with respect to each other, therefore $\theta_{b,2} = 120°$ and $\theta_{b,3} = 240°$. The construction of the DHPMS imposes constraints on opening and closing of all valves as follows:

- The pressure line can be opened if $\theta \in [\theta_{b,k}, \theta_{b,k} + 90°)$ and closed if $\theta \in [\theta_{b,k} + 90°, \theta_{b,k} + 180°)$.
- The tank line can be opened if $\theta \in [\theta_{b,k} + 180°, \theta_{b,k} + 270°)$ and closed if $\theta \in [\theta_{b,k} + 270°, \theta_{b,k} + 360°)$.

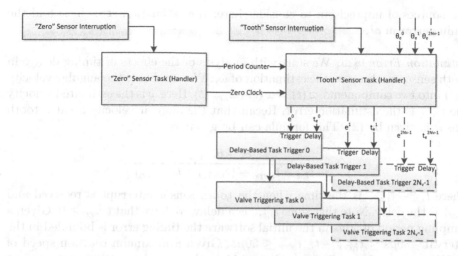

Fig. 3. The proposed architecture of the software of the DHPMS

2.1 Software Architecture

The proposed architecture of the DHPMS software is presented in 3. This architecture is based on interrupt handling and use of timer-triggered (delayed) tasks. There are two main interrupt handlers:

- The zero sensor handler is needed to determine the moment for starting of a new period of rotating shaft. This allows to define reference points of the time t_e^j and to reset tooth index (counter) i.
- The tooth sensor handler increments i, estimates θ_i and $\hat{\omega}_i$ with formulas (1) and (2), and calculates both angles θ_e^j and correspondent time delays t_e^j for each triggering event e^j.

The tooth sensor handler enables delay-based triggering of valve triggering tasks. The task for event e^j is triggered if θ_e^j is expected to be between current and next tooth of the rotating shaft: $\theta_i \le \theta_e^j \wedge \theta_e^j < \theta_{i+1}$.

The proposed software architecture was examined with both simulation and in workbench experiments. The software of the whole DHPMS was designed in Simulink with further automated generation of the real-time software code. This allowed to avoid manual code development and to simulate execution of the same model before experimenting with a real hydraulics of the workbench. The computation part of the workbench was based on a dSpace real-time hardware/software platform.

2.2 Analysis

The aim of the software is to open or close the valves as accurately as possible with respect to a given desired angle θ_e^j. To do this, we first need to analyse how different factors influence the actual opening angle θ_e^j for an event e^j. There are two sources of imprecision to consider here: the estimation error in ω and the timing error in e^j.

Estimation Error in ω. We start with analysis of the effects of timing delays in tooth sensor readings on the estimation of $\hat{\omega}_i$. We can divide the angular velocity $\omega(t)$ into two components, $\omega(t) = \hat{\omega}(t) + \omega_{err}(t)$. Here $\hat{\omega}$ is the estimated velocity and ω_{err} is the estimation error. Recall that the angular velocity $\hat{\omega}_i$ at a tooth sensor is given by (2). This formula can be given as:

$$\hat{\omega}_i = \frac{\theta_i - \theta_{i-1}}{t_{i,a} + t_{i,err} - (t_{i-1,a} + t_{i-1,err})}$$

where $t_{i,a} + t_{i,err}$ is the time when the tooth sensor interrupt is received and $t_{i,err}$ is the delay. Note that since $t_{i,err}$ is a delay, we have that $t_{i,err} \geq 0$. Given a sampling period of $50\mu s$ in the initial software the timing error is bounded in the interval $-50\mu s \leq t_{i,err} - t_{i-1,err} \leq 50\mu s$. Given a maximum rotation speed of 12.5Hz, $\omega_{max} = 25\pi \approx 78.5s^{-1}$. Given 144 teeth, a maximum timing error gives $\hat{\omega} = 72.1s^{-1}$. This means about 8.3% error in the angular velocity estimate.

Note that we have not considered changes in the angular velocity of the shaft. The estimate of the angular velocity $\hat{\omega}$ is accurate only if ω is constant, which is not typically the case. However, due to the short time intervals between tooth interrupts, we can assume the variation in ω between them is negligibly small.

Worst Case Timing of e^j. We can model the position error of valve openings or closings analytically based on the angular velocity and timing error. This gives a model of how imprecision in timing and angular velocity estimates affects the opening and closing position of valves. Let $t^j_{e,ref}$ denote the reference valve opening or closing time and t^j_e the actual opening or closing time of an event e^j. Both times are relative to the time of the last tooth sensor event. We then have that $\theta^j_{e,ref} = \theta_i + \hat{\omega} t^j_{e,ref}$. We have two cases: either $t^j_{e,ref} \leq t^j_e$ or $t^j_{e,ref} > t^j_e$. In the first case we have the position (angle) error θ^j_{err}.

$$\theta^j_{err} = \int_{t^j_{e,ref}}^{t^j_e} \hat{\omega}(t)\, dt + \int_0^{t^j_e} \omega_{err}(t)\, dt \qquad (3)$$

The first term takes into account only the error in time given the estimated angular velocity. Recall we had the maximum angular velocity of $\omega_{max} = 25\pi s^{-1}$. For a maximum timing error $t^j_e - t^j_{e,ref} = 50\mu s$ in the initial system, according to (3) then $\theta^j_{err} = 0.23°$. If the angular velocity is estimated accurately then the second term is small. For a 10% error in the velocity estimate then we get the same position error only at $t^j_e = 500\mu s$. This is close to the time between tooth interrupts, and we will show that this long delays are not possible in Section 5. The second case when $t^j_{e,ref} > t^j_e$ is analogous.

From this analysis one can conclude that a delay in handling valve events gives a larger error than imprecision in the estimation of ω here. Short worst-case response times are hence important for the system to work properly. Note that for system safety, it is more important to minimise response times for opening valves than for closing them.

3   Tools

The actions in the DHPMS are sporadic. Estimation of the worst-case response time with classical real-time scheduling theory [5] for sporadic tasks is safe but usually pessimistic. Therefore we have used the TIMES modelling and analysis tool [1,2] to apply tight bounds on the worst-case response times. The TIMES tool is based on timed automata [4] with tasks. The verification backend is based on the Uppaal [3] model-checking framework for timed automata. This tool is suitable to analyse schedulability on single-core processors. Several scheduling policies, like Rate Monotonic (RM), Earliest Deadline First (EDF), FIFO and fixed priority scheduling (FPS) are supported. It also allows verification of tasks with precedence constraints. The tool can be used to model systems having both sporadic and periodic tasks. The activation of sporadic (controlled) tasks can be described using timed automata.

3.1   The TIMES Modelling Environment

A system in TIMES consists of set of concurrent processes that are described by timed automata. Tasks represent executable code with known properties, such as worst case execution time (WCET). The arrival pattern of tasks can be either periodic or controlled. For each periodic task the following parameters can be provided for the framework: initial offset, period, deadline, WCET and priority (for schedules with fixed priorities). For controlled tasks their arrival pattern is controlled with timed automata similar to the ones in Uppaal.

A timed automaton consists of a set of locations, a set of transitions between locations, a set of clocks, a set of communication channels and a set of (data) variables. Each location has an invariant, describing the possible values of clocks in the location. A transition can have a guard, a communication on a channel and a statement. The guard can state restrictions on both clocks and variable values. The statements can update data variables and reset clocks. The communication on channels is synchronous point-to-point communication. An example of timed automaton is shown in Fig. 4.

As shown in Fig. 4, each location is shown as a rectangle with rounded corners. Locations can be named, e.g., *ZeroActive* is the name of the topmost location. The letter "c" in the top left corner of a location rectangle denotes a committed location. While a non-committed location is active all clocks associated with the automaton progress. All clocks in the system progress at the same rate. Time does not progress in a committed locations, and the system cannot stay in such a state. Tasks can be associated with locations. The task will then arrive before the location is exited. The name of a task is displayed with bold font within the location, e.g., *Zero* and *Tooth* are tasks in locations *ZeroActive* and *ToothActive* respectively. Each location can be associated with an invariant on

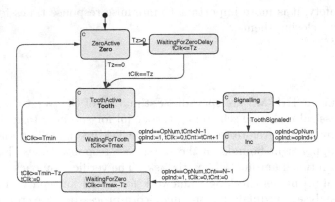

Fig. 4. The timed automaton describing triggering of zero sensor and tooth sensor handling tasks

the clocks of the timed automaton. The invariant of state *WaitingForTooth* is $tClk \leq T_{max}$. If the invariant does not hold and there are no enabled transitions, the automaton deadlocks. Sending on a channel is denoted with an exclamation mark and receiving by a question mark. Here e.g. the transition from location *Signalling* to *Inc*, sends a message on channel *ToothSignalled*. Communication is synchronous, e.g., a message can only be sent if there is a receiver ready to receive the message otherwise the transition is not enabled. Guards, channels and assignments are displayed with a text close to the arrow of the transition.

4   Modelling the DHPMS

We have modelled the handling of interrupts and the triggering of valve tasks in TIMES, to analyse the delays that can occur. The modelled system has the architecture shown in Fig. 3. However, several valve events are handled by the same task. In the model we have the tasks *Tooth, Zero, Valve1Open, Valve2Open* and *Valve1Close, Valve2Close*. The task *Valve1Open* opens the valve on the pressure lines for all cylinders and *Valve2Open* opens the valve on the tank line for all cylinders. The tasks for closing valves are used analogously. This simplification is possible, as we do not make any difference in priorities between tasks for different cylinders. The highest priority is assigned to *Zero*, the second highest priority is assigned to *Tooth*, while all other tasks have lower priorities. Tasks that open valves have higher priority than tasks for closing valves. We are interested in the worst-case response time for the different tasks. All timing properties are measured in a given time unit, which is here $1\mu s$. As this is a single-core system only the Worst-Case Execution Time (WCET) is needed in the schedulability analysis. The WCET for the tooth sensor task was estimated to $20\mu s$, while WCET for zero sensor and valve triggering tasks was estimated to $10\mu s$.

The model in Fig. 4 describes the arrival pattern of the task for handling the Zero sensor and the task for handling the Tooth sensor. We make the simplification that tooth 0 of the first cylinder is at θ_0 of the axle. This makes the accounting of events easier. There are 144 tooth events for every zero event. However, to make the model suitable for model-checking we need to have a model with fewer number of teeth. We shrink the model to only consider a system with 12 teeth ($N = 12$). This means there are 30° between the the teeth. As each cylinder is shifted from each other by 120° and each valve can be opened or closed in a 90° sector, the change of which valve can be opened or closed will also occur every 30°.

Lemma 1. *The worst-case response times will occur after tooth events on a multiple of 30 degrees.*

Proof. 30 is the greatest common divisor of 120 and 90. Hence, the valve tasks that can be released in each 30° sector are fixed. All tasks have time to run between tooth signals. The worst case response time for a task occurs if it is delayed by all tasks released in its sector and all tasks possible released in the preceding sector. Interference from the preceding sector can only occur after a tooth signal on a multiple of 30°. Hence, the worst-case response time of a valve task can only occur after a tooth signal at a multiple of 30°.

The sporadic nature of tasks is modelled using the pattern from [15]. E.g. the system is allowed to stay in a location *WaitingForTooth* until $tClk > T_{max}$ and is enabled to leave the location via a transition after $tClk \geq T_{min}$. Each time the tooth task has run then it possibly enables some valve events in all three cylinders. This is modelled by sending a message on the channel *ToothSignalled* to all cylinders. This is also done utilizing the pattern for synchronizing several processes in [15]. Here we introduce intermediate committed locations, in order to signal many other processes without time progressing in between. The automaton describing each cylinder is then enabled for a given value on *opInd*.

The model in Fig. 5 describes the arrival pattern of tasks for triggering opening and closing of valves for one cylinder. The template is instantiated three times with different parameters for the three cylinders. One cycle in the model describes one revolution of the shaft, where each valve can be opened and closed in a 90° sector. In the figure, the start of a sector i is given by the tooth $tCnt = (tInd + Si) \bmod N$. The valve on the pressure line of the first cylinder can be opened between teeth 0 and 3 (in the interval $[\theta_{b,1}, \theta_{b,1} + 90°)$) and then closed between teeth 3 and 6 (in the interval $[\theta_{b,1} + 90, \theta_{b,1} + 180°)$). The tank line can then be opened between teeth 6 and 9 and closed between 9 and 0. The valves actions for the second cylinder are then shifted 120° and 240° for the third cylinder. Valve tasks are triggered at some time point between tooth events. This is modelled by introducing a non-deterministic delay of a maximum of D_{max} time units before triggering a valve task.

Note that we are interested in the error in θ_{err} estimated with (3) for each valve. This is not modelled here, due to scalability reasons. The desired angle is calculated and the valve tasks scheduled in the task *Tooth*. Hence, if the tooth

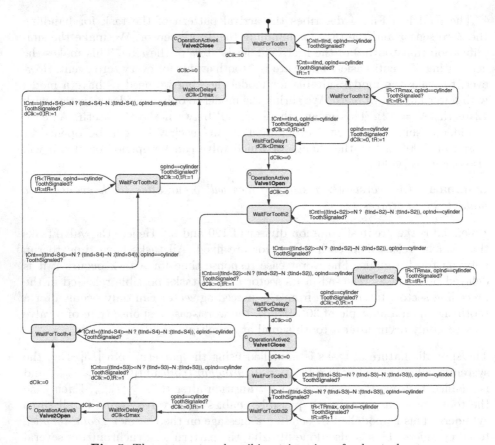

Fig. 5. The automaton describing triggering of valve tasks

task has higher priority than the valve tasks, the worst case response times for the valve tasks can directly be used as the delay for valve. This is the case in the model. Furthermore, as the task *Tooth* actually triggers the valve tasks in the implementation, our model only correctly models the system in this case.

An example schedule of the system is shown in Fig. 6. The schedule shows how all valve tasks are released three times in one rotation of the shaft. Note that for readability, the times between events are shorter than in the real system.

4.1   Extension to Four Cylinders

The DHPMS will perform better with more cylinders. An extension to four cylinders with $\theta_{b,i}$ shifted 90° in each cylinder is straightforward. By the same reasoning as in the proof of Lemma 1, the worst case response time will occur every 90°. The automaton for describing the releases of valve tasks in a cylinder in Fig. 5 can be used directly here, but it is instantiated four times with appropriate

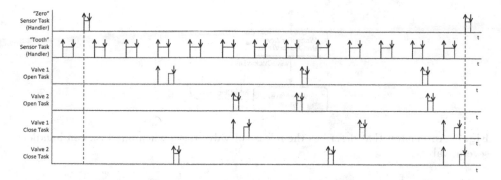

Fig. 6. Example of resulting real-time schedule for three cylinders. Dashed lines denote limits of period of the shaft, up arrows denotes release time, down arrows denote completion time.

parameters. The goal is to extend the DHPMS to many more cylinders (more than 10 cylinders), in order to achieve high performance. As can be seen from the response times for four cylinders in Table 1, the approach does not scale.

4.2   Grouping Several Valve Events into the Same Task

One obvious optimisation for the control software is to have one task to trigger several closely occurring valve events. Instead of having one task for handling each event e_j with times $t + \epsilon_1, \ldots, t + \epsilon_n$, we could have one task that trigger them all at time t. This would create the maximum error of $\max\left(\{\, |\epsilon_i - t_d| \; |i \in [1..n]\,\}\right)$, where t_d is the delay of the triggering task. If one would group events e_j if the difference in ϵ_j is smaller than the worst case execution time of valve triggering tasks of $10\mu s$, then this would clearly be an improvement over scheduling individual tasks.

The timed automaton in Figure 7 describes the release of a task *ValveTask* that handles all valve actions. Here the minimum time interval between task releases is $vTmin = 40\mu s$. E.g., we group n tasks with release times $t + \epsilon_k$ such that $\max(\{\epsilon_k | k \in 1..n\}) \le 40\mu s$. A number greater than the WCET of the task *Tooth* and the task itself is needed for $vTmin$ in this case in order to ensure that the task is not released when it is already running.

5   Results

We analysed the worst case response times of all tasks. Also we checked that the models were deadlock free in order to ensure that the response time analysis is accurate, as deadlocks might hide delays of tasks. The obtained worst case response times for the case of three cylinders are given in Table 1. Here C denotes the (worst-case) computation time, priority is the fixed priority of the task and WCRT is the worst case response time. Due to constraints on the sectors where

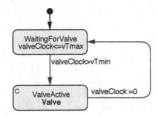

Fig. 7. Automaton that describes the release of valve tasks when one task can handle several valves

Table 1. Worst case response times for tasks in the system with three cylinders to the left and for the system with four cylinders to the right

Task	C (μs)	Priority	WCRT (μs)
Zero	10	8	10
Tooth	20	7	20
Valve1Open	10	6	30
Valve1Close	10	5	50
Valve2Open	10	6	40
Valve2Close	10	5	60

Task	C(μs)	Priority	WCRT(μs)
Zero	10	8	10
Tooth	20	7	20
Valve1Open	10	6	30
Valve1Close	10	5	70
Valve2Open	10	6	40
Valve2Close	10	5	80
Valve3Open	10	6	50
Valve3Close	10	5	90
Valve4Open	10	6	60
Valve4Close	10	5	100

valves can be opened and closed, at most two valve tasks from other cylinders and one task from the same cylinder can delay a task. Given these computation times, the maximum response time is $60\mu s$. This is not better than polling with the period of $50\mu s$. However, the WCRT for the valve opening tasks, which are the most critical, is lower and the processor utilisation is significantly lower, which releases CPU for other computations. The worst case response times for the case of four cylinders is also given in Table 1. In this case the set of valves that can be released are fixed in all 90 degree sectors. This means that a tasks can in the worst case be delayed by four valve tasks left from the previous sector and four tasks from the current sector. Note that all tasks with the same priority also have a fixed priority among themselves in TIMES.

The result of the response time analysis for the case when only one task is used to handle all valve actions is shown in Table 2. The minimum time between task releases is $40\mu s$. If all valve actions handled by a task with release time t_r

Table 2. Worst case response times when only one task is used to handle valve actions

Task	C (μs)	Priority	WCRT (μs)
Zero	10	8	10
Tooth	20	7	20
ValveTask	20	6	40

have times t within the interval $[t_r, t_r + 40]\mu s$ then the maximum delay t_e is $40\mu s$. Hence, this approach can lead to significant reductions in latency especially if there are many events that can occur simultaneously, as in this system.

From a scalability point of view, the main challenge in the analysis is to verify deadlock freedom. TIMES support queries in TCTL like Uppaal and the query "$A[]$ not deadlock" can be used to verify deadlock freedom. However, checking deadlock freedom is very expensive and the models had to be carefully crafted to verify this property. The models of the systems discussed above can now be checked using over approximation in a few seconds. Response time analysis seems to scale much better to larger models.

6   Discussion and Lessons Learned

TIMES is a powerful and easy to use tool for schedulability analysis. However, there are some limitation in TIMES when modelling the type of systems in the paper. A process controlling sporadic tasks cannot synchronise on a channel in a state where a task is also released, as that can result in a deadlock. This is due to how task release is encoded in the verifier. The verifier can also not handle tasks that are scheduled while they are already running, which is probably also due to the encoding. However, in both cases the tool can still calculate WCRT for tasks (which are potentially meaningless due to deadlocks). The TIMES tool cannot be used for multi-processor systems. A framework for schedulability analysis exists for Uppaal that can be used also in this case [9]. This framework could be used here also, but TIMES handles scheduling of tasks automatically, while it would have to be modelled manually following the patterns in the Uppaal schedulability framework. However, when manually modelling the system, we can also workaround the limitation in TIMES mentioned above. SymTA/S [14,10] is a tool for symbolically analysing timing properties of systems that could also be used. However, it is more aimed at analysing component interactions, where the scheduling on individual components is handled using classical real-time scheduling techniques [5]. Real-time scheduling of periodic and semi-periodic tasks on uni-processor systems have been studied extensively [5]. For systems like ours where tasks have complex arrival patterns, the methods are difficult to apply and might yield unnecessarily pessimistic results.

Scalability of the verification is an issue and we have analysed the problem in order to allow simpler models, while still verifying that the properties of interest hold. Obtaining a model that can be efficiently checked and where worst-case response times that are not too pessimistic can be challenging. Here we first analysed how latencies would impact the system, we did not model those effects. Additionally the continuous time dynamics was abstracted so that events can occur non-deterministically at any time within the given boundaries. Then we also decreased the number of teeth while preserving the worst-case behaviour. This makes the model tractable for model checking, although the results can be more pessimistic than necessary. The same style of modelling and verification seems applicable for other similar systems.

Some deadline misses can be tolerated in the system as long as they do not occur too often. Using statistical model checking (SMC) of timed systems [8,7,6] we can statistically analyse the probability of events to occur, which allows handling soft real-time systems where deadlines are allowed to be missed as long as the probability that it occurs is sufficiently small. However, for reliable analysis results, the inputs to the model need to be representative of the real workload of the system. Additionally, e.g., execution times need to be represented by suitable probability distribution. In [7,6] only uniform and exponential distributions are supported, neither provides accurate representations. This could lead to results that are not realistic. In [7] schedulability analysis in this setting using duration probabilistic automata (PDA) [13] is considered. However, PDA only seem to concern acyclic behaviour or periodic systems where the period is fixed. Deadlock freedom, which is also the most computationally heavy property to verify in our model, need to hold always in order for the model to be valid. This suggests that it would still be necessary to ensure that certain properties such as, e.g., deadlock freedom and non-Zenoness hold for sure.

The system in this case study is a hybrid system where the scheduling of tasks is dependent on the physical process. However, the only continuous behaviour in timed automata is the progress of time. We would need to express more complex dynamics to model the system accurately. The model-checking approach in [8,7] only supports priced timed automata. Even in that case most verification problems become undecidable or intractable [8,7,6]. Statistical model checking allows complex continuous dynamics than clocks [16]. However, they analyse systems over finite time intervals and it is not clear how this would be directly used for analysing response times in an accurate way.

7   Conclusion

This paper presented timing analysis for the control software of a Digital Hydraulic Power Management System (DHPMS). We first analysed how different delays affect the performance and safety of the system. Based on this information we modelled the timing of tasks in TIMES, and analysed their worst-case response times. We showed how the functionality of the system can be extended while preserving desirable timing properties.

Timed automata based schedulability analysis and analysis of other real-time properties have been applied in many case studies earlier. The Uppaal website lists case studies from diverse application domains such as communication protocols and robotics applications. However, none of the case studies have considered schedulability analysis of sporadic tasks in cyber-physical systems, where properties of the system need to be considered in the analysis. As computer controlled systems become more prevalent, this is becoming more common. The paper addresses these issues in one important class of systems. We believe that our approach used for the case study can be a good inspiration when solving other similar problems.

References

1. Amnell, T., Fersman, E., Mokrushin, L., Pettersson, P., Yi, W.: TIMES - A tool for modelling and implementation of embedded systems. In: Katoen, J.-P., Stevens, P. (eds.) TACAS 2002. LNCS, vol. 2280, pp. 460–464. Springer, Heidelberg (2002)
2. Amnell, T., Fersman, E., Mokrushin, L., Pettersson, P., Yi, W.: TIMES: a tool for schedulability analysis and code generation of real-time systems. In: Larsen, K.G., Niebert, P. (eds.) FORMATS 2003. LNCS, vol. 2791, pp. 60–72. Springer, Heidelberg (2004)
3. Behrmann, G., David, A., Larsen, K.G.: A tutorial on UPPAAL. In: Bernardo, M., Corradini, F. (eds.) SFM-RT 2004. LNCS, vol. 3185, pp. 200–236. Springer, Heidelberg (2004)
4. Bengtsson, J., Yi, W.: Timed automata: Semantics, algorithms and tools. In: Desel, J., Reisig, W., Rozenberg, G. (eds.) ACPN 2003. LNCS, vol. 3098, pp. 87–124. Springer, Heidelberg (2004)
5. Buttazzo, G.C.: Hard Real-Time Computing Systems. Springer (2011)
6. David, A., Larsen, K.G., Legay, A., Mikučionis, M.: Schedulability of Herschel-Planck revisited using statistical model checking. In: Margaria, T., Steffen, B. (eds.) ISoLA 2012, Part II. LNCS, vol. 7610, pp. 293–307. Springer, Heidelberg (2012)
7. David, A., Larsen, K.G., Legay, A., Mikučionis, M., Poulsen, D.B., van Vliet, J., Wang, Z.: Statistical model checking for networks of priced timed automata. In: Fahrenberg, U., Tripakis, S. (eds.) FORMATS 2011. LNCS, vol. 6919, pp. 80–96. Springer, Heidelberg (2011)
8. David, A., Larsen, K.G., Legay, A., Mikučionis, M., Wang, Z.: Time for statistical model checking of real-time systems. In: Gopalakrishnan, G., Qadeer, S. (eds.) CAV 2011. LNCS, vol. 6806, pp. 349–355. Springer, Heidelberg (2011)
9. David, A., Illum, J., Larsen, K.G., Skou, A.: Model-based framework for schedulability analysis using UPPAAL 4.1. In: Nicolescu, G., Mosterman, P.J. (eds.) Model-Based Design for Embedded Systems. CRC Press (2010)
10. Hamann, A., Henia, R., Racu, R., Jersak, M., Richter, K., Ernst, R.: SymTA/S - symbolic timing analysis for systems. In: WIP Proc. Euromicro Conference on Real-Time Systems 2004 (ECRTS 2004). IEEE Computer Society (2004)
11. Heikkilä, M., Tammisto, J., Huova, M., Huhtala, K., Linjama, M.: Experimental evaluation of a piston-type digital pump-motor-transformer with two independent outlets. In: Bath/ASME Symposium on Fluid Power and Motion Control (2010)
12. Linjama, M., Huhtala, K.: Digital pump-motor with independent outlets. In: The 11th Scandinavian International Conference on Fluid Power, SICFP 2009 (2009)
13. Maler, O., Larsen, K.G., Krogh, B.H.: On zone-based analysis of duration probabilistic automata. In: INFINITY 2010. EPTCS, vol. 39 (2010)
14. Richter, K., Racu, R., Ernst, R.: Scheduling analysis integration for heterogeneous multiprocessor SoC. In: Proceedings of the 24th International Real-Time Systems Symposium (RTSS 2003). IEEE Computer Society (2003)
15. The DARTS team: Modelling tips for TIMES (2004), http://www.it.uu.se/edu/course/homepage/realtid/H04/ass3/modellingtips.pdf
16. Zuliani, P., Platzer, A., Clarke, E.M.: Bayesian statistical model checking with application to Stateflow/Simulink verification. Formal Methods in System Design 43 (2013)

Formal Analysis of a Fault-Tolerant Routing Algorithm for a Network-on-Chip*

Zhen Zhang[1], Wendelin Serwe[2], Jian Wu[3],
Tomohiro Yoneda[4], Hao Zheng[5], and Chris Myers[1]

[1] Dept. of Elec. & Comp. Eng., Univ. of Utah, Salt Lake City, UT, USA
zhen.zhang@utah.edu, myers@ece.utah.edu,
[2] INRIA & Univ. of Grenoble, LIG, Grenoble, France
Wendelin.Serwe@inria.fr
[3] Marvell Technology Group Ltd., Santa Clara, CA, USA
jianwu@marvell.com
[4] National Institute of Informatics, Tokyo, Japan
yoneda@nii.ac.jp
[5] Dept. of Comp. Sci. and Eng., Univ. of S. Florida, Tampa, FL, USA
zheng@cse.usf.edu

Abstract. A fault-tolerant routing algorithm in Network-on-Chip architectures provides adaptivity for on-chip communications. Adding fault-tolerance adaptivity to a routing algorithm increases its design complexity and makes it prone to deadlock and other problems if improperly implemented. Formal verification techniques are needed to check the correctness of the design. This paper performs formal analysis on an extension of the link-fault tolerant Network-on-Chip architecture introduced by Wu *et al* that supports multiflit wormhole routing. This paper describes several lessons learned during the process of constructing a formal model of this routing architecture. Finally, this paper presents how the deadlock freedom and tolerance to a single-link fault is verified for a two-by-two mesh version of this routing architecture.

Keywords: LNT, process algebra, fault-tolerant routing, Network-on-Chip, formal verification.

1 Introduction

Cyber-physical systems (CPS) nowadays have ubiquitous applications in many safety critical areas such as avionics, traffic control, robust medical devices, etc. As an example, the automotive industry makes active use of CPS: modern vehicles can have up to 80 *electronic control units* (ECUs), which control and operate everything from the engine and breaks to door locks and electric windows. Currently, each ECU is statically tied to its specific sensors and actuators. This

---

* This work is supported by the National Science Foundation under Grants CNS-0930510 and CNS-0930225. Part of this work was performed during a visit of the first author at INRIA Grenoble Rhône-Alpes.

F. Lang and F. Flammini (Eds.): FMICS 2014, LNCS 8718, pp. 48–62, 2014.

means that processing power between different ECUs cannot be shared, which degrades the performance of the chip due to imbalanced workload on each ECU. More importantly, this structure is susceptible to faults in that if an ECU fails, it causes a malfunction in the corresponding sensor and/or actuator. With the advances in semiconductor technology, it is now possible to have multiple cores on a single chip which communicate using a *Network-on-Chip* (NoC) paradigm. A NoC approach allows flexible mapping between ECUs and sensors/actuators, which makes it possible for ECUs to share processing power and tolerate faults by having spare units. Some example fault-tolerant NoC architectures currently being developed include those described in [1] and [2].

This paper presents the verification of a NoC architecture that supports the link-fault tolerant routing algorithm [3] extended to a multiflit wormhole routing setting. In particular, deadlock freedom and single link-fault tolerance are formally verified using the CADP toolbox. This paper also presents several key lessons that are learned during the evolution of the model of the NoC architecture. Finally, this paper describes several remaining challenges to the verification of this and similar systems.

This paper is organized as follows. Section 2 surveys related work. Section 3 describes the extended NoC architecture and routing algorithm. Section 4 presents several case studies of the process that led to the final NoC model. Section 5 presents verification results for deadlock freedom and the single-link fault tolerance property. Section 6 discusses the insights obtained from using model checking in the design of the NoC behavior and some future research directions.

2 Related Work

A fully functional NoC system has to be fault-tolerant and free of deadlocks. A variety of approaches have been proposed for fault-tolerant NoC routing. One approach is to use a reconfigurable routing table in which pre-computed routes are stored to avoid faulty links [4]. This method, however, is not adaptive, so it can only avoid permanent faults. An example of a dynamic faulty link detection mechanism is described in [5], but this method only avoids deadlocks rather than ensuring they cannot occur. The Glass/Ni fault-tolerant routing algorithm, on the other hand, guarantees deadlock freedom by disallowing certain turns in the network [6], so that communication cycles cannot occur. This algorithm, however, uses the *node-fault model*, where a fault in an incoming link is interpreted as the complete node failing. Not only does this mean losing the ability to route to an otherwise functional node, but if the node does not actually stop operating, it can potentially introduce deadlock in the network. A modified version proposed in [7] achieves one link-fault tolerance by introducing a mechanism to forward link fault locations to a neighboring routing node allowing for a route selection that avoids the faulty link. This fault forwarding method though can still result in a deadlock at the edges of the mesh network, so in these cases, it must revert to the node-fault model. An improvement proposed in [3] is capable of handling link faults anywhere in the network. Potential deadlock is avoided by allowing a router to drop a packet to prevent the occurrence of a communication cycle, and it is an extended version of this algorithm that this paper attempts to formally verify.

Concerning NoC verification, [8] proposed GeNoC (*Generic Network-on-Chip*), a formal NoC model implemented in the ACL2 theorem prover. Its extension in [9] verifies a non-minimal adaptive routing algorithm. These techniques, however, require user assistance on writing proof obligations. On the other hand, to facilitate the use of model checking techniques, automatic translations are developed from the asynchronous hardware description language CHP (*Communicating Hardware Processes*) to networks of automata [10] and to the process algebraic language LOTOS [11,12]. The latter approach is applied to verify two complex asynchronous designs, one of which is an input controller of an asynchronous NoC [13] that implements a deadlock-free routing algorithm based on the odd-even turn model [14]. However, this NoC does not handle failures.

3   Network-on-Chip Architecture and Routing Algorithm

Figure 1 shows an architecture for a two-by-two mesh composed of four corner routing nodes, all with a similar structure. This architecture implements an extended version of the routing algorithm described in [3]. The original algorithm assumed single-flit packets and that each node could route only a single packet at a time, while this modified architecture allows each node to potentially have multiple multi-flit packets in flight at a time. For example, node 00 may be routing a packet from node 01 to node 10, while simultaneously routing a packet from node 10 to node 01. These extensions though complicate the algorithm, so it is desirable to be able to prove that this extended architecture is still deadlock-free and continues to achieve fault tolerance to a single-link failure, which is the goal of this paper.

The routing algorithm works as follows. Each node communicates with its corresponding *processing element* (PE), and when a PE xy wishes to send a packet to another node $x'y'$, it injects that packet into the network via its router (r_PE_xy). Based upon the intended destination of the packet, the router determines a direction to forward the packet. To guarantee deadlock freedom, the routing algorithm disallows certain turns in the network. Namely, a packet that is moving north in the network is not allowed to turn to the west, and a packet moving east in the network is not allowed to turn to the south. Hence, in order to avoid "illegal turns", each router sends packets south and west, as needed, before sending them north and east. After selecting a direction, the router attempts to communicate with the arbiter in charge of the desired link. At this point, one of three things can occur. First, the link may be busy, and the router must wait its turn to use the link. Second, the link may be faulty, and the router is instructed to find an alternate route. Finally, the link may be free, and the arbiter may non-deterministically select to communicate with this router over any other routers that may be trying to obtain this link. The arbiter then forwards the packet one flit at a time to the succeeding router (i.e., the router the

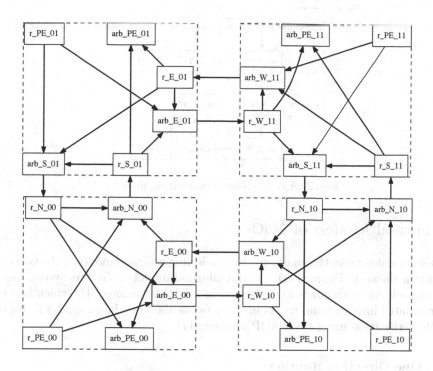

Fig. 1. Architecture of the four routing nodes in a two-by-two mesh

output of the arbiter is connected to), which then executes the same algorithm. Once a packet reaches its destination $x'y'$, the packet is absorbed by the arbiter connected to its PE (arb_PE_$x'y'$).

Assuming there is at most one link-fault, an alternate route always exists, but it may require an illegal turn. For example, assume that node 10 wishes to send a packet to node 01. In this case, a west then north route is desired, but let us assume that arb_W_10 reports a fault on its link to r_E_00. In this case, r_PE_10 must communicate with arb_N_10 instead. Once the packet reaches r_S_11, this router must make the illegal turn and route the packet west through arb_W_11. However, arb_W_11 may be busy routing a packet from node 11 to node 00. This packet though may be blocked because arb_S_01 is busy routing a packet from node 01 to node 10. Similarly, this packet may be blocked because arb_E_00 is busy routing a packet from node 00 to node 11. Finally, this packet is blocked because arb_N_10 is busy due to the packet from node 10 to node 01. Therefore, there is a communication cycle causing a deadlock. In this case, arb_W_11 sends a *negative acknowledgement* to r_S_11 to tell this router to drop the incoming packet, which removes the communication cycle and the potential for deadlock.

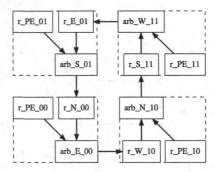

Fig. 2. A counterclockwise routing model

4   Formal Models of NoCs

This section describes the challenges in developing a formal model of the two-by-two mesh shown in Figure 1. Our initial informal model of the two-by-two mesh uses asynchronous channels implemented in a VHDL package [15] which had to be translated into a formal model in the process algebraic language LNT [16] to enable verification using the CADP toolbox [17].

4.1   One Direction Routing

The first model developed and verified is the simple one direction routing model shown in Figure 2. It is advantageous to construct a model with one complete cycle consisting of partial components from each node, since the model is simple enough for testing asynchronous communications between any two components. Also, the resultant state space is manageable, which enables the efficient checking for deadlock and packet loss without having to abstract the model. Since this model only has the counterclockwise routing direction, there are no alternative routes available, avoiding the need to model route forwarding computation in each router. Having only the counterclockwise routing direction also forces the north-to-west illegal turn to occur on the northeast node. In this first model, each PE router only generates one single-flit packet destined to the node in its diagonal direction. For example, the PE connected to node 01 sends a packet to node 10. After emitting one packet, each PE router becomes inactive. No components absorb any packets and it is assumed that no link fault exists in the network. The expected behavior is that the packet from node 10 to node 01 gets dropped due to deadlock avoidance, and the remaining three packets keep cycling through nodes in the network forever, and no deadlock exists.

The arbiter, arb_W_11, on the northeast corner is responsible for detecting the potential deadlock by checking availability of its succeeding router r_E_01. To avoid deadlock, it informs its preceding router r_S_11 to drop the packet when router r_E_01 is not available. The LNT descriptions of arb_W_11 and r_S_11 are shown in Figure 3. The three gates "PEr_Wa_11", "Sr_Wa_11", and "n11_n01" (between square brackets) of the "`arbiter_nack`" process correspond to the three links (r_PE_11 → arb_W_11), (r_S_11 → arb_W_11), and (arb_W_11 → r_E_01) in Figure 2, respectively. The contents of each flit is represented by a natural number, and the arbiter process uses the variable "`one_flit`" of type `Nat` to store the flit travelling through it. The behavior of this process is a non-terminating loop with two nested choices (`select`[1]). The outer choice decides whether the arbiter is ready to receive a packet[2]: if its preceding router r_E_01 confirms its availability by synchronizing on the "`n11_n01`" gate with the arbiter, then it starts to receive the packet; or the arbiter issues a negative acknowledgement "`Sr_Wa_11(false)`" to r_S_11 indicating that its output is blocked by another packet. If both options are available, one is chosen nondeterministically. When the arbiter is ready to receive a packet, it nondeterministically chooses between the PE router, r_PE_11, and the south router, r_S_01. Since taking a packet from r_S_01 effectively makes an illegal turn, this arbiter first sends an acknowledgement "`Sr_Wa_11(true)`" to r_S_11. The router r_S_11 (represented by the LNT process "`router_drop_pkt`") checks the received status of arb_W_11, and a false status leads to a packet drop: r_S_11 is ready to receive the next packet which overwrites the current one that needs to be dropped.

The generated state space for the counterclockwise routing model contains terminal states, indicating deadlocks in the model. Analysis of the diagnostic sequences of transitions reveals that all four packets can get dropped by the r_S_11 router, which is an unexpected behavior. According to the routing protocol, r_S_11 should drop a packet when arb_W_11 returns a false status, and the arbiter should do so only when its output, r_E_01, is busy serving other packets. As mentioned previously, it is possible that one packet is dropped for this reason, but the remaining three should stay in the network as the network is not congested anymore. Analysis of the outer choice on the arbiter's specification shows that there always exists a path where it sends a negative acknowledgement to tell the router r_S_11 to drop its packet. The nondeterministic choice enables sending both, a true and a false acknowledgement to the router, and as long as the gate rendezvous for sending a false acknowledgement is possible, it gets a chance to occur. Therefore, arb_W_11 can always send a false acknowledgment regardless of potential deadlocks.

One possible improvement is to have a prioritized choice: the option of sending a positive acknowledgement is always the preferred one. Ideally, availability of the preferred positive option should prevent the option of sending the negative acknowledgement. To implement this priority would require that the "`select`" operator could probe the possibility of a gate rendezvous on the preferred choice. Implementing the priority choice in LNT requires additional processes [18], which may lead to state explosion. Even if it can be verified, the packet leakage path

---

[1] The LNT construction "`select A [] B end select`" is a non-deterministic choice between A and B.

[2] In LNT, comments start with "`--`" and extend to the end of the line.

```
process arbiter_nack [PEr_Wa_11 , Sr_Wa_11 , n11_n01 : any] is
var one_flit : Nat in loop
  select
      n11_n01; -- Router r_E_01 is ready to accept packet
      select
          PEr_Wa_11(?one_flit); -- Receive packet from r_PE_11
          n11_n01(one_flit) -- Send packet to r_E_01
      [] Sr_Wa_11(true); -- Send positive ack. to r_S_11
          Sr_Wa_11(?one_flit); -- Receive packet from r_S_11
          n11_n01(one_flit) -- Send packet to r_E_01
      end select
  [] Sr_Wa_11(false) -- Send negative ack. to r_S_11
  end select
end loop end var end process

process router_drop_pkt [n10_n11 , Sr_Wa_11 : any] is
var status : Bool, one_flit : Nat in loop
  n10_n11; -- Ready to accept packet from arb_N_10
  n10_n11(?one_flit); -- Receive packet from arb_N_10
  Sr_Wa_11(?status); -- Request arb_W_11's status
  -- Send packet to arb_W_11 ONLY on TRUE status
  if status then Sr_Wa_11(one_flit) end if
end loop end var end process
```

Fig. 3. The LNT processes for arb_W_11 and r_S_11

may not get removed due to the timing of when the probes are executed. Another option is to prune the unwanted execution paths from the generated state space using the priority operator in EXP.OPEN/SVL [19]. However, since the state space of the entire model is generated compositionally using branching bisimulation, which is not a congruence for the priority operator [20].

4.2   Removing Arbiter's Buffering Ability

After all components on the two-by-two mesh are built and connected as shown in Figure 1, the state space generation quickly becomes a challenge due to the state explosion problem. After only 10 of the 24 LNT processes are composed during verification, the state space already has reached 679,284 states, and then adding one more process leads to a state space in excess of 3 million states. Clearly, this state space growth is unmanageable. As mentioned previously, this new architecture allows multiple packets to go through one node at the same time, and the interleavings of gate rendezvous among different routing nodes is a major contributor to the exponential increase of state count. Moreover, in most cases, gate rendezvous happens with offers, which are the concrete data packets. Since there are four different packet data values, each representing the destination location information as described in Section 4.1, interleaving of gate rendezvous is a significant source of this state explosion.

One improvement investigated to alleviate the state explosion problem is to reduce gate rendezvous between arbiters and routers in each node. This means that on the LNT model level, routers and arbiters in one node are merged into one process, removing the need for gate rendezvous between them. The resultant northwest routing node has the following behavior. It nondeterministically selects one among the following three operations: generating its own packet, receiving a packet from the northeast node, or receiving one from the southeast node. Once the node has a packet, based on the packet's destination, it attempts to send out the packet to the first choice of route, and tries alternative routes if the first one is not available. All the other three nodes have a similar behavior.

This simplification of the routing nodes indeed helps to reduce the state space. However, it removes the buffering capacity in each arbiter, and consequently causes deadlocks. A typical deadlock scenario is that initially the four routing nodes generate their own packets at the same time, between the northwest and southwest nodes, and between the northeast and southeast nodes, the packet in one node tries to go the other. No nodes can make progress in this situation. To send a packet, a node needs its neighboring node to communicate on the same gate. It is required because the node's own arbiter, which connects to the neighboring node, cannot store anything, and only the neighboring node has the storing capacity. However, if the neighboring node is trying to do the same thing to this node in the mean time, neither one can succeed in delivering packets because both are waiting for the other to accept their own packets. Removal of the arbiter's buffering ability also renders it impossible for one node to have multiple packets passing through it at the same time.

From this experiment, we conclude that arbiters in the network need storage capacity in order to relay a packet, freeing up their corresponding routing nodes to handle other communications. It also implies that simplifications on the node architecture without modifying the routing algorithm can introduce deadlocks in the system behavior. Therefore, removing interleavings of gate rendezvous on the LNT models is unsuccessful.

4.3   Finding Proper Data Abstractions

As mentioned earlier, another major contributor to the large state space is the existence of many data values in the model. The previous experiments do not consider data abstraction of a packet's content, because a router requires the packet's destination to decide its next forwarding direction: it is impossible for a router to perform routing computation without the destination information, although this information is only needed by the routers. In theory, all except the PE routers can receive packets destined to all node locations in a mesh. Since our link-fault tolerant routing algorithm allows illegal turns (c.f. Section 3), it means that a router may potentially direct packets to all of its viable directions. The idea is, thus, to abstract the routing algorithm using nondeterministic choice. In other words, after receiving a packet, a router nondeterministically selects either its own node, indicating that the packet has reached its destination, or one of the (many) forwarding directions for the packet, without the need to examine the packet's destination. This abstraction enables us to eliminate a packet's destination information. Moreover, since every packet is provided with a preferred route and at least one alternative route for the purpose of fault-tolerance, the router's model should provide, in the non-deterministic choice, the possibility for every forwarding direction as the preferred route for a randomly destined packet, assuming the router does not perform an illegal turn. From the analysis of the routing algorithm, it is obvious that making an illegal turn is never a preferred choice for a route unless all forwarding routes of a router are illegal. For example, the north-to-east legal turn is always a preferred choice over the illegal north-to-south turn at router r_S_01 in Figure 1.

In a two-by-two mesh, there are three types of routers. First, there are routers r_S_11 and r_W_11 that can make two illegal turns (RI2). Next, there are routers r_W_10 and r_S_01 which can make one illegal turn (RI1). Finally, there are all other routers which never make illegal turns. Since routers in each of the three categories have the same abstract behavior, the rest of this section uses representatives, i.e., RI2, RI1, and RI0, to refer to routers in each category.

The next question is whether packets need to be modeled at all. Our first experiment shows that the model without packet information exhibits the packet leakage problem. As discussed in Section 4.1, the reason is an intrinsic feature of RI2, which has a nondeterministic choice where to send a packet: either to RI2 itself or to an illegal forwarding direction. Without any packet information, taking an illegal forwarding direction is always possible, regardless of deadlock avoidance, effectively creating a leakage path. To fix this problem, an abstraction of a packet has to be included such that an illegal turn in RI2 is not always possible. An important feature of the routing pattern is that a packet takes an illegal turn only after its attempt to the preferred route fails due to a failure on the route. In other words, when a packet makes an illegal turn, it must have been diverted at least once before. Thus, a packet can be modeled as a single-bit Boolean variable, indicating whether the packet has been diverted or not. In the LNT process "router_two_illegal" modeling RI2 shown in Figure 4, only a diverted packet can take illegal turns. This restriction rules out the possibility of dropping packets which have not taken an alternate route yet.

Comparing the precise routing decision computation with the nondeterministic choice in the abstract model, a packet destined to one forwarding direction in the concrete model has the possibility to be forwarded to any routing direction in the abstract model. Therefore the abstraction is conservative in that it preserves all transition sequences in its corresponding concrete model. One subtle difference introduced in the abstract model is the notion of a diverted packet, which does not exist in the concrete model. It is, however, a feature that implicitly exists in the concrete model's routing behavior.

There are also three categories of arbiters, corresponding to the router categories. Figure 5 shows the arbiter corresponding to RI2. It selects between its PE router and two routers, flits from which may just have made an illegal turn. For each option the arbiter takes, after receiving a flit, it keeps rejecting requests from RI2 routers until it delivers the flit. When receiving rejections on

```
process router_two_illegal [input, out_arb_PE, out1_illegal,
                            out2_illegal, drop : any] is
var one_flit, arb_status : Bool in loop
  input(?one_flit);
  select
     out_arb_PE(one_flit)
  []
     if one_flit == true then -- packet is diverted
        -- first try out1_illegal, then out2_illegal
        out1_illegal(?arb_status);
        if arb_status == true then
          out1_illegal(one_flit)
        else
          out2_illegal(?arb_status);
          if arb_status == true then
            out2_illegal(one_flit)
          else
            drop -- both illegal turns impossible
          end if
        end if
     end if
  end select
end loop end var end process
```

Fig. 4. The LNT process for the RI2 router

all its illegal forwarding routes, RI2 drops the packet to prevent potential deadlock. The complete LNT specification for the two-by-two NoC is available at
http://www.async.ece.utah.edu/~zhangz/research/lnt_modeling/.

5   Verification Results

Verification of the NoC model consists of two steps: generating the *Labeled Transition System* (LTS) from the LNT specification, and then analyzing the LTS
to verify properties of interest. The LTS for each investigated model is generated compositionally, i.e., by generating and minimizing the LTSs for each process separately before combining them to the LTS of the complete system. For
the combination steps, our verification applied smart reduction [21], which uses
heuristics to find an optimal ordering of composition and minimization steps to
keep the intermediate state spaces manageable. Minimization is performed with
respect to divergence-sensitive branching bisimulation equivalence [22]. Thus,
any livelocks found are preserved during composition, whereas using standard
branching bisimulation would collapse every livelock into a deadlock. In other
words, divergence-sensitive branching bisimulation can reveal true deadlock scenarios. The three properties of interest are: (1) the link-fault tolerant routing
algorithm is free of deadlocks; (2) given at most one failure link, it is never the

```
process arbiter_nack_2 [in_PE_router, in1_illegal,
                         in2_illegal, arb_out : any] is
var one_flit : Bool in loop
  select
      in_PE_router(true); in_PE_router(?one_flit);
      loop L1 in select
         arb_out(one_flit); break L1
      [] in1_illegal(false)
      [] in2_illegal(false)
      end select end loop -- L1
  []
      in1_illegal(true); in1_illegal(?one_flit);
      loop L2 in select
         arb_out(one_flit); break L2
      [] in1_illegal(false)
      [] in2_illegal(false)
      end select end loop -- L2
  []
      in2_illegal(true); in2_illegal(?one_flit);
      loop L3 in select
         arb_out(one_flit); break L3
      [] in1_illegal(false)
      [] in2_illegal(false)
      end select end loop -- L3
  end select
end loop end var end process
```

Fig. 5. The LNT process for the arbiter corresponding to RI2

case that a router is unable to route a packet; and (3) given at most one failure link, a packet never gets dropped when there is only one packet in the network.

Table 1 shows the LTS information for nine two-by-two mesh models: the first row represents a mesh without any link failure, and the remaining eight rows each represent the same NoC with one failure link whose location is shown in the first column. The columns under "Intermediate LTS" show the number of states and transitions of the largest intermediate LTS, and the columns under "Final LTS" show those of the final LTS. The two columns under "Performance" display the maximal amount of allocated virtual memory (in MB) and the total execution time (in s) to generate each LTS. A desktop machine with a CPU of eight 3.60 GHz cores and 16GB of available RAM is used to generate the results listed in this table. One core is used at any time for the parallel composition and state minimization steps. The last column shows the labels of each LTS.

The final LTS for each model is generated by hiding all gates that represent the links between the routers and the arbiters. The only two visible types of gates are the route-failure gates and the packet-drop gates. Rendezvous on the former happen when a router has exhausted all options to forward a packet; rendezvous on the latter occur when a router drops a packet. These gates are left visible to

Table 1. LTS's for two-by-two NoCs

Failure Link	Interm. LTS Size States	Transitions	Final LTS St.	Tr.	Performance RAM	Time	Labels
none	6,295,773	83,386,208	1	1	32,945	5,976	i
01 → 00	20,340	193,726	41	224	111	83	i, drop_Sr_11, drop_Wr_11
01 → 11	1,369,068	18,221,153	1	3	4,039	499	i, drop_Sr_01, drop_Sr_11
00 → 10	6,560	50,688	21	104	111	80	i, drop_Sr_11, drop_Wr_11
00 → 01	6,560	50,688	21	104	111	81	i, drop_Wr_11, drop_Sr_11
10 → 11	122,724	1,269,981	1	3	111	89	i, drop_Wr_10, drop_Wr_11
10 → 00	20,340	193,726	41	224	111	80	i, drop_Wr_11, drop_Sr_11
11 → 01	367,200	4,172,652	1	3	111	106	i, drop_Sr_11, drop_Wr_11
11 → 10	367,200	4,172,652	1	3	111	105	i, drop_Sr_11, drop_Wr_11

facilitate the verification tasks (2) and (3) described above. To model a single link fault in LNT, a working arbiter process is replaced by an arbiter that sends false status to all its connected input routers.

The final LTSs show similarities between the following pairs: (01 → 00, 10 → 00),(01 → 11, 10 → 11), (00 → 10, 00 → 01), (11 → 01, 11 → 10). All visible labels on these LTSs are packet-drop labels. Based on the three types of the router introduced previously, renaming these labels to "drop-at-RI2", and "drop-at-RI1" produces bisimilarity between the two LTSs in each pair.

Since deadlock freedom is a global property and is not always possible to be inferred from local LTS states, generating the global LTS is necessary. A system has a deadlock if its LTS contains a state/transition sequence that starts from the initial state and ends in a terminal state, i.e., a state without outgoing transitions. Deadlock detection then becomes a search for such states in the LTS. Using the CADP toolbox, it is found that no such sequence exists in any NoC's LTS in Table 1. Since the entries in this table cover all possible one-link fault configurations, we can conclude that the link-fault tolerant algorithm is free of deadlock for a two-by-two mesh.

To prove that a router is always able to route a packet, it is necessary to verify that no route-failure gate rendezvous occurs. Since these gates are not hidden during parallel composition, it is straightforward to check their existence in each LTS. Table 1 shows that no transitions are labeled with route-failure labels, which proves verification task (2).

The transition labels in Table 1 show that with one failure link in the network, packets may be dropped, namely when the attempt to make an illegal turn potentially could cause a deadlock. Therefore, in a highly congested network, dropping packets is likely to happen. On the other hand, the routing algorithm should not drop any packets if making an illegal turn is safe. One simplification for checking this property is to have only one node generate only one packet, and verify that no packet-drop labels exist on each model's LTS. For each link failure location shown in Table 1, the packet can be generated in any of the four nodes.

Therefore, this property is thoroughly checked in all 36 possible models. No drop-packet label is found in all LTS's, which proves that no packet is dropped when there is only one packet in the network.

6 Discussion

The construction and refinement of the two-by-two NoC model taught us several valuable lessons. The counterclockwise routing example reveals a packet leakage path in the arbiters that instructs their preceding routers to drop the packet. This leakage stems from the arbiter's specification, in that each arbiter must check its succeeding router's availability before it can receive a packet from another router. For example, arb_W_11 must check with r_E_01 before it receives a packet from either r_PE_11 or r_S_11. Otherwise, if the arbiter does not receive its succeeding router's acknowledgement, it sends a "drop" signal to its preceding router. This option is modeled simply as the arbiter sending back the "drop" signal, which opens the path for packet leakage. The second lesson is that it is necessary for an arbiter to have a buffering capacity for the proposed routing architecture because an arbiter does not need to guarantee the availability of its succeeding router before it receives a packet. It is this idea that leads us to redesign the arbiters, such as the one shown in Figure 5. Without formal analysis, it would have been very challenging to discover the diagnostic information that shows these flaws in our arbiter design.

The state explosion problem encountered during the evolutions of our NoC models inspired us to come up with an adequate data abstraction. This process provided us with a deeper understanding of the routing algorithm. The resultant changes on the router and arbiter models show interesting symmetries that we thought did not exist before. Previous attempts to find symmetries between two nodes did not succeed due to the mismatch in terms of illegal turns made in different nodes. With the data abstraction, routers can be categorized into RI0, RI1, and RI2, as described previously, and each category corresponds to one type of arbiter, as well. The relative positions and connections between these routers and arbiters in Figure 1 show strong symmetries between the clockwise and counterclockwise cycles. Experiences gained in this process may help us to develop heuristics to automate the search for symmetries in the LNT model description so that the model checking effort can be reduced by focussing on representatives from each symmetry group. Efficient state reduction techniques can potentially allow us to perform model checking on larger-scale networks.

With the data abstraction presented in this paper, our results verify deadlock freedom and one-link-fault tolerance of the proposed routing algorithm, demonstrating its robustness. As for its efficiency, our results prove that a packet never gets dropped when it is the only one in the network. Our preliminary experiments show that even when one node generates only two packets, it is possible that the first packet occupies the output link of the second, which attempts to make an illegal turn and gets dropped due to deadlock avoidance. Therefore, it is a challenging task to justify the performance of the routing algorithm in terms of packet drop rate due to deadlock avoidance in the current setting. Since it is directly related to the link failure probability, performance evaluation requires annotations of link failure probability in the model and stochastic model checking techniques are needed to provide a quantitative measure of its performance. Another challenge is that with the current data abstraction, proving delivery of every packet is difficult, since it is possible that some, if not all, packets produced get continuously dropped in the network. A simple solution would be to allocate a unique identifier to each packet and check them on both the production and absorption ends, but the resultant state space is likely to become unmanageable. A more suitable data abstraction scheme and more advanced state reduction techniques, such as on-the-fly model checking [23], are needed to meet this challenge.

References

1. Vivet, P., Lattard, D., Clermidy, F., Beigne, E., Bernard, C., Durand, Y., Durupt, J., Varreau, D.: Faust, an asynchronous network-on-chip based architecture for telecom applications. In: Proc. 2007 Design, Automation and Test in Europe, DATE 2007 (2007)
2. Hoskote, Y., Vangal, S., Singh, A., Borkar, N., Borkar, S.: A 5-ghz mesh interconnect for a teraflops processor. IEEE Micro 27(5), 51–61 (2007)
3. Wu, J., Zhang, Z., Myers, C.: A fault-tolerant routing algorithm for a network-on-chip using a link fault model. Virtual Worldwide Forum for PhD Researchers in Electronic Design Automation (2011)
4. Fick, D., DeOrio, A., Chen, G., Bertacco, V., Sylvester, D., Blaauw, D.: A Highly Resilient Routing Algorithm for Fault-tolerant NoCs. In: Proceedings of the Conference on Design, Automation and Test in Europe, pp. 21–26. European Design and Automation Association (2009)
5. Hosseini, A., Ragheb, T., Massoud, Y.: A fault-aware dynamic routing algorithm for on-chip networks. In: ISCAS, pp. 2653–2656. IEEE (2008)
6. Glass, C.J., Ni, L.M.: Fault-tolerant wormhole routing in meshes. In: FTCS, pp. 240–249. IEEE Computer Society (1993)
7. Imai, M., Yoneda, T.: Improving dependability and performance of fully asynchronous on-chip networks. In: Proceedings of the 2011 17th IEEE International Symposium on Asynchronous Circuits and Systems, ASYNC 2011, pp. 65–76. IEEE Computer Society (2011)
8. Borrione, D., Helmy, A., Pierre, L., Schmaltz, J.: A formal approach to the verification of networks on chip. EURASIP J. Embedded Syst. 2009, 2:1–2:14 (2009)
9. Helmy, A., Pierre, L., Jantsch, A.: Theorem proving techniques for the formal verification of NoC communications with non-minimal adaptive routing. In: DDECS, pp. 221–224. IEEE (2010)
10. Borrione, D., Boubekeur, M., Mounier, L., Renaudin, M., Siriani, A.: Validation of asynchronous circuit specifications using IF/CADP. In: Glesner, M., Reis, R., Indrusiak, L., Mooney, V., Eveking, H. (eds.) VLSI-SOC: From Systems to Chips. IFIP, vol. 200, pp. 85–100. Springer, Boston (2006)
11. Salaün, G., Serwe, W.: Translating Hardware Process Algebras into Standard Process Algebras: Illustration with CHP and LOTOS. Technical Report RR-5666, INRIA (September 2005)

12. Salaün, G., Serwe, W., Thonnart, Y., Vivet, P.: Formal verification of CHP specifications with CADP illustration on an asynchronous Network-on-Chip. In: 13th IEEE International Symposium on Asynchronous Circuits and Systems, ASYNC 2007, pp. 73–82 (March 2007)
13. Beigné, E., Clermidy, F., Vivet, P., Clouard, A., Renaudin, M.: An Asynchronous NOC Architecture Providing Low Latency Service and Its Multi-Level Design Framework. In: ASYNC, pp. 54–63. IEEE Computer Society (2005)
14. Chiu, G.M.: The odd-even turn model for adaptive routing. IEEE Trans. Parallel Distrib. Syst. 11(7), 729–738 (2000)
15. Myers, C.J.: Asynchronous circuit design. Wiley (2001)
16. Champelovier, D., Clerc, X., Garavel, H., Guerte, Y., McKinty, C., Powazny, V., Lang, F., Serwe, W., Smeding, G.: Reference manual of the LNT to LOTOS translator (version 6.0). INRIA/VASY/CONVECS (June 2014)
17. Garavel, H., Lang, F., Mateescu, R., Serwe, W.: CADP 2011: a toolbox for the construction and analysis of distributed processes. STTT 15(2), 89–107 (2013)
18. Garavel, H., Salaün, G., Serwe, W.: On the Semantics of Communicating Hardware Processes and their Translation into LOTOS for the Verification of Asynchronous Circuits with CADP. Science of Computer Programming (2009)
19. Garavel, H., Lang, F.: SVL: a Scripting Language for Compositional Verification. In: Proceedings of the 21st IFIP WG 6.1 International Conference on Formal Techniques for Networked and Distributed Systems, FORTE 2001, pp. 377–392. Kluwer Academic Publishers (August 2001); Full version available as INRIA Research Report RR-4223
20. Gazda, M., Fokkink, W.: Congruence from the operator's point of view: Compositionality requirements on process semantics. In: SOS. EPTCS, vol. 32, pp. 15–25 (2010)
21. Crouzen, P., Lang, F.: Smart Reduction. In: Giannakopoulou, D., Orejas, F. (eds.) FASE 2011. LNCS, vol. 6603, pp. 111–126. Springer, Heidelberg (2011)
22. van Glabbeek, R.J., Luttik, B., Trcka, N.: Branching bisimilarity with explicit divergence. Fundam. Inform. 93(4), 371–392 (2009)
23. Mateescu, R., Thivolle, D.: A model checking language for concurrent value-passing systems. In: Cuellar, J., Sere, K. (eds.) FM 2008. LNCS, vol. 5014, pp. 148–164. Springer, Heidelberg (2008)

Formal Specification and Verification
of TCP Extended with the Window Scale Option

Lars Lockefeer, David M. Williams, and Wan J. Fokkink

VU University Amsterdam, The Netherlands
info@larslockefeer.nl,
{d.m.williams,w.j.fokkink}@vu.nl

Abstract. We formally verify that TCP satisfies its requirements when extended with the Window Scale Option. With the aid of our μCRL specification and the ltsmin toolset, we verified that our specification of unidirectional TCP extended with the Window Scale Option does not deadlock, and that its external behaviour is branching bisimilar to a FIFO queue for a significantly large instance. Finally, we recommend a rewording of the specification regarding how a zero window is probed, ensuring deadlocks do not arise as a result of misinterpretation.

1 Introduction

The Transmission Control Protocol (TCP) plays an important role in the internet, providing reliable transport of messages through a possibly faulty medium to many of its applications. The original protocol (RFC 793 [17]), specified in natural language, required improvement to clarify various ambiguities and identify and address several issues resulting in the publication of a supplemental specification (RFC 1122 [8]), which also refers to numerous other documents.

Our primary contribution is the formal verification of TCP extended with the Window Scale Option, addressing the lack of consideration paid to this option in earlier verification efforts. We take care to extract our formal specification directly from the original specifications of TCP and the Window Scale Option, i.e., RFCs 793, 1122 and 1323. This work was initially triggered by a concern of Dr. Barry M. Cook, CTO at 4Links Limited, regarding the Window Scale Option proposed in RFC 1323 [14]. Specifically, he was worried that the window size being reportable only in units of 2^n bytes may conflict with a requirement that the receive buffer space available should not change downward.

We adopt the process algebra μCRL as our formal specification language. Based on ACP, μCRL is enriched with the algebraic specification of abstract data types. We found μCRL's treatment of data as a first class citizen essential for specifying TCP, and were encouraged by its previous success in verifying the Sliding Window Protocol [1, 2]. We utilise the μCRL toolset and ltsmin [7] to explicitly generate the statespace and perform the automated verification.

Section 2 relates our verification effort to those that precede it. Section 3 aims to bridge the gap between the RFCs and our μCRL specification. The structure

F. Lang and F. Flammini (Eds.): FMICS 2014, LNCS 8718, pp. 63–77, 2014.

Table 1. Comparison of earlier verifications of TCP

Authors	RFC 793	RFC 1122	RFC 1323	Other extensions	Conn management	Data transfer	Message Loss	Duplication	Reordering	Message direction	Conn incarnations	Window Scale
Murphy & Shankar [16]	✓				✓		✓	✓	✓	⇔	n	
Smith [21, 22], Smith & Ramakrishnan [20]	✓			✓	✓	✓	✓	✓	✓	⇒	n	
Schieferdecker [19]	✓	✓		✓	✓					⇔	2	
Billington & Han [4, 11–13]	✓	✓			✓	✓	✓			⇔	1	
Bishop et al. [5], Ridge et al. [18]	✓	✓	✓	✓	✓	✓	✓	✓	✓	⇔	n	
Our verification	✓	✓	✓			✓	✓	✓	✓	⇒	1	✓

of Section 3 mirrors the structure of the μCRL process, which is illustrated more prominently in Figures 1 and 2. We describe our verification approach in Section 4 and conclude that the Window Scale Option does not adversely impact TCP. However, using μCRL we identified deadlocks that may arise due to the ambiguous formulation of how to probe zero windows in RFC 793. Finally, we give a recommendation how this RFC could be reformulated to avoid such misinterpretations.

2   Related Work

Our formal verification of TCP shall address the lack of consideration paid to the Window Scale option in earlier verification efforts. Several publications aim to formally specify and verify the correctness of TCP; Table 1 shows an overview. Murphy & Shankar [16] specified a protocol with a similar service specification to TCP as defined in RFC 793. By a method of step-wise refinement, a protocol specification is defined while maintaining several correctness properties. The need for a three-way handshake and strictly increasing incarnation numbers becomes apparent with the introduction of each fault in the medium, explicitly showing why these facilities are present in TCP. Similarly, by means of a refinement mapping, Smith [21, 22] has shown that the protocol specification satisfies the specification of the user-visible behaviour. Selective acknowledgements were added in [20]. Schieferdecker [19] shows that there is an error in TCP's handling of the ABORT call. After stating a possible solution, a LOTOS specification of TCP is given and several μ-calculus properties verified using CADP. Bishop et al. [5] considered whether execution traces generated from real-world implementations of TCP, were accepted by a protocol specification of TCP in Higher Order Logic (HOL), which includes PAWS, the window scale option and congestion control algorithms. Of the test traces generated, the specification accepted 91.7%.

   Billington & Han have studied TCP extensively considering both RFC 793 and RFC 1122 using Coloured Petri Nets. A concise overview of their TCP service specification is given in [4] and includes connection establishment, normal data transfer, urgent data transfer, graceful connection release and abortion of connections. In [11], they give a model of the connection management service, which is further refined in [12]. This revised specification is used as a basis for a verification of connection management [13] considering a model without retransmissions and a model with retransmissions. As a result of their verification efforts, Billington & Han find several issues within connection management. For example, a deadlock may occur when one entity opens the connection passively and, after receiving and acknowledging a connection request, immediately closes the connection again. However, the work by Billington & Han on data transfer has not yet led to a verification.

As the Sliding Window Protocol (SWP) underlies TCP (see Section 3) we also compare our verification to those of SWP. We, like Bezem & Groote [3] and Badban *et al.* [1], use μCRL for our specification. Bezem & Groote and Badban *et al.* consider bidirectional communication across a medium that can lose but not duplicate nor reorder messages. Our verification considers a medium that can lose, duplicate and reorder messages, but does so only in a unidirectional setting. Whereas we, like Bezem & Groote, consider a finite window size (namely 2^2), Badban *et al.* performed the verification on an arbitrarily large window. Madelaine & Vergamini [15] modelled and verified SWP using LOTOS and AUTO. They, like us, consider the unidirectional case across a medium that can lose, duplicate and reorder messages. Finally, Chkliaev et al. [9] specify an amended version of SWP, in which the sender and receiver need not synchronise on the sequence number initially.

3 Specification

In this section we present the overall structure of our μCRL specification of TCP, which includes the core functionality specified in RFCs 793, 1122 and 1323, extended to include the window scale option. It is the aim of this section to relate the RFCs to the μCRL specification[1], assisting the reader in bridging the gap between the two. Although our μCRL specification incorporates Connection Teardown we omit discussion of this procedure for brevity. For an overview of the most prominent formal verification techniques for communication protocols using μCRL, the reader is referred to [10].

TCP receives data from some application and packages this into segments to be handed to the network layer. The TCP instance of the receiver receives segments from the network layer and should ensure the data is delivered to the receiver's application in the same order as it was sent. The purpose of a segment is twofold: (i) a segment may contain zero or more octets of data that the sender's application wishes to relay to an application at the receiver; and, (ii) a segment communicates control information between the two entities.

---

[1] The complete μCRL specification can be found in the Master's thesis entitled *Formal Specification and Verification of TCP Extended with the Window Scale Option* by L. Lockefeer, VU University Amsterdam, 2013, available at http://www.cs.vu.nl/~wanf/theses/lockefeer.pdf

TCP begins by establishing a connection with both entities reaching agreement on the configuration to use for the connection that is stored in their Transmission Control Block (TCB). This data includes the initial sequence number that the entity will use for outgoing data (ISS), the size of the send window for the entity (SND.WND), indicating the maximum number of octets that it may send at once, and the size of the receive window for the entity (RCV.WND), indicating the maximum number of octets that it is prepared to accept at once. We shall take as the initial state of our model, the ESTABLISHED state. We encourage readers unfamiliar with the TCP specifications to refer to Page 23 of RFC 793 and the amendments thereof on Page 86 of RFC 1122, which provides an illustration of all possible states of TCP. Such states include the CLOSE_WAIT, FIN_WAIT_1 and FIN_WAIT_2 states discussed in Section 3.1.

TCP uses the Sliding Window Protocol (SWP) for its data transfer. Both sender and receiver maintain a window of n sequence numbers, ranging from 0 to $n-1$, that they are allowed to send or receive, respectively. The sender may send as many octets as the size of its window before it has to wait for an acknowledgement from the receiver. Once the receiver sends an acknowledgement for m octets, its window *slides* forward m sequence numbers. Likewise, the sender's window *slides* m sequence numbers if this acknowledgement arrives. To function correctly over mediums that may lose data, the maximum size of the window is $\frac{n}{2}$ [23]. In the implementation of SWP underlying TCP, octets may be acknowledged before they are forwarded to the application layer (AL) and therefore still occupy a position in the receive buffer. In this case, the receiving entity reduces the window size by returning an acknowledgement segment, ensuring the sending entity does not send new data that will overflow its buffer. Once the octets are forwarded to the application layer, it may reopen the window.

The receiver may adjust the size of the sender's window at any time, through the value of SEG.WND set in acknowledgement segments. As the size of this field is limited to 16 bits, TCP can send at most 2^{16} octets into the medium before having to wait for an acknowledgement and, if the medium can hold octets, unnecessary delay will be incurred. To resolve this, RFC 1323 [14] proposes the Window Scale Option. If implemented, the send and receive windows are maintained as 32-bit numbers in the TCB of the sender and receiver, which is also extended to include variables SND.WND.SCALE and RCV.WND.SCALE. Whenever an entity receives an acknowledgement, it left-shifts the value of SEG.WND by the value of SND.WND.SCALE before it updates its send window. Likewise, whenever an entity sends an acknowledgement it sets the window field of the outgoing segment to the size of its receive window, right-shifted by the scale factor RCV.WND.SCALE.

We do not validate Connection Establishment, firstly because it has been well studied in the literature as discussed in Section 2 and, secondly, RFC 1323 adds no functionality to connection establishment that we expect to refute earlier verification efforts concerning this phase. We instead specify data transfer, taking care to include the core TCP functionality as well as any peripheral functionality that is potentially influenced by the Window Scale Option, in which two TCP instances (*TCP1* and *TCP2*) communicate data over a possibly faulty medium.

In this section we shall focus most of our attention on the process modelling the TCP instance as this was the primary exercise in modelling TCP. Although our μCRL specification also incorporates Connection Teardown we have omitted discussion of this procedure for brevity. In any case, in order to keep the verification tractable, the actions included to model Connection Teardown are encapsulated before instantiating the statespace in Section 4. Likewise, although we specify a generic TCP process that executes the responsibilities of the sending and receiving instances, when we come to compose our model of unidirectional TCP, including processes modelling the Application and Network layers, some actions must be encapsulated in TCP1 and TCP2 to instantiate them as the sending and receiving entities, respectively.

3.1   The TCP Instance

To avoid discussing abstract notions such as connections (at the TCP level) and sessions (at the application level) that are rather detached from their contexts of sending and receiving entities in a network, we will take the point of view that we have modelled a TCP instance which only has one connection with one remote entity. This TCP instance maintains the state of the connection and the TCB. To manage its window, the sender maintains the variables SND.UNA, SND.NXT and SND.WND in the TCB. SND.UNA holds the sequence number of the first segment in the sequence number space that was sent, for which an acknowledgement has not yet been received. SND.NXT holds the sequence number of the next segment that the sender will send. Finally, SND.WND holds the number of octets that TCP may send at most before it should wait for an acknowledgement.

Some ambiguity surrounds the specification of the sequence number, as both octets and segments are assigned one. In principle, TCP numbers each octet with a unique sequence number, modulo the size of the sequence number space. A segment inherits its sequence number from the first octet it contains. However, a segment containing no octets still requires a sequence number. Here, it is still numbered with the sequence number maintained in SND.NXT, but SND.NXT is not updated. Henceforth, we adopt the convention of denoting SND.NXT as SND_NXT in μCRL, and likewise for other variables/states of the RFCs.

AL Calls SEND. The first call discussed in [17], SEND, may only be issued if the connection is in the ESTABLISHED or CLOSE_WAIT state. As long as there remains capacity in the send buffer, the TCP instance accepts SEND calls from the application layer via the tcp_rcv_SND event, adding its octets to the buffer.

Octets in Send Buffer? If the connection is in the ESTABLISHED or CLOSE_WAIT state and TCP is allowed to send one or more octets, a segment containing the eligible to be sent octets is passed to the network layer by issuing the call tcp_call_SND. This segment is labelled with the next sequence number to be used as maintained in SND_NXT. After the sequence number, the acknowledgement number and advertised window are included, followed by the number of

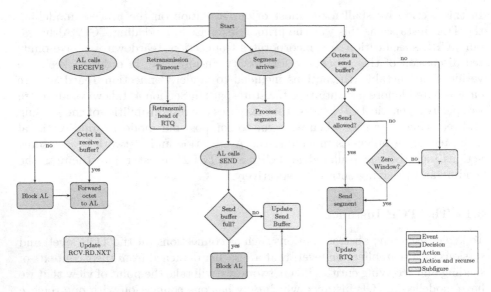

Fig. 1. Abstract overview of our specification of TCP Data Transfer

octets included in the segment and the values of the `ACK` and `FIN` flag. The actual
number of octets that TCP can send at a certain time is calculated by taking the
difference m between `SND.UNA` and `SND.NXT`. If $m <$ `SND.WND`, TCP may package
any number of octets $n \leq m$ into a segment and send it into the medium. Note
that the receive window size relayed in the segment is calculated by applying
the scale factor `RCV.WND.SCALE` to the actual receive window size. Subsequently,
the octets included in the segment are removed from the send buffer and the
segment is added to the retransmission queue (rtq). Finally, `SND_NXT` is updated
to reflect the next sequence number to be used.

In our model, the `ACK` flag will always be set to false in segments carrying
data octets and therefore, the value of the acknowledgement field in the segment
will not be processed by the receiver of the segment. The specification dictates
that the `ACK` flag is always set to true and that the latest acknowledgement
information is always included in each data segment. However, this would greatly
complicate the processing of incoming segments in our model and would only be
of use in case of a bidirectional connection, that we do not consider to limit the
size of our state space. In a unidirectional setting, the sender's value of `RCV_NXT`
will always be the same since it never receives data. Likewise, the receiver's
values of `SND_NXT` and `SND_UNA` will remain constant since it never sends data.
Hence, at all times during the execution of the protocol, if we have a sender
A and a receiver B that have agreed on initial sequence number x, it will hold
that $A_{\texttt{RCV\_NXT}} = B_{\texttt{SND\_NXT}} \land B_{\texttt{SND\_NXT}} = B_{\texttt{SND\_UNA}} = x$. Acknowledgement
processing will not take place since $\neg(B_{\texttt{SND\_UNA}} < A_{\texttt{RCV\_NXT}})$.

More can be said about the octets that are eligible to be sent. If it holds that
`SND_UNA` $\leq$ `SND_NXT` $<$ (`SND_UNA` + `SND_WND`), then the sender is allowed to send

$x = (\text{SND\_UNA} + \text{SND\_WND}) - \text{SND\_NXT}$ octets. To this end, we specified a function *can_send* that returns x if the length of the buffer is greater than x, or the length of the buffer otherwise. No octets may be sent if $\neg(\text{SND\_UNA} \leq \text{SND\_NXT} < (\text{SND\_UNA} + \text{SND\_WND}))$. From a modelling perspective, this solves an ambiguity in [17], namely that TCP may send octets *at its own will*.

A TCP instance must regularly transmit something to the remote entity if the variable SND_WND is set to 0 to prevent a potential deadlock. If the send window is 0 and the retransmission queue is empty, but octets are available in the send buffer, the sender will send a segment containing one octet. This segment is taken from the send buffer, put on the retransmission queue and the variable SND_NXT is updated. Note that this is the only major difference between our model and the behaviour specified in RFC 793; we delay further explanation and justification of this important revision until Section 4.

AL Calls RECEIVE. The second call from the application layer that the TCP instance must process is RECEIVE [17]. By issuing a `tcp_rcv_RECEIVE` call, parameterised with the octet pointed at by RCV_RD_NXT maintained in the TCB, that octet is offered to the application layer. The octet is removed from the receive buffer and RCV_RD_NXT is incremented. The call may only be issued if the connection is in an ESTABLISHED, FIN_WAIT_1, FIN_WAIT_2 or CLOSE_WAIT state, if $(\text{RCV\_NXT} - \text{RCV\_RD\_NXT}) \bmod n > 0$ and if the octet with sequence number RCV_RD_NXT is available in the receive buffer. The variable RCV_RD_NXT is not mentioned in [17]. Instead, the size of the receive window, stored as RCV_WND in the TCB, is updated every time the receive buffer is manipulated. However, page 74 strictly requires the total of RCV_WND and RCV_NXT not to be reduced. It is unclear whether the total may not be reduced when an incoming segment is processed, or not at all. Either way, we believe that it relates to the requirement that the right edge of the window should never be moved to the left. To simplify the implementation but ensure this requirement we maintain RCV_WND at its initial value, and introduce the variable RCV_RD_NXT that is always the sequence number of the next octet to be forwarded to the application layer. At all times it holds that $\text{RCV\_NXT} \leq \text{RCV\_RD\_NXT} \leq (\text{RCV\_NXT} + \text{RCV\_WND})$.

Segment Arrives. A segment received from the network layer is deemed acceptable in the following situations [17]:

1. If the segment does not contain data octets:
    (a) If RCV.WND=0, it is required that SEG.SEQ=RCV.NXT
    (b) If RCV.WND>0, it is required that RCV.NXT≤SEG.SEQ<RCV.NXT+RCV.WND
2. If the segment does contain data octets
    (a) If RCV.WND=0, the segment is not acceptable.
    (b) If RCV.WND>0, it is required that
        – Either RCV.NXT≤SEG.SEQ<RCV.NXT+RCV.WND
        – Or: RCV.NXT≤SEG.SEQ+SEG.LEN−1<RCV.NXT+RCV.WND

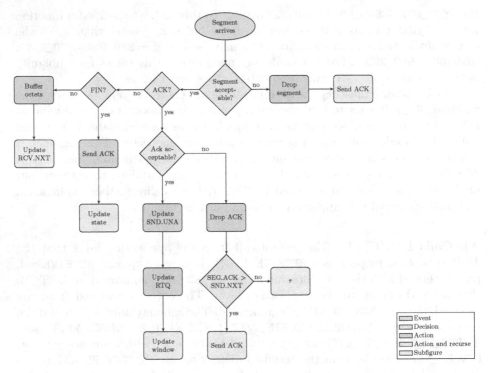

Fig. 2. Abstract overview of our specification of TCP Segment Processing

RFC 793 states that segments arriving out of order may be dropped by the receiver or suggests, to improve performance, that these segments are held in a special buffer to be processed regularly as soon as their turn arrives. In our model an unacceptable segment is dropped and an acknowledgement is sent to the sender containing the current value of `RCV.NXT`; from a modelling point of view, it makes no significant difference whether the segment is later taken from a special buffer or it is received again. Otherwise, segments continue to be processed in order of their sequence numbers. An acknowledgement is constructed including the sequence number of the octet that the TCP instance expects to receive next, the acknowledgement number and the advertised window. The `ACK`-flag of the acknowledgement segment is set to `T` while the `FIN`-flag is set to `F`.

We already stated that, in our model, a segment that carries data always has the `ACK` flag set to false. Additionally, we specify `FIN` segments to not contain acknowledgement information or data. We distinguish between segments carrying data, carrying acknowledgement information and carrying `FIN` information; we determine the type of a segment using functions *is_ack* and *fin_flag_set*.

If the incoming segment m is an acknowledgement, the TCP instance first checks that it is acceptable. This is done by verifying whether the acknowledgement number extracted from the segment is strictly between `SND_UNA` and `SND_NXT`, or indeed equal to `SND_NXT`. If so, `SND_WND` is updated to be the size of the window contained in the segment, multiplied by the scale factor, SND_WND_SCALE. Moreover, SND_UNA is updated and segments containing octets with a sequence number of at most i are removed from the retransmission queue, where i is strictly between SND_UNA and the acknowledgement number extracted from the segment, or equal to SND_UNA. Note that, in [14] the scale factor is defined as n, resulting in integer division/multiplication by 2^n via bit shifting, whereas we maintain the scale factor as 2^n and apply scaling using division and multiplication. Where a scale factor of 1 is stated in [14], we write $2 = 2^1$.

Finally, if the acknowledgement is not acceptable it is dropped and the TCP instance remains in the same state. The official specification states that in response to an unacceptable acknowledgement an acknowledgement must be sent back if SEG.ACK > SND.NXT. In a unidirectional setting, such a situation will never occur so we exclude such behaviour from our model.

If the incoming segment is acceptable, for which (SEG_SEQ=RCV_NXT), and for which both *is_ack* and *fin_flag_set* return false, it is processed as a data segment. Its octets are added to the receive buffer and RCV_NXT is updated to reflect the next sequence number that the receiver expects to receive. Furthermore, the RCV_ACK_QUEUED flag in the TCB, which indicates that an acknowledgement should be sent, is set to true. This sets the SWP implementation of TCP apart, as an acknowledgement is sent while the octets may not yet be forwarded to the application layer and therefore occupy a position in the receive buffer. Therefore, the size of the window that is reported back represents the available capacity in the receive buffer if less than the difference between RCV.NXT and the size of the receive window that was originally agreed upon.

In [8], it states: *"a host [...] can increase efficiency [...] by sending fewer than one ACK (acknowledgement) segment per data segment received"*. We include this behaviour by setting a flag that an acknowledgement should be sent. We then enable the TCP instance to send an acknowledgement whenever the RCV_ACK_QUEUED flag in the TCB is set to true. To prevent sending an acknowledgement multiple times, this flag is then set to false again.

Retransmission Timeout. For each segment the TCP instance puts on the retransmission queue, it starts a timer. When a timer expires, its segment must be retransmitted. To avoid modelling time explicitly, we allow a TCP instance to retransmit the first element on the retransmission queue at its own convenience.

3.2   The Complete System

We obtain the complete system by putting two TCP instances in parallel with additional processes modeling the Application and Network Layers. The application layer continuously offers octets to the TCP instance by issuing the call al_call_SEND. Receiving data is modelled by having the application layer call al_call_RECEIVE for an arbitrary octet. Finally, we specify a network layer that may duplicate, reorder and lose data. General action names are renamed into action names specific for each component. We assume the variables to be set as a result of the connection establishment procedure including the scale factor that each of the TCP instances will apply to their outgoing segments.

When instantiating processes for unidirectional TCP, we encapsulated (i.e., blocked) both `AL2_call_SEND` and `TCP2_rcv_SEND` to prevent AL2 from issuing the `SEND` call. Similarly, `AL1_call_RECEIVE` and `TCP1_rcv_RECEIVE` were encapsulated to prevent AL1 from issuing the `RECEIVE` call. The approach to exclude connection termination from our model is similar: by encapsulating actions `AL1_call_CLOSE`, `AL2_call_CLOSE`, `TCP1_rcv_CLOSE` and `TCP2_rcv_CLOSE`, we ensured that they will not be called in our model. Taken together, these modifications ensured that we were able to obtain a non-terminating model $TCP_{\rightarrow}$ of the data-transfer phase for a unidirectional TCP connection from our specification.

We also had to prevent deadlocks and undesired behaviour as a result of the reuse of sequence numbers. Whilst the introduction of PAWS [14] helps alleviate this problem when networks get faster (by increasing the size of the sequence number space) no protection is proposed other than to assume a limit on the time a segment can reside in the medium, namely the Maximum Segment Lifetime (MSL). Strictly speaking, this means that TCP cycles through all of its sequence numbers, waits until all segments have been acknowledged and all duplicates have drained from the network and starts a new run. The only reason that in practice there is no actual waiting period, is that data transfer speeds are guaranteed to be so 'slow' that it takes more than the MSL to send out octets with sequence numbers $i + 1 \ldots (i + (n - 1)) \bmod n$ after an octet with sequence number i is sent. Likewise, we ensure our specification does not get overly complex due to the addition of timing restrictions, by limiting our verification to one run of sequence numbers. We may still start anywhere in the sequence number space, since all calculations are defined modulo the size of this space.

However, the following problem remains. Assume a sequence number space ranging from $m \ldots n$. The receiving TCP instance will still accept an octet with sequence number m after receiving the octet with sequence number n. Hence, if such an octet is still in the medium as the result of duplication or retransmission, it will be accepted by the receiving TCP instance upon receipt and subsequently delivered to the application layer. Given that the assumption on the MSL holds, such behaviour cannot occur in a real-world situation. To model this we ensure that the global variable maintaining the total number of sequence numbers is greater than the number of octets, as the sequence number space is guaranteed to be larger than the number of octets sent and the problem will not occur.

4   Verification

Our verification focused on two aspects of our model: (i) we verified that its state space is deadlock free, and (ii) we compared the external behaviour of our model, defined in terms of the `SEND` and `RECEIVE` calls issued by the application layers, to the external behaviour of a FIFO queue. One can consider the `SEND` call of TCP as putting something into a queue and `RECEIVE` as taking something from it: the sender puts data elements into the transport medium and the

Table 2. Statistics of the state space generation for our model

Octets Sent	Window Size	Window Scale	Medium Capacity	Levels	States	Transitions	Exploration Time
4	2	1	2	36	881.043	3.910.863	21 sec
			3	40	11.490.716	53.137.488	104 sec
			4	44	91.821.900	434.372.541	7.5 min
8	2	1	2	54	16.126.380	76.356.475	3 min
			3	58	823.501.590	4.031.264.559	49 min
	4	2	2	49	98.697.902	473.332.511	15 min
			3	56	3.505.654.685	Buffer Overflow	3 hrs, 40 min
16	4	2	2	77	3.255.174.492	3.444.088.224	4 hrs, 40 min

receiver takes them all out of this medium in precisely the same order. We first specified a behavioural specification B, then we generated an LTS from both B and $TCP_{\rightarrow}$. All actions in $TCP_{\rightarrow}$, other than SEND and RECEIVE, were defined as internal behaviour. We minimised the LTS of $TCP_{\rightarrow}$ and verified it was branching bisimilar to the LTS of B: $TCP_{\rightarrow} \Leftrightarrow_B B$. Note that a fairness assumption is enforced by the minimisation algorithm; τ-loops from which an 'exit' is possible were eliminated from our minimised state space. Such τ-loops arise from segments that are continuously dropped by the network layer or a sequence of repeated retransmissions, behaviour that we can safely abstract from.

For both $TCP_{\rightarrow}$ and B, we generated a state space using the distributed state space generation tool `lps2lts-dist` of the ltsmin toolset [7]. By using the `--deadlock` option, absence of deadlocks could be checked during state space generation. In addition, we used the `--cache` option to speed up state space generation. State space generation was run on the DAS-4 cluster, more specifically on 8 nodes equipped with an Intel Sandy Bridge E5-2620 processor clocked at 2.0 GHz, 64 gigabytes of memory and a K20m Kepler GPU with 6 gigabytes of on-board memory. At each node, we utilised only 1 core to prevent the process from running out of memory. Table 2 shows some benchmarks of the state space generation for $TCP_{\rightarrow}$ for several different parameterisations. Subsequently, the state space of $TCP_{\rightarrow}$ was minimised with the `lts-reduce-dist` tool of the `ltsmin` toolset, which uses the distributed minimisation algorithm as described in [6]. Finally, the `ltsmin-compare` was used to verify that $TCP_{\rightarrow} \Leftrightarrow_B B$.

As illustrated in Table 2, the capacity of the medium significantly impacts the size of the state space. We settled for a medium capacity of two segments. Since one segment may contain at most as many segments as the size of the window, a medium capacity of 2 means that a TCP instance can send at most two windows of data segments into the medium before it must 'wait' for the medium to either lose or deliver a segment. For the window scaling to be non-trivial, the size of the window should be at least 2^2 with a scale factor of 2^1 allowing three possible window sizes: zero, two and four that allow for interesting scenarios where the reported size of the window is shrunken to half of its original size.

We performed our verification assuming a sequence number space of size 2^3+1, a window size of 2^2, a scale factor of 2^1 and a medium capacity of 2^1 segments, in which the sending TCP sends 2^3 octets. With these parameters, we obtained a model that was small enough to verify within reasonable time, with characteristics that are representative for a real-world implementation of TCP. If the size of the model increases, all relevant buffers and calculations will simply scale with this increase; it is unlikely that errors are introduced as a result.

Correctness of the Window Scale Option. Our initial hypothesis was that as the size of the window could only be reported in units of 2^n, problems could arise when a single octet is sent and the window that the receiving TCP entity reports must be adapted. Conceivably, situations could arise where a sending entity has a view of the size of the window at the receiving end that exceeds the maximum buffer space available. With the aid of our formal specification, we find that this is not the case. Both entities maintain the send and receive window as 32-bit numbers and maintain a scale factor by which they right/left-shift the value reported in/taken from an acknowledgement segment. Note that this shift by a factor k, has the same effect as a floored division or multiplication by a factor 2^k. Assume a receive buffer of capacity 2^{n+1} and, therefore, a window size of at most 2^n and a scale factor k, where $0 < k \leq (n-1)$, resulting in a division or multiplication by 2^k. Now, if the receiver receives a segment carrying $0 < m \leq 2^n$ bytes, two scenarios may occur: (i) the reduced buffer space (receive window) is reported in the acknowledgement segment; or, (ii) the old buffer space is reported. If (i), then the reported window size is $\lfloor (2^n - m)/2^k \rfloor < 2^{n-k} < 2^n$ else if (ii) then nothing changes and therefore the reported window size is $\lfloor 2^n/2^k \rfloor \leq 2^{n-k} < 2^n$. The reported buffer size is always $\leq 2^{n-k}$ and can never become greater than $2^{(n-k)+k} = 2^n$ when it is left-shifted at the remote end. Hence, a sending entity never views the receive buffer space available at a receiving entity to exceed the maximum buffer space available.

A second conceivable problem relates to the explicit statement in [17] that a TCP instance should not 'shrink' its receive window, meaning that the buffer capacity is reduced, i.e., the right edge of the window is moved to the left. Assume a sender and receiver have agreed upon a window size of 4. The sender sends two octets and immediately then sends another two octets. By the arrival of the first segment at the receiver, the octets are put in its receive buffer and, unfortunately, at the same time the capacity of the buffer is also reduced by one octet, causing the receiving entity to report a window of size 1 to the sender rather than 2. As the second segment, carrying two octets, is already in transit it will be discarded upon arrival at the receiver because it contains more octets than the receiver may accept. The sender will keep retransmitting this segment and it will be discarded as long as no octets are taken from the receive buffer. If window sizes get bigger, the delay incurred may significantly impact the performance of the protocol. Eventually, however, the octet will be accepted when buffer space becomes available as octets that arrived earlier are taken from the receive buffer.

When window scaling is in effect, one might expect such a scenario to occur every time an odd number of bytes is sent, due to the size of the window being reported only in multiples of 2^n. However, in this case the actual capacity of the receive buffer is not reduced and the receiver maintains the window size as a 32-bit not a 16-bit number. Therefore, the second segment that may have been in transit already, will still be accepted and an acknowledgement containing the latest size of the window will be sent back within reasonable time. In a situation where the segment was not yet sent, the difference in the number of octets that may be sent is only 1, causing a performance rather than a correctness issue.

Recommended Revision of RFC 793. During our verification using μCRL, we identified a possibility of deadlock when strictly following the RFC 793 specification as we will show below. Therefore, we recommend revising the specification in its dealing with zero windows; requiring that *whenever the sender (i) has data on its send buffer, (ii) has a zero window and (iii) has an empty retransmission queue, a segment is sent to probe the zero window containing at least one octet of data from the send buffer.* This behaviour was included in our model as stated in Section 3.1 but we withheld explanation and justification until now.

Instead, the current specification states on page 42 that: *"The sending TCP must be prepared to accept from the user and send at least one octet of new data even if the send window is zero. The sending TCP must regularly retransmit to the receiving TCP even when the window is zero. [...] This retransmission is essential to guarantee that when either TCP has a zero window the re-opening of the window will be reliably reported to the other."* The latter part of this statement is confusing. It is not the *retransmission* that is essential, but rather the *transmission* of a segment (whether taken from the send buffer or the retransmission queue) when the send window is zero.

To see why, suppose that the sender has two octets on its send buffer and sends only the first of these. The receiver then acknowledges this octet, but does not yet take it from its buffer. As a result of this, both the send and receive window are now 0. In this scenario, there is still data to be sent, but the retransmission queue is empty. If the requirements above are strictly followed, the zero window will never be probed as long as the user does not provide *new data* for the sender to *accept and send at least one octet of* and therefore leads to deadlock. Implicitly, the reader may expect data on the send buffer to be sent in this case, regardless. However, this is certainly contradicted by the suggestion to *"avoid sending small segments by waiting until the window is large enough before sending data"*. Note that care should be taken when implementing this feature, since as a result of waiting to send something, no new acknowledgements will arrive to update the window information, again leading to deadlock.

Requiring the sender to be prepared to send at least one octet of new data even when the retransmission queue is non-empty also ensures that the window will be reopened, but not how one would expect. The new data is sent to the receiver, which will reject the segment since it is out of sequence. However, as a result of this rejection, the receiver sends an acknowledgement containing up-to-date window information, potentially reopening the window. Our proposed revision intentionally does not attend to the case of the retransmission queue being non-empty; it is already covered by the requirement that *"if the retransmission timeout expires on a segment in the retransmission queue, send the segment at the front of the retransmission queue again, reinitialize the retransmission time and return"* on page 77. As an advantage, whenever the retransmission queue is non-empty an in-sequence segment will be sent and therefore accepted while its acknowledgement may also reopen the window. Only if the retransmission queue is empty, a segment containing new data probes the zero window. This segment is then guaranteed to be accepted if the receiver has reopened its window.

It may be that our revision matches the interpretation intended of the original specification, but we have shown that the wording of the specification can lead to implementations where deadlocks occur. A formal specification, given here in μCRL, leaves less scope for erroneous implementations due to misinterpretation.

5   Conclusion

TCP plays an important role in the internet, providing reliable transport of data over possibly faulty networks. The protocol is complex and its specification consists of many documents that mainly describe the proposed functioning of the protocol in natural language. We set out to formally specify TCP extended with the Window Scale Option and verify its correctness, redressing the lack of consideration paid to this option in earlier verification efforts.

Whilst formally specifying TCP, we traversed several ambiguities in RFC 793; the modelling decisions we made in this regard were stated in Section 3. Due to its formal nature, our specification may serve as a useful reference for implementors of the protocol. Moreover, our recommendation for revising RFC 793 brings attention to the potential misinterpretations of how and when to probe the zero window, which we have shown may lead to deadlock.

The process algebra that we used for our specification, μCRL, turned out to be powerful enough to mimic the required features. The size of the state space, however, was a limiting factor that forced us to split our verification efforts into a verification of TCP data transfer and a separate verification of connection teardown; the latter was omitted from this paper.

Using the ltsmin toolset, we were able to formally verify that our μCRL specification of unidirectional TCP extended with the Window Scale Option does not contain deadlocks, and that its external behaviour is branching bisimilar to a FIFO queue for a significantly large instance. In addition, we believe that the specification is general enough to make the introduction of errors as parameters are increased highly unlikely. Whilst our specification also supports bidirectional data transfer, only unidirectional instances were verified to avoid intractable state space explosion; a point we aim to redress in subsequent work.

Acknowledgments. The authors are indebted to Dr. Barry M. Cook, for posing the initial research question, and Dr. Kees Verstoep, for essential support in using the DAS-4 cluster. We also thank the anonymous reviewers for their insightful suggestions.

References

1. Badban, B., Fokkink, W.J., Groote, J.F., Pang, J., van de Pol, J.: Verification of a sliding window protocol in μCRL and PVS. Formal Aspects of Computing 17(3), 342–388 (2005)

2. Badban, B., Fokkink, W.J., van de Pol, J.: Mechanical verification of a two-way sliding window protocol. In: CPA. CSE, vol. 66, pp. 179–202. IOS Press (2008)
3. Bezem, M., Groote, J.F.: A correctness proof of a one-bit sliding window protocol in μCRL. The Computer Journal 37(4), 289–307 (1994)
4. Billington, J., Han, B.: On defining the service provided by TCP. In: ACSC. CR-PIT, vol. 16, pp. 129–138. ACS (2003)
5. Bishop, S., Fairbairn, M., Norrish, M., Sewell, P., Smith, M., Wansbrough, K.: Rigorous specification and conformance testing techniques for network protocols, as applied to TCP, UDP, and sockets. In: SIGCOMM, pp. 265–276. ACM (2005)
6. Blom, S., Orzan, S.: Distributed state space minimization. Software Tools for Technology Transfer 7(3), 280–291 (2005)
7. Blom, S., van de Pol, J., Weber, M.: LTSMIN: distributed and symbolic reachability. In: Touili, T., Cook, B., Jackson, P. (eds.) CAV 2010. LNCS, vol. 6174, pp. 354–359. Springer, Heidelberg (2010)
8. Braden, R.: Requirements for Internet hosts-communication layers. RFC 1122 (1989)
9. Chkliaev, D., Hooman, J., de Vink, E.P.: Verification and improvement of the sliding window protocol. In: Garavel, H., Hatcliff, J. (eds.) TACAS 2003. LNCS, vol. 2619, pp. 113–127. Springer, Heidelberg (2003)
10. Fokkink, W.J.: Modelling Distributed Systems. Texts in theoretical computer science, An EATCS Series. Springer (2007)
11. Han, B., Billington, J.: Validating TCP connection management. In: SEFW, pp. 47–55. ACS (2002)
12. Han, B., Billington, J.: Experience using coloured Petri nets to model TCP's connection management procedures. In: CPN, pp. 57–76 (2004)
13. Han, B., Billington, J.: Termination properties of TCP's connection management procedures. In: Ciardo, G., Darondeau, P. (eds.) ICATPN 2005. LNCS, vol. 3536, pp. 228–249. Springer, Heidelberg (2005)
14. Jacobson, V., Braden, R., Borman, D.: TCP extensions for high performance. RFC 1323 (1992)
15. Madelaine, E., Vergamini, D.: Specification and verification of a sliding window protocol in LOTOS. In: FORTE. IFIP Trans., vol. C-2, pp. 495–510 (1991)
16. Murphy, S.L., Shankar, A.U.: Service specification and protocol construction for the transport layer. In: SIGCOMM, pp. 88–97. ACM (1988)
17. Postel, J.: Transmission control protocol. RFC 793 (1981)
18. Ridge, T., Norrish, M., Sewell, P.: A rigorous approach to networking: TCP, from implementation to protocol to service. In: Cuellar, J., Sere, K. (eds.) FM 2008. LNCS, vol. 5014, pp. 294–309. Springer, Heidelberg (2008)
19. Schieferdecker, I.: Abruptly terminated connections in TCP - a verification example. In: Applied Formal Methods in System Design, pp. 136–145 (1996)
20. Smith, M.A.S., Ramakrishnan, K.K.: Formal specification and verification of safety and performance of TCP selective acknowledgement. Trans. on Networking 10(2), 193–207 (2002)
21. Smith, M.A.S.: Formal verification of communication protocols. In: FORTE. IFIP Conf. Proc., vol. 69, pp. 129–144. Chapman & Hall (1996)
22. Smith, M.A.S.: Formal verification of TCP and T/TCP. PhD thesis, Massachusetts Institute of Technology (1997)
23. Tanenbaum, A.S.: Computer Networks, 4th edn. Prentice Hall (2002)

Learning Fragments
of the TCP Network Protocol

Paul Fiterău-Broştean*, Ramon Janssen, and Frits Vaandrager

Institute for Computing and Information Sciences
Radboud University Nijmegen
P.O. Box 9010, 6500 GL Nijmegen, The Netherlands
{P.FiterauBrostean,f.vaandrager}@cs.ru.nl, ramon.janssen@student.ru.nl

Abstract. We apply automata learning techniques to learn fragments of
the TCP network protocol by observing its external behaviour. We show
that different implementations of TCP in Windows 8 and Ubuntu induce
different automata models, thus allowing for fingerprinting of these implementations. In order to infer our models we use the notion of a mapper
component introduced by Aarts, Jonsson and Uijen, which abstracts the
large number of possible TCP packets into a limited number of abstract
actions that can be handled by the regular inference tool LearnLib. Inspection of the learned models reveals that both Windows 8 and Ubuntu
13.10 violate RFC 793.

1 Introduction

Our society has become reliant on the security and application of protocols,
which are used for various operations. Standards describing these protocols typically fail to specify what an agent should do in case another agent does not
follow the rules of the protocol, which can result in exploits by hackers. Moreover, implementations of these standards can differ, and may deviate slightly
from the official standard, resulting in security vulnerabilities. Automata learning techniques can help expose and/or mitigate such problems through tools
that help generate state models for these systems.

Learning techniques enable the inference of state models for systems available
as black boxes. Inferring such models is important not only for understanding
these systems, but also for model checking and model based testing. To this
end, several learning algorithms and tools have been developed, such as those
presented in [4,19,17,2,20,12].

Whereas learning algorithms such as L* [4], work for systems with limited
numbers of abstract inputs and outputs, many protocols make use of messages
with parameters, for instance sequence numbers or flags. Moreover, network
protocols may have variables. As an example, the TCP protocol maintains several
variables for connection initialization and synchronization. Efforts have been

---

* Supported by NWO project 612.001.216: Active Learning of Security Protocols
  (ALSEP).

F. Lang and F. Flammini (Eds.): FMICS 2014, LNCS 8718, pp. 78–93, 2014.

made to develop techniques to learn these more complex systems. In particular, building on the extension of the L* algorithm used to learn Mealy machines (Niese [11]), F. Aarts et al. describe in [3] a methodology for learning systems via abstraction. This method entails introducing a *mapper* component in-between the protocol and the learner. The *mapper* reduces the parameters and state variables implied by the protocol to a small number of abstract values, on which learning algorithms can then be applied. By using this technique, they were able to infer state models of simulated versions of the Transmission Control Protocol (TCP) and the Session Initiation Protocol (SIP).

In this work we use abstraction to learn implementations of the TCP-protocol for different operating systems. We then highlight a situation where these implementations do not adhere to the standard. We use the abstraction based on the approach described in [22], but extend it to include the increment operator which is needed to learn the TCP protocol. While the learning setup used specifically targets TCP, it can be adapted to learn other protocols.

Related Work. In recent years, there have been many applications of automata learning to protocol analysis. We mention here only a few selected references and refer to these works for a more extensive overview of the literature. In [21], automata learning was used to establish that implementations of SSH violate the standard. In [6], automata learning was used to reproduce a widely publicized mistake in a protocol for electronic banking. The methodology described by Aarts et al. [3] was also used to infer state diagrams of banking cards in [1]. Dawn Song et al. [7] developed techniques to learn the state diagram of a network protocol used to control botnets. Learning techniques were also used to automatically infer HTTP interaction models for web applications, as part of the SPaCIoS Project [5].

Organization. The paper is structured as follows: Section 2 gives a brief description of the TCP network protocol, Section 3 sets the context of regular inference with abstraction. Section 4 presents the framework we implemented to learn the TCP network protocol. Section 5 explains how the setup implements abstraction. Section 6 explains difficulties encountered and how we managed them. Section 7 presents experiments carried out to learn TCP. Section 8 outlines conclusions and future work.

2   The TCP Network Protocol

The transmission control protocol [16], or TCP, is a connection-based network protocol that allows two application programs to transfer data bidirectionally in a reliable and orderly manner. The programs can run on the same or on separate machines. TCP supports data transfer through the *connection* abstraction where a *connection* comprises two endpoints associated with each of the two programs. A connection progresses from one state to the next following events. Possible events are user actions, receipt of TCP *segments*, which are network packets containing flags and register data, and timeouts. Connection progression is depicted in Figure 1.

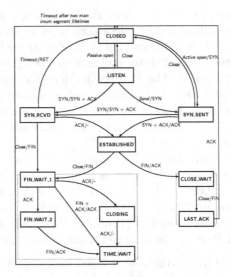

Fig. 1. A state diagram describing TCP[1]

We give a brief example of how the protocol functions from connection initiation to termination. For brevity, we use FLAGS-segment as shorthands for segments having the mentioned control flags activated.

The two systems communicating through TCP have different roles: one system acts as a *server* and the other as a *client*. Connection between *server* and *client* is established through the three-way handshake. Assuming the *server* is in the LISTEN-state, waiting for a *client* to connect to it, the *client* sends a SYN-segment on an ACTIVE OPEN-action and transitions to the SYN_SENT-state. On receiving this segment, the *server* responds with a SYN+ACK-segment, transitioning to the SYN_RCVD-state. The *client* then acknowledges the *server*'s segment with an ACK-segment and transitions to the ESTABLISHED-state. On receiving this segment, the *server* also transitions to the ESTABLISHED-state, connection is established and data can be transferred, thus concluding the three-way handshake.

When either side has finished sending data, that side sends a segment with a FIN-flag on an ACTIVE CLOSE-action, signaling that it has no more data left to send. This can be acknowledged with a FIN+ACK-segment if the other device also wants to close the connection, or with a ACK-segment if that device still wants to send data. Once the device has sent all data, it sends a FIN-message, closing the connection.

Notice that the state diagram in Figure 1 does not fully specify the behaviour of the TCP-implementation. More specifically, the model does not reveal what response is given in case either side receives a segment for which no transition is defined (for instance, if a RST-segment is received in the SYN_RCVD-state).

---

[1] Retrieved from http://www.texample.net/tikz/examples/tcp-state-machine/. Copyright 2009 Ivan Griffin. Reprinted under the LaTeX Project Public License, version 1.3.

Moreover, the model abstracts away from register data such as the sequence and acknowledgment numbers found in TCP packets. Many of these details can be inferred from the protocol standard. There are, however, some details which are implementation specific, with each operating system providing its own TCP implementation. Moreover, such implementations do not always adhere to the prescribed standards. Such was the case for HTTP, as shown in [15]. Hence, inferring models of these TCP implementations represents a valuable asset in analyzing their concrete behavior.

3 Regular Inference Using Abstraction

In this section, we recall the definition of a Mealy machine, the basic ideas of regular inference in Angluin-style, and the notion of a mapper which allows us to learn "large" models with data parameters.

3.1 Learning Mealy Machines

We will use Mealy machines to model TCP protocol entities. A Mealy machine $\mathcal{M}$ is the tuple $\mathcal{M} = \langle I, O, Q, q_0, \rightarrow \rangle$, where

- I, O, and Q are nonempty sets of *input symbols, output symbols,* and *states,* respectively,
- $q_0 \in Q$ is the *initial state,* and
- $\rightarrow \subseteq Q \times I \times O \times Q$ is the *transition relation.*

Transitions are tuples of the form $(q, i, o, q') \in \rightarrow$. A transition implies that, on receiving an input $i \in I$, when in the state $q \in Q$, the machine jumps to the state $q' \in Q$, producing the output $o \in O$. Mealy machines are deterministic if for every state and input, there is exactly one transition. A Mealy machine is finite if I and Q are finite sets.

Angluin described L* in [4], an algorithm to learn deterministic finite automata. Niese [11] adapted this algorithm to learning deterministic Mealy machines. Improved versions of the L* algorithm were implemented in the LearnLib tool [17,13]. A graphical model of the basic learning setup is given in Figure 2.

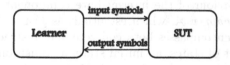

Fig. 2. Overview of the learner and the SUT

We assume an implementation, or <u>System Under Test</u> (*SUT*), and postulate that its behaviour can be described by a deterministic Mealy Machine $\mathcal{M}$. The *learner,* connected to the *SUT,* sends *inputs* (or queries) to the *SUT* and observes resulting *outputs*. After each observation, the *learner* sends a special *reset* message, prompting the reset of the implementation. Based on the observation of the outputs, it builds a hypothesis $\mathcal{H}$. The hypothesis is then tested against the implementation. Testing involves running a number of test sequences which determine whether the hypothesis conforms to the *SUT*. The hypothesis is returned if all test sequences show conformation, otherwise it is further refined on the basis of the new counterexample. This process is repeated until all equivalence queries are passed.

3.2   Inference Using Abstraction

Existing implementations of inference algorithms only proved effective when applied to machines with small alphabets (sets of input and output symbols). Practical systems like the TCP protocol, however, typically have large alphabets, e.g. inputs and outputs with data parameters of type integer or string.

A solution to this problem was proposed by Aarts et al in [3]. In this work, the concrete values of every parameter are mapped to a small domain of abstract values in a history-dependent manner. A *mapper component* is placed in-between the *learner* and the *SUT*. The *learner* sends abstract inputs comprising abstract parameter values to this component. The mapper component then turns the abstract values into concrete values (by taking the inverse of the abstraction function), forming concrete inputs, and sends them to the *SUT*. The concrete outputs received from the *SUT* are subsequently transformed back to abstract outputs and are returned to the *learner*. Reset messages sent by the *learner* to the *SUT* also reset the mapper component. A graphical overview of the *learner* and mapper component is given in Figure 3.

Fig. 3. Overview of the learner, the mapper and the SUT

Formally, the behaviour of the intermediate component is fully determined by the notion of a *mapper* $\mathcal{A}$, which essentially is just a deterministic Mealy machine. A mapper encompasses both concrete and abstract sets of input and output symbols, a set of states, an initial state, a transition function that tells us how the occurrence of a concrete symbol affects the state, and an abstraction function which, depending on the state, maps concrete to abstract symbols. Each mapper $\mathcal{A}$ induces an abstraction operator $\alpha_{\mathcal{A}}$, which transforms a concrete Mealy machine with concrete inputs I and outputs O into an abstract Mealy machine with abstract inputs X and outputs Y. If the behaviour of the *SUT* is described by a Mealy machine $\mathcal{M}$ then the *SUT* and the mapper component together are described by the Mealy machine $\alpha_{\mathcal{A}}(\mathcal{M})$. Dually, each mapper also induces a concretization operator γ_A, which transforms an abstract hypothesis Mealy machine $\mathcal{H}$ with inputs X and outputs Y into a concrete Mealy machine with inputs I and outputs O. A key result proved by Aarts et al [3] is that $\alpha_A(\mathcal{M}) \leq \mathcal{H}$ implies $\mathcal{M} \leq \gamma_A(\mathcal{H})$, where $\leq$ denotes behavioural inclusion of Mealy machines. This result allows us to transform an abstract model $\mathcal{H}$, inferred through interaction with a mapper component, into a concrete model that over-approximates the behaviour of the SUT.

4   Learning Setup

In the case of TCP, the SUT is the *server* in the TCP communication. On the other side, the *learner* and *mapper* simulate the *client*. On the client side we also introduce the *adapter*, a component that performs a 1 to 1 translation of messages to segments sent over the network. More specifically, it builds request segments from concrete inputs, sends them to the *server*, retrieves the response segments and infers the respective concrete outputs, which it delivers to the *learner-mapper* assembly. The *adapter* is also responsible for detecting system timeouts. It is important to make distinction between the *mapper* and *adapter*. Whereas the *mapper* implements mapping between abstract and concrete messages, the *adapter* transforms these concrete messages to a format that is readable by the SUT.

With that said, we present in Figure 4 the framework implemented to learn fragments of the TCP implementation. On the learner side, we use *LearnLib* [17] and *Tomte* [22], two Java based learning tools. LearnLib provides the Java implementation of the L* based learning algorithm, while we use some of Tomte's libraries to connect the *learner* to a Java based *mapper* via direct method calls. A Python adapter based on *Scapy* [18] is used to craft, send request packets and retrieve response packets. Communication between the *mapper* and *adapter* is done over sockets.

We conducted our experiments on both a single and on two separate machines. The *client* and *server* reside in separate operating systems. The model which is inferred via learning describes the TCP implementation for the operating system on which the *server* resides. Each operating system enables the user to configure parameters involved in TCP. These parameters can also have an influence over the resulting model. We used *Wireshark* to monitor communication between *client* and *server*.

The experiments were carried out with the *server* deployed on Windows 8 and Ubuntu 13.10 respectively. The *server* passively listens for incoming connections on a port while the *learner*, acting as a "fake client", sends messages to the *server* through its own port. The source code of the learning setup, along with some documentation on usage, is available at [10]. With virtualization, the experiments can be run on a personal PC.

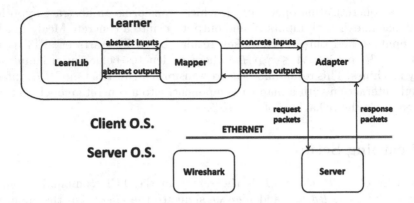

Fig. 4. Overview of the experimental setup

5   Messages and Abstraction

5.1   Mapper Description

As mentioned previously, the *mapper* component translates abstract input messages into concrete input messages, and concrete output messages into abstract output messages. More specifically, parameters contained in messages are mapped from a concrete to an abstract domain, and vice versa. Figure 5 shows the concrete and abstract parameters used in learning. Also shown is how the concrete parameters are then associated with fields within TCP segments by the *adapter*. Our message selection is based on the work of Aarts et al. in [3]. Like in their work, both inputs and outputs are generated based on the sequence number, acknowledgement number and flags found in each TCP segment.

Both the concrete and the abstract alphabets comprise *Request* inputs and *Response* outputs. Each of these inputs and outputs takes 3 parameters corresponding to the sequence number, acknowledgment number and the TCP flags. The concrete parameters *SeqNr* and *AckNr* are defined as 32 bit unsigned integers, while their corresponding abstract parameters *SeqV* and *AckV* are either *valid* or *invalid*. The *Flags* parameter can have the values ACK, SYN, FIN, RST, or any valid combination as listed in Figure 5. These flags correspond to bitfields of the control register in the TCP-frame, in which flags are either set or unset. In other words, each element of *flags* defines which flags have been set: all flags mentioned are set, all other flags are not.

We abstract away from the sequence and acknowledgement numbers sent to the *server* by way of validity. We define validity based on whether the sequence and acknowledgement numbers comply to the standard TCP flow. Here the sequence number sent is equal to the last acknowledgement number received while the acknowledgement number sent is equal to the last sequence number received (the server sequence number) plus the length of the data that the *client* expects to receive (which in our case is 0, no data is transferred) plus 1 in case the segment carries a SYN or a FIN flag. ACK flags do not lead to any increase.

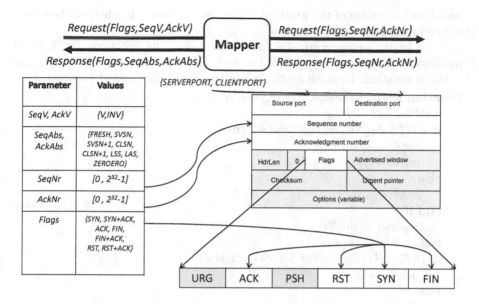

Fig. 5. Message scheme

Numbers that comply to this standard are *valid*, those that do not are *invalid*. We except from this rule whenever the *server* is in the LISTENING-state with no connection set up. In this case, fresh sequence numbers are generated by a number generation algorithm. We abstract away from this algorithm by deeming all generated numbers *valid* and none *invalid* at this stage. Consequently, we surpress any messages containing *invalid* parameters that the *learner* generates at this point. (we do not create nor send segments for these inputs)

We abstract away from the sequence and acknoweldgement numbers received from the *server* by comparing them with values encountered in the communication up to that point. These values are stored in state variables which are maintained by the *mapper*. We also define the abstract output *timeout* for the case when no response segment is received.

In order to map between abstract and concrete the *mapper* maintains the following state variables:

- $\{lastFlagSent, lastAckSent, lastSeqSent\}$ store the last flag, acknowledgement and sequence numbers sent by the client
- $\{lastAbsSeq, lastAbsAck\}$ store the last sequence and acknowledgement abstractions sent by the client
- *valClientSeq* stores the last *valid* sequence number sent by the client
- *InitServSeq* stores the server's initial sequence number
- *INIT* records whether the server is in its initial state.

Variables *lastSeqSent*, *lastAckSent*, *lastFlagSent*, *lastAbsSeq*, *lastAbsAck* and *InitServSeq* store the first or most recent occurrence of certain message parameters. Variable *valClientSeq* stores the last valid sequence number: its definition is based on knowledge of the protocol. Variable *INIT* records whether the server is in the initial state.

On the basis of these variables, we define below the functions for *Request* transmission, *Response* receipt, and *Timeout*. For symmetry, we use *SeqAbs* and *AckAbs* as notations for both abstract input and abstract output parameters.

function REQUEST(*Flags, SeqNr, AckNr*)
    lastFlagSent ← *Flags*
    if *INIT* ∨ *SeqNr* == *valClientSeq* **then**
        SeqAbs ← *valid*
        valClientSeq ← *SeqNr*
    else
        SeqAbs ← *invalid*
    end if
    lastSeqSent ← *SeqNr*
    lastAbsSeq ← *SeqAbs*
    if *INIT* ∨ *AckNr* == *InitServSeq* + 1 **then**
        AckAbs ← *valid*
    else
        AckAbs ← *invalid*
    end if
    lastAckSent ← *AckNr*
    lastAbsAck ← *AckAbs*
      return *Request*(*Flags, SeqAbs, AckAbs*)
end function

In the context of *Response* outputs, we compare values found in server responses to a set of reference values. Note the similarity between the conditions we chose and the conditions used in nmap [14] to perform OS fingerprinting. Also note that we assume no collision between different reference values. It is indeed possible that the client sequence number is equal to the server sequence number. However, the likelihood is very low due to the extended range these numbers can take values in.

function RESPONSE(*Flags, SeqNr, AckNr*)
    if *INIT* **then**
        SeqAbs ← **FRESH**
        InitServSeq ← *SeqNr*
    else
        SeqAbs ← ABSTRACT(*SeqNr*)
    end if
    AckAbs ← ABSTRACT(*AckNr*)
    if *AckAbs* == **CLSN** + 1 **then**
        InitServSeq ← *SeqNr*
    end if
    INIT ← *IsInitial*()
      return *Response*(*Flags, SeqAbs, AckAbs*)
end function

function ABSTRACT(*concVal*)
   if *concVal* −− *valClientSeq* | 1 **then**
     absVal ← **CLSN** + 1
   else if *concVal* == *valClientSeq* **then**
     absVal ← **CLSN**
   else if *concVal* == *InitServSeq* **then**
     absVal == **SVSN**
   else if *concVal* == *InitServSeq* + 1 **then**
     absVal ← **SVSN** + 1
   else if *concVal* == *lastSeqSent* **then**
     absVal ← **LSS**
   else if *concVal* == *lastAckSent* **then**
     absVal ← **LAS**
   else if *concVal* == 0 **then**
     absVal ← **ZERO**
   else
     absVal ← **INV**
   end if
   return *absVal*
end function
function TIMEOUT
   INIT ← *IsInitial*()
end function

5.2 Initial State Detection

One important aspect is the detection of the initial state (ie. the LISTENING-state in the TCP protocol, *INIT* in the mapper definition). This is necessary in order to follow the TCP flow, wherein transitions from this state imply that new sequence numbers are generated for both *client* and *server*. The server and client sequence number variables (*clientSN* and *serverSN*) must be updated accordingly. For this purpose, we defined an oracle which tells whether the system is in the initial state. We found that such an oracle for Windows 8 can be implemented by a function over the state variables stored in the mapper and the output parameters. For Ubuntu 13.10, definition of such a function was made difficult by the fact that, depending on the system's current state, the abstract input *Request*(ACK+RST, *valid*, *invalid*) either resets the system or is ignored. If the oracle is defined via a function, definition of this function depends on the operating system for which TCP is learned. We show the definition of *INIT* for Windows 8 below.

function IsINITIAL
   if *IsResponse* **then**
     INIT ← *RST* ∈ *Flags* ∧ *SeqAbs* = *valid* ∧ *SYN* ∈ *lastFlagSent*
   else if *IsTimeout* **then**
     INIT ← *INIT* ∨ (*lastAbsSeq* = *valid* ∧ *RST* ∈ *lastFlagSent*)
   end if
end function

Obviously, such a function would have to be inferred manually for every implementation of TCP that is learned. To circumvent this, we implemented a mechanism that automatically checks whether a trace (sequence of inputs) triggers a return to the initial state. This verification relies on distinguishing inputs to signal whether the LISTENING-state is reached and consequently, whether fresh values can be accepted by the mapper. For TCP, we assume, based on the protocol specification, that a SYN-segment with fresh register values is a distinguishing input for the initial state, as only in the LISTENING-state state does a SYN-segment yield a SYN+ACK-segment which acknowledges the sequence number sent. A valid implementation of TCP should always adhere to this condition, otherwise connections could easily be interrupted by spurious SYN-segments. Addition of this automatic mechanism enables us to learn TCP implementations without changing the *mapper* to fit the operating system.

This mechanism is embedded into the learning process as follows: for each input sent, we check if the trace leading up to and including that input, is a resetting trace, that is, it prompts the transition to the initial state. This information is then fed to the $IsInitial()$ function, for proper update of the mapper. After each check, the SUT must return to the state it had previously to the check being done. In the case of TCP, this can only be done by re-running the whole trace. Information accumulated on the resetting property of traces is stored after each check, so next time the same trace is checked, we have a direct result and do not have to reapply the whole trace. There is of course, considerable overhead since a trace of n inputs now entails feeding $\frac{(n+1)*(n+2)}{2}$ inputs. This number grows if we consider the additional RST-segments we have to send. But such overhead is acceptable in a setting where a small maximum trace length is still adequate for learning.

6   Complications Encountered

To learn the system, several issues had to be addressed. Firstly, we had to implement resetting mechanisms that would prompt the TCP connection to return to the start state. We implemented two approaches, one by opening a new connection to the *server* on a different port each time we started a new query, the other by resetting the connection via a valid RST-segment. In the first case, we were hit by thresholds on the number of connections allowed. For Ubuntu, each connection is associated with a file descriptor. Not closing the file descriptor on the *server* side as not to interfere with learning means that the default limit, 1024, can be reached using relatively few inputs. This limit can be increased to 4096 for Ubuntu 13.10 32-bit version using *ulimit*, which is still not sufficient for learning using a alphabet. The solution was using garbage collection to clear out these unused descriptors. In Java, this is done automatically. For Windows, we found that once the *server* reaches a certain number of connections left in the CLOSE_WAIT-state, the *server* proceeds to send FIN+ACK-segment to close all connections. The second approach implies sending a RST-segment with a *valid* sequence number, which was possible with the mapper previously described. In our learning experiments we combined the two approaches, that is, we switched ports on every run and each run was ended with a valid RST-segment, leaving no idle connection behind.

We also had to manage the handling of SYN+ACK retransmits. When the *server* is in the SYN_RCVD-state, it expects a corresponding ACK-segment to the SYN+ACK-segment it sent, thus ending the 3 way handshake. In this situation, the TCP protocol specifies that, if the *server* does not receive the expected acknowledgement within a time frame (defined by the initial retransmission timeout or *initialRTO*), it re-sends the SYN+ACK-segment a number of times after which it closes the connection. This behaviour is not accounted for because it would require timer adjustments to fit with the *initialRTO* . All traces must therefore be run within *initialRTO* time. We disabled SYN+ACK retransmission for Ubuntu by setting the *tcp_synack_retries* to 0. Unfortunately, Ubuntu does not allow the user to modify the *initialRTO* since its value is hard coded to around one second(see TCP_INIT_TIMEOUT at [23]). The time window provided by the *initialRTO* forced us to lower the maximum trace length as to fit within this time frame. For Windows 8, *initialRTO* is initially set to 3 seconds (and can be configured, see [24]), which provides sufficient time to execute sequences of long inputs. An alternative approach would have been to ignore the retransmissions of similar SYN+ACK-segments.

We also encountered difficulties with packet receipt. By analyzing packet communication we found that Scapy sometimes misses fast *server* responses, that is, responses sent after a short time span from their corresponding requests. We believe this could be caused by Scapy's slow performance in intercepting responses quick enough. To circumvent this problem, we crafted a network tracking tool based on Impacket [8] and Pcapy [9] which augments Scapy's receipt capabilities. In case Scapy does not receive any responses back, the tracking tool either confirms that no response was intercepted or returns the response that Scapy missed.

Our experiments were also affected by the operating system on which the *learner* setup was deployed. The Ubuntu operating systems the *learner* was run on are unaware of what network packets are sent by Scapy, and therefore cannot recognize the response packets sent by the *server*. More specifically, as a TCP-connection is set up by the *learner*, the operating system notices a connection that it has not set up itself. Consequently, it responds with a RST-segment to shut down that connection. The problem was solved by dropping all RST-segments sent by the operating system via a firewall rule. This can be done in Ubuntu using the *iptables* command. Windows required no such tweak.

For Ubuntu 13.10 we also found that, whenever in the ESTABLISHED or CLOSE_WAIT states, the *server* behaved apparently non-deterministically when receiving ACK and FIN+ACK segments with *valid* sequence numbers and *invalid* acknowledgement numbers. On receiving these packets, the *server* either retransmitted an ACK-segment or it gave no answer. This behaviour is partly, but not completely, explained by a fragment in the source code in which invalid acknowledgements are dropped. In order to handle this situation, we split the *invalid* range of numbers for these inputs into three subranges, each exhibiting specific behaviour. These ranges are $[2^{31}, -WIN - 1], [-WIN, -1], [1, 2^{31} - 1]$ where WIN is the window size, which correspond to **B,W** and **A** in the inferred Ubuntu model. The ranges are relative to what a *valid* server sequence number would be.

7   Experimental Results

We learned models for Windows 8 and Ubuntu 13.10 LTS. As mentioned previously, the *client* and *server* reside in different operating systems. Because the *adapter* can only function under Linux, we ran the learner setup (or *client*) on Ubuntu systems.

For Windows 8, the *client* was deployed on a guest virtual machine using the Ubuntu 12.04 LTS operating system, while the *server* resided on the Windows 8 host. We also experimented with the *client* residing on a separate computer running Ubuntu 13.10 that communicated with the same Windows 8 server and obtained identical results. Similarly for Ubuntu 13.10, the *server* and *client* were deployed both on one computer, each in its own Ubuntu virtual machine within the same Windows 8 host, and on separate machines.

In order to reduce the size of the diagram, we eliminate all self loops that have *timeout* outputs. Moreover, we use the initial flag letters as shorthands: *s* for *syn*, *a* for *ack*, *f* for *fin* and *r* for *rst*. We condense *Request/Response(flags, seq, ack)* to *flags(seq, ack)* and we group inputs that have the same abstract output and resulting state. *valid* and *invalid* abstract parameters are shorthanded to *v* and *inv* respectively. In the Ubuntu experiment, we split the *invalid* class in 3 ranges $\{B, W, A\}$ for *ack* and *fin+ack* segments as to handle non determinism. Finally, inputs having the same effect regardless of the *valid* or *invalid* value of a parameter are merged and the parameter is replaced with _.

Figures 6 and 7 show the state models learned for the two operating systems. Both models depict 4 states of the reference model. We can identify handshake and termination on the two diagrams by following the sequence of inputs: S(v,v), A(v,v), AF(v,v). We see that for each input in the sequence the same output is generated. There are, however, notable differences, like the verbosity of the listening state in case of Ubuntu 13.10. RST-segment responses also differ. Whereas in Ubuntu 13.10, a RST-segment response always carries a 0 acknowledgement number, for Windows 8, similar to its joining sequence number, it takes the value of the last acknowledgement number sent resulting in RST(*las,las*) outputs.

Checking the models against the specification reveals non-compliance with the rfc standard [16]. The standard specifies on page 36 (see quotation below) that, when in synchronized states, receiving unacceptable segments should trigger specific ACK-segment sent back. Later, an exception is made for RST-segment, which should be dropped. Our learned models, as well as manual tests show that implementations do not follow this specification.

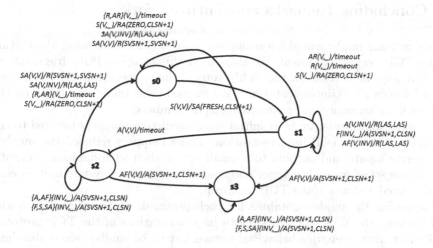

Fig. 6. Learned model for Windows 8 TCP

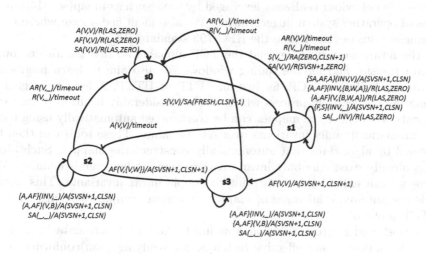

Fig. 7. Learned model for Ubuntu 13.10 TCP

If the connection is in a synchronized state (ESTABLISHED,FIN-WAIT-1, FIN-WAIT-2, CLOSE-WAIT, CLOSING, LAST-ACK, TIME-WAIT), any unacceptable segment (out of window sequence number or unacceptible acknowledgment number) must elicit only an empty acknowledgment segment containing the current send-sequence number and an acknowledgment indicating the next sequence number expected to be received, and the connection remains in the same state.

8   Concluding Remarks and Future Work

We defined and implemented a learning setup for the inference using abstraction of the TCP network protocol. We then used this setup to learn fragments of different implementations of the TCP protocol, more specifically, the Windows 8 and Ubuntu 13.10 implementations. We learned these implementations on the basis of flags, sequence and acknowledgement numbers.

For our experiments, we built initial state predicting mappers tailored to the operating system's TCP implementation. These mappers reduced the number of concrete inputs and outputs to a small set of abstract inputs and outputs. We ran our setup for each mapper and respective operating system and, in each case, covered 4 states of the TCP protocol.

Comparing the models obtained for each protocol, we found a slight variation between the Windows and Ubuntu implementations of the TCP protocol. While in normal scenarios behaviour turned out to be similar, some abnormal scenarios revealed differences in the values of sequence and acknowledgement numbers, as well as the flags found in response packets. This variation results in differing transitions between the state machines inferred for each OS. The difference in behaviour is already leveraged by tools such as nmap(see [14]), as a means of operating system fingerprinting. We also identified a case where both implementations deviated from the RFC 793 standard [16].

In the future we want to extend the TCP alphabet so that we also account for data transfer and for the sliding window. We also aim to learn fragments of protocols built over TCP, for instance FTP or HTTP. A long term goal is automating the learning process which would considerably facilitate future experiments. We believe the mapper can be constructed automatically using tools that automatically infer invariants over sets of values. These tools can then be harnessed by algorithms that automatically construct the mapper. Such algorithms already exist, the only invariant they support however is equality. We believe we can extend this constraint to simple linear invariants. This would enable the automatic inference of mappers for more complex systems, such as the TCP protocol.

Our work and related efforts such as [6,21] show that automata learning is rapidly becoming a very effective technque for studying (non)conformance of implementations to protocol standards.

References

1. Aarts, F., de Ruiter, J., Poll, E.: Formal models of bank cards for free. In: Proceedings of the 4th International Workshop on Security Testing, SECTEST 2013, Luxembourg, March 22 (2013)
2. Aarts, F., Heidarian, F., Kuppens, H., Olsen, P., Vaandrager, F.: Automata learning through counterexample guided abstraction refinement. In: Giannakopoulou, D., Méry, D. (eds.) FM 2012. LNCS, vol. 7436, pp. 10–27. Springer, Heidelberg (2012)

3. Aarts, F., Jonsson, B., Uijen, J.: Generating models of infinite-state communication protocols using regular inference with abstraction. In: Petrenko, A., Simão, A., Maldonado, J.C. (eds.) ICTSS 2010. LNCS, vol. 6435, pp. 188–204. Springer, Heidelberg (2010); Full version avalable at https://pms.cs.ru.nl/iris-diglib/src/getContent.php?id=2013-Aarts-InferenceRegular
4. Angluin, D.: Learning regular sets from queries and counterexamples. Inf. Comput. 75(2), 87–106 (1987)
5. Buchler, M., Hossen, K., Mihancea, P.F., Minea, M., Groz, R., Oriat, C.: Model inference and security testing in the spacios project. In: 2014 Software Evolution Week - IEEE Conference on Software Maintenance, Reengineering and Reverse Engineering (CSMR-WCRE), pp. 411–414 (February 2014)
6. Chalupar, G., Peherstorfer, S., Poll, E., de Ruiter, J.: Automated reverse engineering using lego, http://www.cs.ru.nl/~erikpoll/papers/legopaper.pdf
7. Cho, C.Y., Babić, D., Shin, E.C.R., Song, D.: Inference and analysis of formal models of botnet command and control protocols, New York, NY, USA (2010)
8. Corelabs. Impacket, http://corelabs.coresecurity.com/index.php?module=Wiki&action=view&type=tool&name=Impacket
9. Corelabs. Pcapy, http://corelabs.coresecurity.com/index.php?module=Wiki&action=view&type=tool&name=Pcapy
10. Fiterau, P., Janssen, R.: Experimental learning setup for TCP, https://bitbucket.org/fiteraup/learning-tcp
11. Hagerer, A., Hungar, H., Niese, O., Steffen, B.: Model generation by moderated regular extrapolation. In: Kutsche, R.-D., Weber, H. (eds.) FASE 2002. LNCS, vol. 2306, pp. 80–95. Springer, Heidelberg (2002)
12. Howar, F., Steffen, B., Jonsson, B., Cassel, S.: Inferring canonical register automata. In: Kuncak, V., Rybalchenko, A. (eds.) VMCAI 2012. LNCS, vol. 7148, pp. 251–266. Springer, Heidelberg (2012)
13. Merten, M., Steffen, B., Howar, F., Margaria, T.: Next generation LearnLib. In: Abdulla, P.A., Leino, K.R.M. (eds.) TACAS 2011. LNCS, vol. 6605, pp. 220–223. Springer, Heidelberg (2011)
14. Nmap, http://nmap.org/book/osdetect.html
15. Pahdye, J., Floyd, S.: On inferring tcp behavior. SIGCOMM Comput. Commun. Rev. 31(4), 287–298 (2001)
16. Postel, J. (ed.): Transmission Control Protocol - DARPA Internet Program Protocol Specification, RFC 3261 (September 1981), http://www.ietf.org/rfc/rfc793.txt
17. Raffelt, H., Steffen, B., Berg, T., Margaria, T.: LearnLib: a framework for extrapolating behavioral models. STTT 11(5), 393–407 (2009)
18. Scapy, http://www.secdev.org/projects/scapy/
19. Shahbaz, M., Groz, R.: Inferring mealy machines. In: Cavalcanti, A., Dams, D.R. (eds.) FM 2009. LNCS, vol. 5850, pp. 207–222. Springer, Heidelberg (2009)
20. SPaCIoS. Deliverable 2.2.1: Method for assessing and retrieving models (2013)
21. Tijssen, M.: Automatic modeling of ssh implementations with state machine learning algorithms. Bachelor's thesis, Radboud University Nijmegen (June 2014)
22. Tomte, http://www.italia.cs.ru.nl/tomte/
23. Ubuntu TCP header file, http://lxr.free-electrons.com/source/include/net/tcp.h
24. How to modify the tcp/ip maximum retransmission time-out, http://support.microsoft.com/kb/170359

On the Validation of an Interlocking System by Model-Checking

Andrea Bonacchi and Alessandro Fantechi

DINFO - University of Florence
Via S. Marta 3
Firenze, Italy
{a.bonacchi,alessandro.fantechi}@unifi.it

Abstract. Railway interlocking systems still represent a challenge for formal verification by model checking: the high number of complex interlocking rules that guarantee the safe movements of independent trains in a large station makes the verification of such systems typically incur state space explosion problems. In this paper we describe a study aimed to define a verification process based on commercial modelling and verification tools, for industrially produced interlocking systems, that exploits an appropriate mix of environment abstraction, slicing and CEGAR-like techniques, driven by the low-level knowledge of the interlocking product under verification, in order to support the final validation phase of the implemented products.

1 Introduction

In the railway signalling domain, an *interlocking* is the safety critical system that controls the movement of the trains in a station and between adjacent stations. The interlocking monitors the status of the objects in the railway yard and allows or denies the routing of the trains in accordance with the railway safety and operational regulations that are generic for the region or country where the interlocking is located. The instantiation of these rules on a station topology is stored in the part of the system named *control table.* Control tables of modern computerized interlockings are implemented by means of iteratively executed software controls over the status of the yard objects.

One of the most common ways to describe the interlocking rules given by control tables is through boolean equations or, equivalently, ladder diagrams which are interpreted either by a Programmable Logic Controller (PLC) or by a proper evaluation engine over a standard processor.

Verification of correctness of control tables has been a prolific domain for formal methods practitioners. Model checking in particular has raised the interest of many railway signalling industries, being the most lightweight from the process point of view, and being rather promising in terms of efficiency: safety properties of an interlocking system are quite directly expressed in temporal logic, and their specifications by means of *control tables* can be directly formalized. However, due to the high number of boolean variables involved, automatic

F. Lang and F. Flammini (Eds.): FMICS 2014, LNCS 8718, pp. 94–108, 2014.

verification of sufficiently large stations typically incurs in combinatorial state space explosion problem.

The first applications of model checking have therefore addressed portions of an interlocking system [4,10]; but even recent works [9,21] show that routine verification of interlocking designs for large stations is still a challenge for model checkers, although specific optimizations can help [21].

A recent effort has collected up-to-date reports about interlocking verification [6,11,15,16]. Notwithstanding their different verification aims, one point in common to these works is the use of SAT-based model checking, which appears to be more promising in this respect. We also refer to these works for an extensive bibliographic references about interlocking verification.

In particular, in [6], we have introduced an effort made in a cooperation with our industrial partner[1], with the final aim of reducing the costs of verifying the safety requirements of the produced interlocking systems, in the system validation phase. This validation activity considers the control tables as implemented in the produced interlocking systems, and extracts from legacy control tables a Simulink model made of boolean functions with logical gates. The Simulink model is used in the daily verification activity of the industrial partner to simulate on the model the same test cases foreseen for the produced system, in order to profit from the radically (up to twenty times) shorter time w.r.t. testing.

However, in [6] we also set up a verification framework based on model checking on the extracted model, employing Matlab *Design Verifier* [20], both because it works on Simulink models and to exploit at best its SAT-solving capabilities on the native boolean coding of the control tables.

This paper inherits from [6] the verification framework but presents a separate study aimed to make more precise the kind of verification process that the framework conveniently supports, by considering an appropriate use of environment abstraction, slicing and CEGAR-like techniques, driven by the detailed knowledge of the interlocking product under verification.

The paper is organized as follows: in Section 2 Ladder Logic used to implement control tables is introduced. In Section 3 we discuss the possible different goals of formal verification efforts for interlocking systems. In section 4 slicing and abstraction techniques for attacking state explosion are discussed. Section 5 introduces the proposed iterative verification process, which is applied in section 7 on models obtained with the extraction procedure sketched in Section 6. Section 8 concludes the paper.

2 Ladder Logic Diagrams

In Relay Interlocking Systems (RIS), still operating in several sites, the logical rules of the control tables were implemented by means of physical relay connections. With Computer Interlocking Systems (CIS), in application since 30 years, the control table becomes a set of software equations that are executed by the interlocking. Since the signalling regulations of the various countries were

---

[1] The name is omitted for confidentiality reasons.

already defined in graphical form for the RIS, and also in order to facilitate the representation of control tables by signalling engineers, the design of CISs has usually adopted traditional graphical representations such as *Ladder Logic Diagrams* (LLD) [18] and relay diagrams [13]. These graphical schemata, also called *principle schemata*, are instantiated on a station topology to build the control table, that is then translated into a program for the interlocking.

Correctness of control tables depends also on their model of execution by the interlocking software. In building CISs, the manufacturers adopt the principle of *as safe as the relay based equipment* [1], and often the implemented model of execution is very close to the hardware behaviour of the latter.

Ladder Logic is a graphical language which can represent a set of boolean equations and their execution order (*control cycle*) can be detailed as the following equation system:

$$\tilde{x} = f(\tilde{x}, \tilde{y})$$

where $\tilde{x}, \tilde{y}$ are boolean variable vectors representing respectively state/output variables and input variables: these equations are cyclically executed. Ladder Logic represents the working of relay-based control systems. For this reason the variables on the right hand of the equation are also named *contacts*, while the variables in the left hand are named *coils*. Variables can be distinguished in:

- *Input variables*: the value is assigned by sensor readings or operator commands. These variables are defined in the expressions and cannot be used as coil.
- *Output variables*: can be only coils and their value is determined by means of the assignments of the diagram and is delivered to actuators.
- *Latch variables*: the value is calculated by means of the assignments, but is used only for internal computation of the values of other variables. A latch variable is used as coil in an assignment and is an input variable in other assignments.

With these three kinds of variables, a Ladder Logic Diagram describes a state machine whose memory is represented by the latch variables and the evolution is described by the assignment set. An execution of this state machine, named *control cycle*, involves:

1. Reading input variables; the values of these variables are assumed to be constant for the entire duration of the control cycle.
2. Compute each equation, in sequence, hence assigning values to the output variables and to the latch variables as a function of the current values of the input variables and the values of the latch variables computed at the previous control cycle.
3. Transmission of the values of the output variables.

In this way, the equations can be seen as interpreted by a reasoner engine. The reasoner engine is the same for every plan; the control table is coded as data, actually boolean equations, for the reasoner. Behind this choice is the minimization of certification efforts: the reasoner is certified once for all, the data are considered "easier" to certify if they can be related in some way to the standard principle schemata adopted by railway engineers in the era of relay-based interlockings. For this reason, this approach is also referred as "data-driven".

In order to give a metric to the dimension of the problem in terms of parameters of the control tables, [9] defines the *size* of a control table as the couple (m, n), where m is the maximum number of inter-dependent equations involved, that means equations that, taken in pairs, have at least one variable in common, and n is the number of inputs of the control table. Another used metric is just the size of the layout, given as the number of physical entities that constitute the layout (points, track circuits, signals, ...) and the number of routes that are established on the layout.

An example of a single row of a Ladder Logic Diagram is reported in figure 1, expressing the boolean equation:

$$y = x \wedge (w \vee \sim z)$$

In this graphical language, if x is a boolean variable, an expression e can be defined inductively by means of the following syntax:

- "--]   [--" represents an un-negated variable.
- "--]/ [--" represents a negated variable.
- "--( )" represents a coil.
- To mimic a logical *and* two variables are wired in series.
- To mimic a logical *or* two variables are wired in parallel.

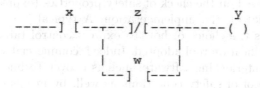

Fig. 1. Equation $y = x \wedge (w \vee \sim z)$ in ladder logic formalism

According to the above representation of the set of boolean equations we can call $\tilde{x}_i, \tilde{y}_i$ the vectors of values taken by such variables in successive executions. From the equations we can define $F(\tilde{x}_i, \tilde{x}_{i+1}, \tilde{y}_i)$ as a boolean function that is true iff $\tilde{x}_{i+1} = f(\tilde{x}_i, \tilde{y}_i)$, representing one execution of the equations. Let $Init(\tilde{x})$ be a predicate which is true for the initial vector value of state and output variables. If $P(\tilde{x})$ is a predicate telling that a desired (safety) property is verified by the vector $\tilde{x}$, then the following expression:

$$\Phi(k) = Init(\tilde{x}_0) \wedge \bigwedge_{i=0}^{k-1} F(\tilde{x}_i, \tilde{x}_{i+1}, \tilde{y}_i) \wedge \bigvee_{i=0}^{k} \sim P(\tilde{x}_i)$$

is a boolean formula that tells that P is not true for the state/output vector for some of the first k execution cycles. According to the Bounded Model Checking (BMC) principles [5], using a SAT-solver to find a satisfying assignment to the boolean variables ends up either in unsatisfiability, which means that the property is satisfied by the first k execution cycles, or in an assignment that can be used as a counterexample for P, in particular showing a k-long sequence of input vectors that cause the safety problem with P. SAT-based Bounded Model Checking has been recently used for the verification of interlocking systems in [11,15].

In Section 6 we focus on the representation in a format suitable for Design Verifier of the legacy control tables that are loaded, in the form of LLDs, in the analysed interlocking systems.

3   Verification Goals

The various attempts to formal verification of interlocking systems that we find in the literature differ in many cases for the actual verification goal, according to the phase of the development process where formal verification is applied, but also to the kind of development process followed.

Control tables may indeed play two main roles (not always both present) in the development of these systems: either as specifications of the interlocking rules [12], often issued by a railway infrastructure company, or as an implementation means, when they come encoded in some executable language, that may be either proprietary or standard, as is the case of ladder diagrams. In the first case, verification of control tables may address self consistency of the specification, or correctness of the implementation w.r.t. the specification, while in the second case it may be focused on the check of safety properties (expressed for example in a temporal logic) on the implementation. A typical issue of any of these verification tasks is the choice of how to express control tables in a language suitable for the verification tool adopted. Indeed, commercial solutions exist for the production of interlocking software, such as Prover Technology's Ilock, that includes formal proof of safety conditions as well, by means of a SAT solving engine. Industrial acceptance of such "black-box" solutions is however sometimes hindered by the fear of vendor lock-in phenomena and by the loss of control over the production process.

In an evolution line of interlocking systems, the so called "geographic" approach departs from the traditional usage of control tables: the interlocking logic is made up by composition of small elements that take care each of the control of a physical element (point, track circuit, signal) and are connected by means of predefined composition rules, mimicking the topology of the specific layout. The global interlocking logic therefore comes out as the result of the composition of the elementary bricks. The geographic approach inherits typical modelling paradigms from computer science, and can be considered as a *model-based approach*, while control tables inherit the criteria of relay-based functional definition. A known example of this approach is the EURIS language [3] developed in the Netherlands, and later adopted by Siemens, for the GRACE toolset of Siemens [17].

The relation between control tables and the geographical modelling has been studied in [2], where automated instantiation of geographical models from control tables has been proposed: this relation can also drive the verification that a geographical implementation satisfies the specifications given as control tables. On the other hand, the trend to formalize interlocking rules also at the specification level in a geographic fashion is exemplified by the INESS project, where UML State Diagrams have been chosen as the modelling language [14].

The context of this paper assumes control tables playing the role of implementation means, and is aimed to support the final system validation activity over railway signalling products coming from different branches of the industrial partner. In particular, the verification process described in the following translates the control tables expressed in the ladder diagrams proprietary format of our industrial partner. We have already mentioned the feasibility study [9], that investigated the actual applicability bounds for explicit and symbolic model checkers on this class of systems, at varying size parameters of control tables. The not encouraging results were in accordance with those obtained by several concurrent studies. Indeed, [23,21,22] show how specifically optimized verification techniques allow the range of verifiable systems to be expanded.

SAT-based verification techniques appear to be more promising, due to the native boolean coding of the control tables. This, combined with a strong indication of the industrial partner to exploit commercial modelling and verification tools, has suggested the adoption of Matlab *Design Verifier* [20] working on Simulink models.

Hence, the study has continued addressing on the one side techniques to constrain the state space size (see Sect. 4), and on the other side a framework for extracting a Simulink model from the implemented control tables, which has been introduced in [6] and summarized in Sect. 6.

4   Environment Assumptions and Slicing

We can observe that the state space of a model of an interlocking system depends on the modelling of its environment as well. Indeed, the study of [9] made no assumption whatsoever on the environment: the study was aimed at finding the limits of verification of a completely unconstrained set of boolean equations, with little attention to realism of the equations set w.r.t. actual interlocking rules. The particularly negative outcomes of that work in terms of size of tractable interlockings were mostly due to the absence of constraints on the external environment, that is to the assumption that the system is open to any behaviour of the environment.

Most works on formal verification of interlocking systems do indeed make assumptions on the behaviour of the environment, in order to constrain the state space, but also because some verification framework can only deal with a closed system. Such assumptions may take the form of an explicit model of the environment: for example, trains moving on the controlled track layout are also modelled, and the trains often obey to some reasonableness constraint, such as trains moving in only one direction, appearing in the layout only at its borders, respecting signals, and so on. Such constraints enforce only particular sequences of events (e.g. track occupancy events) to be possible inputs for the interlocking systems, and consequently limit the state space explosion typical of when considering a fully open environment. It is then a matter of the safety assessment process to demonstrate that the properties proved under given assumptions are maintained in any real situation due to the reasonableness of the environment. For example, it is possible in many cases to show that modelling two trains is enough to cover cases with more trains present in the track layout [8,19].

Such assumptions in general refer to locality properties, that is, for example, *no-derailment* on a point is scarcely related to the position of a distant point on a parallel track. To be more precise, locality is implied by the definition of *routes*, that is, the set of contiguous track elements that need to be granted for a given train movement: the routes insisting on a given track element define the elements that may be directly related to the status of the given element. Locality given by the topological layout of the controlled systems have been used in [23,21,22] to define domain-oriented optimizations of the variable ordering in a BDD-based verification.

Locality can be used also for slicing, as suggested in [9] and [15]. The idea is to consider only the portion of the model that has influence on the property to be verified, by a topological selection of interested track elements: this allows for a much more efficient verification, at the price of repeating the verification activity for each extracted slice and of showing that verifying slices does imply the satisfaction of desired properties for the whole system. Extracting a slice of the model implies to make assumptions on the environment of the slice: either an open, unconstrained environment, or constrained by reasonableness assumptions. Verification of a slice is targeted therefore to the satisfaction of local properties of the slices, under the assumptions (possibly none) given for the environment of the slice. It is therefore needed to show that the satisfaction of local properties under the given environment assumptions imply the satisfaction of global properties of interest.

We recall from [6] that the experience reported in this paper is that of an independent verifier of the interlocking systems produced by other branches of the company, with little insight of the followed process, and focusing on the final product. In this context, the verification process is applied to a low-level implementation, where the only information on the implemented high level functionality is given by the knowledge of the physical track layout and of the naming convention that specifies references given to the layout elements by the names of the boolean variables involved. Indeed, each track element n, where n is a unique identifying number, is associated to several variables whose name contains the number n. This guides the extraction of a slice.

Consider for example a no-derailment property that can be expressed as: by no way point p can move while track circuit t is occupied. A slice can be built by considering only the equations that include variables whose name contains p and t. All the other variables in the left hand of the equations are considered as free variables, and hence constitute the environment of the slice, either open or constrained by some reasonableness assumptions. If it comes out that the slice/environment pair is not suitable for meaningful verification, the pair should be refined in a successive step, giving rise to an iterative verification process.

This reasoning can be extended to any safety property. Consider a safety property ϕ that tells that a dangerous situation referring to the status of some elements $\{t_1, t_2, \ldots t_n\}$ is never reached. Let us build the smallest slice M' containing equations with variables referring $\{t_1, t_2, \ldots t_n\}$: let us call $\{x_1, x_2, \ldots x_m\}$ such variables, and $\{y_1, y_2, \ldots y_p\}$ all the other variables. in this slice all the equations assigning a value not depending from any x_i to a variable y_j is omitted. The values taken by the y_j variables are not defined, hence they can be considered as part of the fully open environment. The states reachable by executing the slice M' with any input are a superset of the states reachable when we add any constraint to the values taken by the y_j variables (e.g., by adding equations not present in M', or constraining the environment). Hence, if $M' \models \phi$, then the property is satisfied by the whole equation system M. Otherwise, a counterexample for $M' \models \phi$ may tell either that the property is not satisfied at all by M, or that M' has too few equations, or that the environment is not sufficiently constrained.

5 CEGAR-Like Verification Process

The proposed iterative verification process is inspired by the CEGAR (CounterExample Guided Abstraction Refinement) paradigm [7], in which the analysis of counterexamples drives the refinement of the model for a further verification cycle.

As shown in Fig. 5, in our case the full model is initially sliced by leaving all its input variables (that is, its environment) as unconstrained. If the property is not verified, a counterexample is generated: the counterexample is examined in order to add constraints on the environment able to remove the occurrence of spurious counterexamples (*model refinement step*).

The initial slice M', chosen on the basis of the required property (see Sect. 4), focuses on a given set of track elements, each uniquely identified by a numeric identifier. Hence the slice is constituted by the equations that refer to variables having those numbers in their identifier. As we have said, all the other variables in the right hand side of the equations are considered as free variables, and hence constitute the fully open environment of the slice. The property P' is also obtained from the desired property P through a consistent slicing mechanism. As discussed in Sect. 4, it is likely that P' is equal to P and P is a safety properties. For the discussion of this section, we just assume that $M' \models P' \Rightarrow M \models P$, that is, slicing preserves P.

The model refinement step, which is executed when P' is not satisfied and a counterexample CE is generated, can exploit different techniques, depending on the results of the analysis conducted on CE. The counterexample analysis is strictly dependent on the functional and safety aspects of system at hand, and

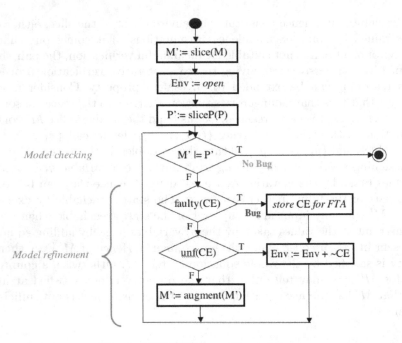

Fig. 2. CEGAR-like verification loop

hence requires some knowledge of the produced system: it is therefore a mostly manual analysis requiring help from signal engineers.

First of all, the analyst can decide that CE is actually related to some fault. The verification process can continue after storing the faulty scenario. The data that have produced the counterexample are then excluded for the next refinement step.

The decision represented in the flow graph by $unf(CE)$ is actually a phase of the counterexample analysis aimed to distinguish counterexamples that can be clearly decided to be unfeasible due to, e.g., physical constraints, from those that may be possibly unfeasible due to the actual behaviour of the environment of the slice, which is constituted by the equations excluded from the slice. In the first case, it is likely that the counterexample is generated by an unfeasible combination of values of input variables, while in the second case it is due to the unconstrained behaviour assumed for the adjacent elements, that is, by unfeasible combination of values of latch variables that are assigned by equations which have been excluded from the slice.

In the first case the analysis continues on the same slice, by excluding the input data that has produced CE, while in the second case the slice is considered too small to continue the verification process, and is augmented by bringing in all the equations that contain free variables of the M' slice[2]. Recall that at the first step the free variables of M' are those that do not contain the identifiers of the track

---

[2] This step can be automated, although in the experience reported in Sect. 7 it has been performed manually.

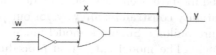

Fig. 3. Equation $y = x \wedge (w \vee \sim z)$ translated in Simulink with logical gates

elements on which the slide was first built: hence this step enlarges the scope of the considered slice to some other track elements, that with high probability are physically adjacent to the original ones due to the locality principles. The property P' needs not to be changed: indeed, $augment(M') \models P'$ means that M' satisfies P' when embedded in its proper environment.

The model refinement cycle terminates when the property is verified (possibly trivially because the model has become over-constrained): at that point the possible faulty counterexamples stored during the process can be subject to further analysis in order to plan corrective action or to support fault analysis (e.g. Fault Tree Analysis) conducted at the system level.

We have verified that the above verification process, with its incremental nature, has helped the verifier to acquire a step-by-step increasing confidence on the system's behaviour. This is expected to be an added value when the approach is adopted within an independent validation division, for which a control table is a very low-level representation of the rules implemented by the system.

We finally note that the presented process is independent from the model checking technique used, although in section 7 we will discuss how the process is applied with a Bounded Model Checker.

6   Model Extraction

One of the most critical steps in the formal verification of interlocking systems is the description of control tables in a suitable format for a model checker. In the particular context of this study, this step was entrusted to a model extraction process which is composed of three phases:

1. **Import Station Data:** all data about a station (equations, timers, interfaces, ...) are imported in Matlab by means of proprietary legacy libraries that read the binary files loaded on the interlocking system.
2. **Model Station Data:** the equations are modelled in a Simulink model by means of a tool named *LLD-Parser* [6]. The example equation of Fig. 1 is modelled, as expected, as the logic gates of Fig. 6, where the gates are actually Simulink blocks.
3. **Linking the Models:** All the equations are then linked between them by means of the latch variables, or by timers when needed; in this way the model of a station is completed. The model has as input and output the input/output variables of the equations.

The details of the procedure have been only partially described in [6], since they are covered by confidentiality constraints; anyway, for our purposes it is enough to say that the procedure builds a Simulink model made of boolean gates that replicates the ladder logic. The model extraction procedure has been applied to equipments containing up to 3500 equations with 500 input variables. This means that the produced Simulink models are very intricate and actually not human-readable.

Note that the model extraction is actually a reverse engineering process, in which some domain knowledge is needed to relate the variables used in the equations to the controlled track layout. Due to independence constraints between the validation team and the design team, this knowledge is not always readily available. In the following, in accordance with Sections 4 and 5, we assume that in the extracted model variables' identifiers refer to specific track layout elements (track circuits, points, etc.). Adjacency of layout elements is inferred from the equations, rather than known in advance. The kind of each element can be instead deduced from the identifier.

7   Verification with Design Verifier

We show in the following an example verification performed on a Computer Interlocking Subsystem that controls a small railway station.

The subsystem has 1038 equations, 321 inputs and 470 outputs; each equation can have from one input to a maximum of 25 inputs. The size of the model is therefore rather large, and slicing is therefore considered according to the iterative process defined in section 5. The verification considers a *no-derailment* property $ND35$ for a chosen point, numbered 35 (referring to the fragment of track layout represented in Fig. 5). The property has been defined as:

"Under the preconditions (which are considered to characterize the state in which the route is granted for the passage of a train):

1. A *route request* for the route 11, that includes switch 35, has been received.
2. In accordance with the route request the switches belonging to the route are in the correct position.
3. The route is reserved.

the switch 35, in the case a *movement request*, $MR35$, is received, must not move either in normal position, $NPM35$, or in reverse position, $RPM35$".

The verification with Design Verifier requires the property $ND35$ to be expressed as a Simulink "observer", as shown in Fig 4.

According to the process described in Section 4, we generate the smallest slice of the Computer Interlocking Subsystem to prove the property $ND35$; this slice includes all the equations referring variables whose identifier contains the number 35: the slice has 16 equations and 70 inputs (see figure 5). The preconditions,on the section 18 variables, have been modelled as a restriction of the station inputs.

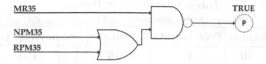

Fig. 4. Rappresentation of the property *ND35* in Simulink

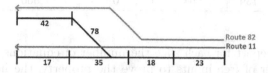

Fig. 5. Fragment of station plan where the property has been proven

The verification on *Slice1* has taken 15 iterations, each producing a new counterexample and requiring the refinement of the preconditions on the input variables to exclude the obtained counterexample. At the end of this phase, when
the property was finally satisfied, the analysis of the counterexamples and of the
input data used to exclude the counterexample in successive steps has shown
that these other preconditions had been actually introduced:

a. No other route request must have been received.
b. The route reservation announces to the adjacent station on the route the
   next arrival of a train, and the station acknowledges this announcement:
   this acknowledgement must be already received.

This consideration has suggested that enlarging the slices as recommended in the
iterative process would have soon given better results. Indeed, we have performed
such enlargement (*Slice2*) that has allowed us to include such preconditions
in the slice itself. The new slice contains all the equations that controls the
sections 17, 18, 42 and 78; finally the new inputs of the slice are the variables or
equations for the section 23. The verification of the same property for this slice
has immediately produced no counterexamples.

In order to test the sensitiveness of the approach to timing issues, we have included in *Slice3* a timer equation which was not included in *Slice2*. The duration
of the timer is set to 5 seconds, while the simulation step (a parameter of Design
Verifier [20]) is 150 milliseconds. With these parameters, the verification was not
concluded in reasonable time (presumably, the property was satisfied, but Design
Verifier was not able to complete the search for non-existing counterexamples)
because much time was spent to wait the firing of the timer.

We therefore decided to adopt a different time scale, by changing the simulation step to half a second, after checking that the different time scale is still
compatible with the functional behaviour of the slice. The property is satisfied
with the compressed time scale, and the computation time has been dramatically
decreased, well beyond expectations.

Table 1. Verification Results

Slice	Equations	Inputs	Free Inputs	Counterex.	Sim. Step (ms)	Time (sec)
$Slice_1$	16	70	42	15	150	60.0
$Slice_2$	64	140	94	0	150	104.0
$Slice_3$	65	139	94	-	150	(> 4 days)
$Slice_3$	65	139	94	0	500	46.0

In Table 1 we report for each slice the number of equations, the number of inputs, the number of free inputs to prove the property, the number of counterexamples produced before proving the property, the simulation step used and the time taken by Design Verifier to complete a single verification step. The entire process of importing data production binary files, modelling the station and proving the property has been run on an DELL XPS L501X 2.67GHz, 4GB of RAM machine with Windows 7, 64 bits, operating system.

8 Conclusion

The conducted verification experiments have shown the feasibility of the proposed iterative approach on slices of models derived by an industrial design of a quite large sized interlocking. Indeed, the whole model consisting of one thousand equations is actually not easy to deal with, although Design Verifier was able to terminate a preliminary verification experiment on the whole model, producing a counterexample with an assignment to a quite large number of input variables. We recall that the validation team, independent from the production team, has limited knowledge of the details of the equipment, and therefore was not able to interpret such a complex counterexample.

Although a systematic study in this direction has not been attempted, the size of the interlocking systems on which the approach has been evaluated is considerably larger than the limits referred in [9,21], which are around a few hundreds of equations.

The choice of Design Verifier as the used model checker, that was strongly suggested by the industrial partner, has not allowed to play with different verification strategies, being a commercial and relatively closed tool. Design Verifier is a SAT-based Bounded Model Checker [5], and hence it is best aimed at verifying that the boolean output of the observer holds for all the states up to a given depth. In the conducted experiments, the default depth of 20 Simulink simulation steps was considered to be enough to prove the above properties, since the slice was starting its behaviour from a known initial state (the route is locked) and has to respond to few stimuli. Enlarging the slice in general may increase the depth needed to prove a meaningful property. In this case, a further cycle aimed to adjust the depth value should be added to the iterative process. Obviously, increasing the depth increases the time taken by a verification step as well, in principle exponentially w.r.t. the depth due to the increase of boolean variables on which a SAT assignment is sought. The results shown in this paper were all obtained within the default bound value of 20 set by Design Verifier. Indeed, by injecting some modifications in *Slice3*, which prevent the satisfaction of *ND35*, we have obtained counterexamples of maximal length 17, so quite close to the bound.

Actually, the experimental framework we have presented in this paper will allow us to perform a comprehensive study of the actual performance of Design Verifier over a set of control tables that implement different stations for which interlocking systems are being produced by the industrial partner. This study will hopefully provide information about the actual effectiveness of performing automatic verification on large interlocking systems, giving indications about the optimal slice size that allows for a meaningful verification within reasonable computation time for the single verification steps, with minimal number of iterations. This study will require a deeper understanding of how a SAT-solver such as that used inside Design Verifier works, in order to explain apparently unusual phenomena such as the dramatic decrease of computation time on *Slice3* experimented when changing the simulation pace.

However, the proposed iterative verification process, independently from the particular model checker used, has shown its capability of refining the knowledge of the validators on the internal working of a complex equipment, due to the incremental information given by the produced counterexamples. This is in our opinion the major contribution of this research.

References

1. Vanit-Anunchai, S.: Modelling Railway Interlocking Tables Using Coloured Petri Nets. In: Clarke, D., Agha, G. (eds.) COORDINATION 2010. LNCS, vol. 6116, pp. 137–151. Springer, Heidelberg (2010)
2. Banci, M., Fantechi, A.: Instantiating Generic Charts for Railway Interlocking Systems. In: Tenth International Workshop on Formal Methods for Industrial Critical Systems (FMICS 2005), Lisbon, Portugal, September 5-6 (2005)
3. Berger, J., Middelraad, P., Smith, A.J.: EURIS, European railway interlocking specification. In: Proceedings of IRSE 1993, pp. 70–82. Institution of Railway Signal Engineers (1993)
4. Bernardeschi, C., Fantechi, A., Gnesi, S., Larosa, S., Mongardi, G., Romano, D.: A Formal Verification Environment for Railway Signaling System Design. Formal Methods in System Design, 139–161 (1998)
5. Biere, A., Cimatti, A., Clarke, E., Zhu, Y.: Symbolic Model Checking without BDDs. In: Cleaveland, W.R. (ed.) TACAS 1999. LNCS, vol. 1579, pp. 193–207. Springer, Heidelberg (1999)
6. Bonacchi, A., Fantechi, A., Bacherini, S., Tempestini, M., Cipriani, L.: Validation of Railway Interlocking Systems by Formal Verification, A Case Study. In: Counsell, S., Núñez, M. (eds.) SEFM 2013 Collocated Workshops. LNCS, vol. 8368, pp. 237–252. Springer, Heidelberg (2014)
7. Clarke, E.M., Grumberg, O., Jha, S., Lu, Y., Veith, H.: Counterexample-Guided Abstraction Refinement. In: Emerson, E.A., Sistla, A.P. (eds.) CAV 2000. LNCS, vol. 1855, pp. 154–169. Springer, Heidelberg (2000)

8. Fantechi, A.: Distributing the Challenge of Model Checking Interlocking Control Tables. In: Margaria, T., Steffen, B. (eds.) ISoLA 2012, Part II. LNCS, vol. 7610, pp. 276–289. Springer, Heidelberg (2012)
9. Ferrari, A., Magnani, G., Grasso, D., Fantechi, A.: Model checking interlocking control tables. In: Proc. 8th FORMS/FORMAT Symposium, pp. 98–107 (2010)
10. Groote, J.F., van Vlijmen, S., Koorn, J.: The Safety Guaranteeing System at Station Hoorn-Kersenboogerd. In: Logic Group Preprint Series 121. Utrecht University (1995)
11. Haxthausen, A.E., Peleska, J., Pinger, R.: Applied Bounded Model Checking for Interlocking System Designs. In: Counsell, S., Núñez, M. (eds.) SEFM 2013 Collocated Workshops. LNCS, vol. 8368, pp. 205–220. Springer, Heidelberg (2014)
12. Haxthausen, A.E., Le Bliguet, M., Kjær, A.A.: Modelling and Verification of Relay Interlocking Systems. In: Choppy, C., Sokolsky, O. (eds.) Monterey Workshop 2008. LNCS, vol. 6028, pp. 141–153. Springer, Heidelberg (2010)
13. Haxthausen, A.E.: Developing a domain model for relay circuits. Int. J. Software and Informatics 3(2-3), 241–272 (2009)
14. FP7 Project INESS - Deliverable D.1.5 Report on translation of requirements from text to UML (2009)
15. James, P., Lawrence, A., Moller, F., Roggenbach, M., Seisenberger, M., Setzer, A., Kanso, K., Chadwick, S.: Verification of Solid State Interlocking Programs. In: Counsell, S., Núñez, M. (eds.) SEFM 2013 Collocated Workshops. LNCS, vol. 8368, pp. 253–268. Springer, Heidelberg (2014)
16. James, P., Moller, F., Nguyen, H.N., Roggenbach, M., Schneider, S., Treharne, H., Trumble, M., Williams, D.: Verification of Scheme Plans using CSP‖B. In: Counsell, S., Núñez, M. (eds.) SEFM 2013 Collocated Workshops. LNCS, vol. 8368, pp. 189–204. Springer, Heidelberg (2014)
17. Jung, B.: Die Methode und Werkzeuge GRACE. In: Formale Techniken für die Eisenbahn-sicherung (FORMS 2000), Fortschritt-Berichte VDI, Reihe 12, Nr. 441. VDI Verlag (2000)
18. Kanso, K., Moller, F., Setzer, A.: Automated verification of signalling principles in railway interlocking systems. Electron. Notes Theor. Comput. Sci. 250(2), 19–31 (2009)
19. Moller, F., Nguyen, H.N., Roggenbach, M., Schneider, S., Treharne, H.: Defining and model checking abstractions of complex railway models using CSP‖B. In: Biere, A., Nahir, A., Vos, T. (eds.) HVC 2012. LNCS, vol. 7857, pp. 193–208. Springer, Heidelberg (2013)
20. Simulink, http://www.mathworks.com/products/simulink/
21. Winter, K., Robinson, N.J.: Modelling Large Railway Interlockings and Model Checking Small Ones. In: Twenty-Fifth (ACSC 2003), pp. 309–316 (2003)
22. Winter, K., Johnston, W., Robinson, P., Strooper, P., van den Berg, L.: Tool support for checking railway interlocking designs. In: Proceedings of the 10th Australian Workshop on Safety Critical Systems and Software, pp. 101–107 (2006)
23. Winter, K.: Symbolic Model Checking for Interlocking Systems. In: Flammini, F. (ed.) Railway Safety, Reliability, and Security: Technologies and Systems Engineering. IGI Global (May 2012)

Deadlock Avoidance in Train Scheduling:
A Model Checking Approach*

Franco Mazzanti, Giorgio Oronzo Spagnolo,
Simone Della Longa, and Alessio Ferrari

Istituto di Scienza e Tecnologie dell'Informazione "A.Faedo",
Consiglio Nazionale delle Ricerche, ISTI-CNR, Pisa, Italy

Abstract. In this paper we present the *deadlock avoidance* approach used
in the design of the scheduling kernel of an Automatic Train Supervision
(ATS) system. The ATS that we have designed prevents the occurrence
of deadlocks by performing a set of runtime checks just before allowing a
train to move further. For each train, the set of checks to be performed
at each step of progress is retrieved from statically generated ATS configuration data. For the verification of the correctness of the logic used
by the ATS and the validation of the constraints verified by the runtime
checks, we define a formal model that represents the ATS behavior, the
railway layout, and the planned service structure. We use this formal
model to verify both the absence of deadlocks and absence of false positives (i.e., cases in which a train is unnecessarily disallowed to proceed).
The verification is carried out by exploiting the UMC model checking
verification framework locally developed at ISTI-CNR.

1 Introduction

One of the pillars of current industry-related research in Europe is the development of intelligent green transport systems managed by smart computer platforms that can automatically move people within the cities, while at the same
time ensuring safety of passengers and personnel. In particular, in the metro
signaling domain, the increasing demand for automation have seen the raise
of Communications-based Train Control (CBTC) systems as a *de-facto* standard for coordinating and protecting the movements of trains within the tracks
of a station, and between different stations. In CBTC platforms, a prominent
role is played by the Automatic Train Supervision (ATS) system, which automatically dispatches and routes trains within the metro network. In absence
of delays, the ATS coordinates the movements of the trains by adhering to the
planned timetable. In presence of delays, the ATS has to provide proper scheduling choices to guarantee a continuous service and ensure that each train reaches
its destination. In particular, this implies that the ATS shall necessarily avoid
the occurrence of *deadlock* situations, i.e., situations where a group of trains
block each other, preventing in this way the completion of their missions.

---

* This work was partially supported by the PAR FAS 2007-2013 (TRACE-IT) project
and by the PRIN 2010-2011 (CINA) project.

F. Lang and F. Flammini (Eds.): FMICS 2014, LNCS 8718, pp. 109–123, 2014.

This paper presents the experience of ISTI-CNR in the design of the scheduling kernel of an ATS system. The component was designed within the framework of an Italian project, namely "Train Control Enhancement via Information Technology" (TRACE-IT) [1]. The project concerns the specification and development of a CBTC platform, and sees the participation of both academic and industrial partners. Within the project, a prototype of the ATS system has been implemented, which operates on a simple but not trivial metro layout with realistic train missions. To address the problem of deadlock avoidance in our ATS prototype, we have decided to develop sound solutions based on formal methods. In a short preliminary work [2], we have outlined a model-checking approach for the problem of deadlock avoidance. Such an approach included several manual steps, and did not consider the presence of *false positives* (i.e., cases in which a train is unnecessarily disallowed to proceed). The approach presented in this paper the principles of the previous work to define a more structured, semi-automated approach that can deal with realistic circular missions. Furthermore, the current strategy exploits the usage of model checking also to address the problem of false positives.

The ATS that we have designed prevents the occurrence of deadlocks by performing a set of runtime checks just before allowing a train to move further. The set of checks to be performed is retrieved from statically generated configuration data that are validated by means of model checking. Our approach to produce valid configuration data starts with the automatic identification of a set of *basic cases* of deadlocks. This goal is achieved by statically analysing the missions of all the trains, and providing a set of preliminary constraints that can be used to address the basic cases of deadlocks. Then, we build a formal model of the scheduling kernel of the ATS that includes the constraints associated to the basic cases of deadlock. We use such a formal model to verify the absence of *complex cases* of deadlocks, and to assess the absence of false positive cases. To this end, we apply model checking by means of the UMC (UML Model Checker) tool, which is a verification environment working on UML-like state machines [3]. When complex cases of deadlock are found, the formal model is updated with additional checks to address such cases. The validation process iterates until the ATS configuration data are proven to avoid all possible cases of deadlocks. The verification of the configuration data for the full railway yard is performed by decomposing it into multiple regions to be analysed separately, and by proving that the adopted decomposition allows extending the results to the full layout.

The paper is structured as follows. In Sect. 2, we illustrate an abstract model of the ATS, together with the metro layout and the missions of our ATS prototype. In Sect. 3, the basic cases of deadlocks are described, and the approach to identify and automatically avoid such cases is outlined. Sect. 4 explains how complex cases of deadlocks can occur, and introduces the problem of false positives. Sect. 5 describes the formal model provided for the ATS and the approach adopted to verify the absence of deadlocks and false positives. In Sect. 6, we describe how we have partitioned the full layout. Sect. 7 reports the most relevant works related to ours, and Sect. 8 draws conclusions and final remarks.

2   An Abstract Model of the System

The abstract behavior of the kernel of the ATS system can be seen as a state machine. This state machine has a local status recording the current progress of the train missions and makes the possible scheduling choices among the trains which are allowed to proceed.

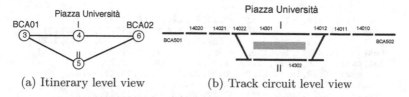

(a) Itinerary level view   (b) Track circuit level view

Fig. 1. The itinerary and track circuit level view of a station

Train movements can be observed and modeled at different levels of abstractions. In Figure 1 we show two levels of abstraction of the train movement, namely the itinerary level view and the track circuit level view. An *itinerary* is constituted by the sequence of track circuits (i.e., independent line segments) that must be traversed for arriving to a station platform from an external entry point, or for leaving from a station platform towards an external exit point. Track circuits are not visible at the itinerary level view, which is our level of observation of the system for the deadlock-avoidance problem. Instead, at the interlocking management level, we would be interested in the more detailed track circuit level view, because we have to deal with the setting of signals and commutation of switches for the preparation of the requested itineraries. Notice that it is task of the interlocking system (IXL) to ensure the safety of the system by preparing and allocating a requested itinerary to a specific train. At the ATS level it is just a performance issue the need to avoid the issuing of requests which would be denied be the IXL, or to avoid sequences of safe (in the sense risk free) train movements but which would disrupt the overall service because of deadlocks.

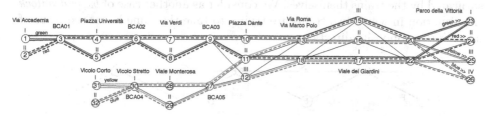

Fig. 2. The yard layout and the missions for the trains of the green, red, yellow and blue lines

In our case, the overall map of the railway yard which describes the various interconnected station platforms and station exit/entry points (itinerary endpoints) is shown in Figure 2. Given our map, the mission of a train can be seen as a sequence of itinerary endpoints. In particular, the service is constituted by eight trains which cyclically start their missions at the extreme points of the layout, traverse the whole layout in one direction and then return to their original departure point. The missions of the eight trains providing the green/red/yellow/blue line services shown in Figure 2, are represented by the data in Table 1.

Table 1. The data for the missions

```
Green1:  [1,3,4,6,7,9,10,13,15,20,23,22,17,18,11,9,8,6,5,3,1]
Green2:  [23,22,17,18,11,9,8,6,5,3,1,3,4,6,7,9,10,13,15,20,23]
Red1:    [2,3,4,6,7,8,9,10,13,15,20,24,22,17,18,11,9,8,6,5,3,2]
Red2:    [24,22,17,18,11,9,8,6,5,3,2,3,4,6,7,8,9,10,13,15,20,24]
Yellow1: [31,30,28,27,11,13,16,20,25,22,18,12,27,29,30,31]
Yellow2: [25,22,18,12,27,29,30,31,30,28,27,11,13,16,20,25]
Blue1:   [32,30,28,27,11,13,16,20,26,22,18,12,27,29,30,32]
Blue2:   [26,22,18,12,27,29,30,32,30,28,27,11,13,16,20,26]
```

In absence of deadlock avoidance checks, in our abstract model, trains are allowed to move from one point to the next under the unique condition that the destination point is not assigned to another train. This transition is modeled as an atomic transition, and only one train can move at each step. We are interested in evaluating the traffic under any possible condition of train delays. Therefore we abstract completely away from any notion of time and from the details of the time schedules. Indeed, if we consider all the possible train delays, the actually planned times of the time table become not relevant.

3   The Basic Cases of Deadlock

A *basic deadlock* occurs when we have a set of trains (each one occupying a point of the layout) waiting to move to a next point that is already occupied by another train of the set. In our railway scenario this means that we have a basic deadlock when two trains are trying to take the same itinerary in opposite directions, or when a set of trains are moving around a ring which is completely saturated by the trains themselves. We consider as another case of *basic deadlock* the situation in which two trains are trying to take the same linear sequence of itineraries in opposite directions.

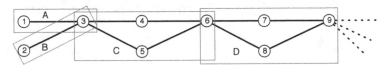

Fig. 3. A a sample selection of four basic critical sections from the full layout

For example, if we look at the top-left side of our yard layout we can easily recognize four of these zones in which the four Green and Red trains might create one of these basic deadlocks (see also Figure 3):

a) The zone A [1-3] when occupied by Green1 and Green2.
b) The zone B [2-3] when occupied by Red1 and Red2.

c) The zone C [3-4-6-5] when occupied by the four Green and Red trains.
d) The zone D [6-7-9-8] when occupied by the four Green and Red trains.

The first step of our approach to the deadlock free scheduling of trains consists in statically identifying all those zones of the railway layout in which a basic deadlock might occur. We call these zones *basic critical sections*. We have already seen the two basic kinds of critical sections, namely *ring sections* and *linear sections*, which are associated to the basic forms of deadlocks mentioned before. Given a set of running trains and their missions, the set of basic sections of a layout are statically and automatically discovered by comparing the various missions of all trains. In particular, linear sections are found by comparing all possible pairs of train missions. For example if we have that:

```
Train1: [ ..., a, x, y, z, b, ...]
Train2: [ ..., c, z, y, x, d, ...]
```

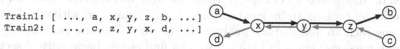

then (x,y,z) constitutes a basic linear section of the layout. Similarly if we have for example three trains such that:

```
Train1: [ ..., x, y, ...]
Train2: [ ..., y, z, ...]
Train3: [ ..., z, x, ...]
```

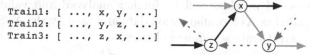

then (x,y,z) constitutes a basic ring section of the layout.

The next step of our approach consists in associating one or more counters to the critical sections in order to monitor at execution time that the access to them will not result in a deadlock. It is indeed evident that if we allow at most N-1 trains to occupy a ring section of size N no deadlock can occur on that ring. Similarly, in the case of linear sections, we could use two counters (each one counting the trains moving in one direction) and make sure that one train enters the section only if there are no trains coming from the opposite side (while still allowing several trains to enter the section from the same side). When a train is allowed to enter a basic critical section the appropriate counter is increased; when the train is no longer a risk for deadlocks (e.g. moves to an exit point of the section) the counter is decreased.

The above policy can be directly encoded in the description of the train missions by associating to each itinerary endpoint the information on which operations on the counters associated to the entered/exited sections should be performed when moving to that endpoint. We call the description of the train missions extended with this kind of information *extended train mission*.

Let S be a generic name of a section. In the following we will use the notation S+ to indicate that a train is reaching an entry point of a ring section S, (correspondingly increasing its counter), and the notation S- to indicate that a train is reaching an exit point of section S (correspondingly decreasing its counter). The notation SR+ (SR-) indicates that a train is reaching the entry (exit) point of a linear section S from when arriving from its right side. The notation SL+ (SL-) indicates that a train is reaching the entry (exit) point of a linear section S from when arriving from its left side.

The cases of deadlocks over the basic sections shown in Figure 3 can be avoided by extending the missions of the trains of the green and red lines (originally shown in Table 1) in the following way:

```
Sections:
  [A, B, C max 3, D max 3]
Train Missions:
  Green1: [ (AL+)1, (AL-,C+)3,4, (C-,D+)6,7, (D-)9,10,13,15,20,23,
              22,17,18,11, (D+)9,  8, (D-,C+)6,5, (C-,AR+)3, (AR-)1 ]
  Green2: [23,22,17,18,11, (D+)9,8, (D-,C+)6,5, (C-,AL+,AR+)3, (AR-)1,
              (AL-,C+)3,4, (C-,D+)6,7, (D-)9,10,13,15,20,23 ]
    Red1: [ (BL+)2, (BL-,C+)3,4, (C-,D+)6,7, (D-)9,10,13,15,20,24,
              17,18,11, (D+)9,8, (D-,C+)6,5, (C-,BR+)3,2 ]
    Red2: [24,22,17,18,11, (D+)9,8, (D-,C+)6,5, (C-,BL+,BR+)3, (BR-)2,
              (BL-,C+)3,4, (C-,D+)6,7, (D-)9,10,13,15,20,24 ]
```

Given the discovered set of basic sections, the description of the extended train missions for all running trains can be automatically computed without effort. By performing such an initial static analysis on the overall service provided by our eight train missions shown in Figure 2 we can find eleven basic critical sections (see Figure 4) and automatically generate the corresponding extended mission descriptions for all trains. All this automatically generated data about critical sections and extended missions will be further analyzed and validated before being finally encoded as ATS configuration data and used by the ATS to perform at runtime the correct train scheduling choices.

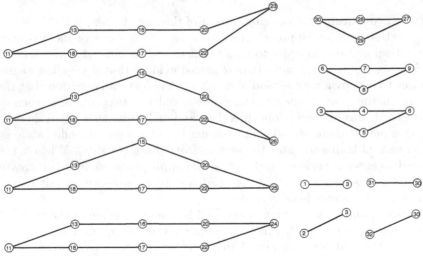

Fig. 4. All the basic critical sections of the overall layout

4   From Basic to Composite Sections

Our set of basic critical sections actually becomes a new kind of resource shared among the trains. When moving from one section to another, a train may have to release one section and acquire the next one. Again, this behavior can be subject to deadlock. Let's consider the example of regions A, B, C shown in Figure 5.

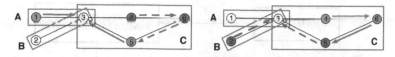

Fig. 5. Deadlock situations over the composition of basic critical sections

In the left case (the right case is just an analogous example), train `Green2` cannot exit from critical section C because it is not allowed to enter critical section A. Moreover, train `Green1` is not allowed to leave critical section A because it is not allowed to enter critical section C. The deadlock situation that is generated in the above case is not a new case of deadlock introduced by our deadlock avoidance mechanism, but just an anticipation of an unavoidable future deadlock (of the basic kind) which would occur if we allow one of the two trains to proceed. To solve these situations, we can introduce two additional composite critical section E and F respectively over the points [1-3-4-6-5], (section A plus section C) and [2-3-4-6-5] (section B plus section C), which are allowed to contain at most three of the trains `Green1`, `Green2`, `Red1`, `Red2`). These new sections are shown in Figure 6a. The missions of the Green and Red trains are correspondingly updated to take into consideration also these new sections.

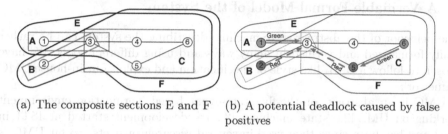

(a) The composite sections E and F   (b) A potential deadlock caused by false
                                        positives

Fig. 6. Composite sections and new deadlock case

It is very important that our mechanism does not give raise to false positive situations, i.e, situations in which a train is unnecessarily disallowed to proceed. False positive situations, in fact, not only decrease the efficiency of the scheduling but also risk to propagate to wider composite sections, creating even further cases of false positives or deadlocks.

Let us consider the situation shown in Figure 6b. The red train in 2 is not allowed to proceed in point 3 because section E already contains its maximum of three trains. The same occurs for the green train in point 1 (section F already has three trains). As a consequence nobody can progress, while, on the contrary, nothing bad would occur if the red train in 2 was allowed to proceed.

As we build greater composite sections it becomes extremely difficult to manually analyze the possible effects of the choices. We need a mechanical help for exhaustively evaluating the consequences of our choices, discover possible new cases of deadlock involving contiguous or overlapping critical sections, and completely eliminate potential false positives situations from the newly introduced composite critical sections. As shown in Figure 7, we will rely on model checking

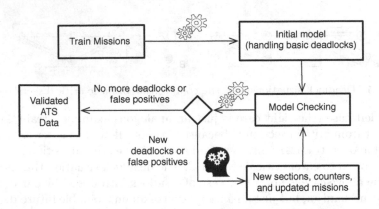

Fig. 7. The ATS configuration data validation process

approach for starting a sequence of iterations in which new problems in terms of deadlocks are found are resolved by creating and managing new sections in an incremental way.

5   A Verifiable Formal Model of the System

The behavior of the abstract state machine describing the system can be rather easily formalized and verified in many ways and using different tools. We have chosen to follow a UML-like style of specification and exploit our in-house UMC framework.

UMC is an abstract, on-the-fly, state-event based, verification environment working on UML-like state machines [3]. Its development started at ISTI in 2003 and has been since then used in several research projects. So far UMC is not really an industrial scale project but more an (open source) experimental research framework. It is actively maintained and is publicly usable through its web interface (https://fmt.isti.cnr.it/umc).

In UMC a system is described as a set of communicating UML-like state machines. In our particular case the system is constituted by a unique state machine. The structure of a state machine in UMC is defined by a Class declaration which in general has the following structure:

```
class <name> is
    Signals:
        <list of asynchronous signals managed by the objects of the class>
    Operations:
        <list of synchronous call ops managed by the objects of the class>
    Vars:
        <list of local vars belonging to the state of the objects of the class>
    Behavior:
        <list of rules defining the state evolutions of the objects of the class>
end <name>
```

The Behavior part of a class definition describes the possible evolutions of the system. This part contains a list of transition rules which have the generic form:

```
<SourceState> --> <TargetState> {<EventTrigger>[<Guard> ] /<Actions> }
```

Each rule intuitively states that when the system is in the state SourceState, the specified EventTrigger is available, and all the Guards are satisfied, then all the Actions of the transition are executed and the system state passes from SourceState to TargetState (we refer to the UML2.0 [4] definition for a more rigorous definition of the run-to-completion step).

In UMC the actual structure of the system is defined by a set of active object instantiations. A full UMC model is defined by a sequence of Class and Objects declarations and by a final definition of a set of Abstraction rules. The overall behavior of a system is in fact formalized as an abstract doubly labelled transition system (L2TS), and the Abstraction rules allow to define what we want see as labels of the states and edges of the L2TS. The temporal logic supported by UMC (which has the power of full μ-calculus but also supports the more high level operators of CTL/ACTL uses this abstract L2TS as semantic model and allows to specify abstract properties in a way that is rather independent from the internal implementation details of the system [5].

It is outside the purpose of the paper to give a comprehensive description of the UMC framework (we refer to the online documentation for more details). We believe instead that a detailed description of fragment of the overall system can give a rather precise idea of how the system is specified. To this purpose, we take into consideration just the top leftmost region of the railway yard as show by Figure 8, which is traversed only by the four trains of the green and red lines.

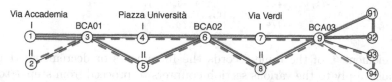

Fig. 8. The top-left region of the full railway yard

Our UMC model is composed of a single class REGION1 and a single object SYS.

```
class REGION1 is
    ...
end REGION1
SYS: REGION1  -- a single active object
Abstractions {
    <observation rules>
    }
```

In our case the class REGION1 does not handle any external event, therefore the Signals and Operations parts are absent. The Vars part, in our case contains, for each train, the vector describing its mission, and a counter recording the current progress of the train (an index of the previous vector). E.g.

```
G1M: int[]:= [1,3,4,6,7,9,92,91,9,8,6,5,3,1];  --mission of train Green1
G1P: int  := 0;  --progress inside mission of train Green1, i.e. index inside G1M
```

Similar mission and progress data is defined for the other trains as G2M, G2P (train Green2), R1M, R1P (train Red1), R2M, R2P (train Red2).

As we have seen in the previous sections, in this area we have to handle six critical sections, called A, B, C, D, E, F. For the sake of simplicity, in in this case we handle the linear A and B critical sections as if they were rings of size 2 (which allow at most one train inside them). We use six variables to record the limits of each section, and other six variables to record the current status of the various sections, properly initialized with the number of the trains initially inside them.

```
MAXSA: int :=1;    -- section A: [1,3] (see Figures 3, 6a and 8)
MAXSB: int :=1;    -- section B: [2,3]
MAXSC: int :=3;    -- section C: [3,4,5,6]
MAXSD: int :=3;    -- section D: [6,7,9,8]
MAXSE: int :=3;    -- section E: [1,3,4,5,6]
MAXSF: int :=3;    -- section F: [2,3,4,5,6]
SA: int :=1;    SB: int :=1;    SC: int :=0;
SD: int :=0;    SE: int :=1;    SF: int :=1;
```

For each train, the set of section updates to be performed at each step is recorded into another table which has the same size of the train mission. We show below the table G1C which describes the section operations to be performed by train Green1 during its progress:

```
G1C: int[] :=  -- Section counters updates to be performed by train Green1
  --A,B,C,D,E,F
  [[1,0,0,0,1,0],      --1       [0,0,0,0,0,0],       --92-91
   [-1,0,1,0,0,1],     --1-3     [0,0,0,1,0,0],       --11-9
   [0,0,0,0,0,0],      --3-4     [0,0,0,0,0,0],       --9-8
   [0,0,-1,1,-1,-1],   --4-6     [0,0,1,-1,1,1],      --8-6
   [0,0,0,0,0,0],      --6-7     [0,0,0,0,0,-1],      --6-5
   [0,0,0,-1,0,0],     --7-9     [1,0,-1,0,0,0],      --5-3
   [0,0,0,0,0,0],      --9-92    [0,0,0,0,0,0]];      --3-1
```

The element i of the table records the increments or decrements that the train must apply to the various section counters to proceed from step i to step i+1 of its mission. For example, in order to proceed, at step 1, from endpoint 1 to endpoint 3, train Green1 must apply the updates described in the element [-1,0,1,0,0,1], i.e., decrement the counter of section A, and increment the counters for sections C and F.

In the Behavior part of our class definition we will have one transition rule for each train, which describes the conditions and the effects of the advancement of the train. In our case there is no external event which triggers the system transitions, therefore they will be controlled only by their guards.

In the case of train Green1, for example, we will have the rule:

```
01:  s1 -> s1
02:  { - [(G1P <13) and  --  13 is the length of the mission for green1
03:      (G1M[G1P+1] /= R1M[R1P]) and                    ----
04:       (G1M[G1P+1] /= G2M[G2P]) and                      |
05:        (G1M[G1P+1] /= R2M[R2P]) and                     |
06:        (SA + G1C[G1P+1][0] <= MAXSA) and                |
07:         (SB + G1C[G1P+1][1] <= MAXSB) and               | Guard
08:          (SC + G1C[G1P+1][2] <= MAXSC) and              |
09:           (SD + G1C[G1P+1][3] <= MAXSD) and             |
10:            (SE + G1C[G1P+1][4] <= MAXSE) and            |
11:             (SF + G1C[G1P+1][5] <= MAXSF)] /       ----
12:      SA := SA + G1C[G1P+1][0];         ----
13:      SB := SB + G1C[G1P+1][1];            |
14:      SC := SC + G1C[G1P+1][2];            |
```

```
15:      SD := SD + G1C[G1P+1][3];          | Actions
16:      SE := SE + G1C[G1P+1][4];          |
17.      SF := SF + G1C[G1P+1][5];          |
18:      G1P := G1P +1;                      ----
19:   }
```

The above rule states that, if train Green1 has not yet completed its mission (line 02), and the next endpoint for its mission is not already assigned to another train (lines 03–05), and for each critical section the update of its associated counter does not exceed the stated limits (lines 06–11), then the train is allowed to proceed: the section counters are updated as requested by the step (lines 12–17) and the train progress is incremented of one step (line 18). Similarly, it is done for all the other four trains.

Finally, we have to define what we want to observe on the abstract L2TS associated to the system evolutions. Actually we are just interested to observe that a certain state is the final one, where all trains have completed all their steps, therefore returning to the point where they started from.

This can be done assigning a label, e.g. ARRIVED to all the system configuration in which the each train is in its final position.

```
Abstractions {
State SYS.G1P=13 and
      SYS.G2P=13 and
      SYS.R1P=13 and
      SYS.R2P=13 -> ARRIVED
}
```

The above abstraction rule specifies that the ARRIVED label should be assigned to a state when the progresses of the four trains reach the value 13 (the last index of all the train missions).

At this point the L2TS associated to our model will be a directed graph which will converge to a final state labelled ARRIVED in the case that no deadlock occurs in the system. This can be easily checked by verifying the CTL-like formula:

AF ARRIVED

The formula states that all paths (A in the formula) starting from the initial state of the system eventually will reach (F) a state labelled HOME. If this property does not hold we observe the generated counterexample and view all the details of the path which leads to the deadlocked state.

In our case the formula is true. The generated statespace has just 10073 configurations, and UMC explores all of them in a few seconds.

But are we sure that we have removed all the possible cases of false positives? One way to verify that is to allow a train to proceed even if its progress violates the constraints of the critical sections, but marking the reached state as DEAD. This is easily done in our model by removing the conditions on the section counters from the guards of the train transitions, and by adding in the Abstraction part the following observation rules:

```
State SYS.SA > MAXSA -> DEAD
State SYS.SB > MAXSB -> DEAD
State SYS.SC > MAXSC -> DEAD
```

```
State SYS.SD > MAXSD -> DEAD
State SYS.SE > MAXSE -> DEAD
State SYS.SF > MAXSF -> DEAD
```

In this way we can check the absence of false positives by verifying the formula:

not EF (DEAD **and EF** ARRIVED)

Which states that does not exists a path (E) which eventually reches (F) a state that labelled DEAD, and from which exists (E) a continuation of the path which eventually reaches (F) a state in which all trains are in their destination.

Unfortunately the above formula false, and that allows discovering several other cases of false positives, (like the one shown in Figure 9) whose removal requires a more refined use of the counters (the final version of the code can be found at http://fmt.isti.cnr.it/umc/examples/traceit/).

If we want to check again the absence of deadlocks in this second kind of model we can now modelcheck the formula:

A[(EF ARRIVED) **U** (DEAD **or** ARRIVED)]

This is a typical branching time formula, which states two things. The first is that all paths will eventually reach a state labelled as DEAD or ARRIVED. The second is that for all intermediate states of these paths there is scheduling choice that allows driving all trains to destination (EF ARRIVED).

In this case the size of the generated statespace is 10493 configurations and the evaluation time is less than two seconds.

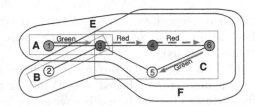

Fig. 9. Another case of false positive for section E

6   Partitioning the Full Model

Sometimes the scheduling problem might be too complex to be handled by the model checker. In these cases, it is useful to split the overall layout into subregions to be analyzed separately. In particular, in the system used as our case study, we have four trains moving along the red-line and green-line service, and four other trains moving along the yellow-line and blue-line service. In we consider all the possible interleavings of eight trains each one performing about 20 steps, we get a system with about 20^8 configurations. Most model checkers (and UMC among them) may have difficulties in performing an exhaustive analysis over a system of this size, therefore it is useful to consider a possible splitting of the overall layout. In our case we have considered a partitioning of the system as shown in Figure 10. The analysis of region 1 has been performed following the approach outlined in the previous sections, and has led to the management of six critical sections.

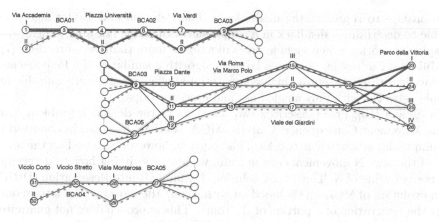

Fig. 10. The three regions partitioning the full layout

The analysis of region 3 is similar to the previous one, and leads to the introduction of further four critical sections. The analysis of region 2 is more complex, being bigger and with 8 trains inside it. The analysis does not reveals any new cases of deadlocks or false positives, therefore the critical section remain the basic sections already discovered with our static analysis (shown in Figure 11). The statespace size of the model for region 2 is 6,820,504 configurations and its verification takes a few minutes.

In general, it is not true that the separate analysis of the single regions in which a layout is partitioned actually reveals all the possible deadlocks of the full system. For this being true it is necessary that the adopted partitioning does not cut (hiding it from the analysis) any critical section that overlaps two regions. Since we know from our static analysis were are positioned the basic critical sections for the layout, and we know that composite sections can only extend over contiguous/overapping basic sections, it is sufficient to partition the system in such a way that each region encloses completely a closed group of connected basic sections.

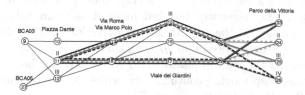

Fig. 11. Four critical sections in region 2

7   Related Work

The problem of deadlock avoidance in train scheduling has been studied since the 80s. In one of the first works on the subject, Petersen and Taylor [6] propose a solution based on dividing the line into track segments and using algebraic relationships to represent the model logic. The Petersen and Taylor algorithm is able to determine a deadlock in a simple network but is not able to deal with complex networks, which include fleets moving in more than two directions [7].

Mills and Pudney [8] propose a labeling algorithm similar to the Petersen and Taylor algorithm, presenting high computational efficiency but only suitable for simple networks with only single lines and crossing loops.

In [9] and [10], Pachl describes two solutions to the deadlock problem. One is the Movement Consequence Analysis (MCA), derived from studies on routing techniques for stochastic networks. This solution, however, is based on the analysis of the next N movements of the train, without specifying how to determine the correct value of N. The second solution, Dynamic Route Reservation (DRR), is an evolution of MCA and is based on authorizing the movement of a train only after the reservation of a portion of the route. This approach does not guarantee the absence of deadlock and can lead to false positives.

In [7], Cui describes an application of the Bankers Algorithm to the deadlock problem. Movement tasks are modeled as processes and track segments as resources. Requests are approved if all the processes can obtain all the required resources. The algorithm can lead to false positives and it is time-consuming. The author proposes various improvements to reduce false positives and improve general performance.

Mittermayr [11] uses Kronecker Algebra to model the train routes and build an evolution graph, subsequently reduced to the relevant synchronizing nodes. This approach has been used to model additional constraints such as alternative routes, long trains that occupy more than one track circuit, synchronization in case of route overtaking and connection. The solution avoids false positives and false negatives. This approach, however, requires the Scheduler to have access to the evolution graph in order to successfully schedule trains dynamically.

8 Conclusions

The development of solutions to the problem of deadlock avoidance in train scheduling is a complex and still open task [12]. Many studies have been carried out on the subject since the early '80s, but most of them are related to normal railway traffic, and not to the special case of driverless metropolitan systems. Automatic metro systems indeed may express some original properties, e.g., the difficulty of changing the station platform on which a train should stop, or the fact that all trains keep moving continuously, which makes the problem rather different from the classical railway case. The project under which this study has been carried out is still in progress, and the actual ATS prototype in under development. There are many directions in which this work is going to proceed. For example, we want to see if the model checking / model refinement cycles for the detection and management of critical sections could be in some way fully automatized removing the human intervention for the generation of the final validated ATS configuration data. A further interesting evolution would be the generation and validation of the critical sections data directly from the inside of the ATS. This would allow to automatically handle at run time also the dynamic change of the itinerary of the trains. The current metro-line oriented approach could be further generalized to a wider railway oriented setting by taking into consideration the train and platform lengths, or the possibility of specifying connections and overtakings among trains. At a first look the handling of these aspects should require only minor updates of our current approach.

References

1. Ferrari, A., Spagnolo, G.O., Martelli, G., Menabeni, S.: From commercial documents to system requirements: an approach for the engineering of novel CBTC solutions. Int. Journal on STTT, 1–21 (2014)
2. Mazzanti, F., Spagnolo, G.O., Ferrari, A.: Designing a deadlock-free train scheduler: A model checking approach. In: Badger, J.M., Rozier, K.Y. (eds.) NFM 2014. LNCS, vol. 8430, pp. 264–269. Springer, Heidelberg (2014)
3. Gnesi, S., Mazzanti, F.: An abstract, on the fly framework for the verification of service-oriented systems. In: Wirsing, M., Hölzl, M. (eds.) SENSORIA Project. LNCS, vol. 6582, pp. 390–407. Springer, Heidelberg (2011)
4. OMG: Object Management Group, UML Superstructure Specification (2006), http://www.omg.org/spec/UML/2.4.1
5. ter Beek, M.H., Mazzanti, F., Gnesi, S.: CMC-UMC: A Framework for the Verification of abstract Service-Oriented Properties. In: Proceedings of the 2009 ACM Symposium on Applied Computing, pp. 2111–2117. ACM (2009)
6. Petersen, E., Taylor, A.: Line Block Prevention in Rail Line Dispatch and Simulation Models. INFOR Journal (21), 46–51 (1983)
7. Cui, Y.: Simulation-based hybrid model for a partially-automatic dispatching of railway operation. Ph.D. Thesis Universitat Stuttgart (2009)
8. Mills, R., Pudney, P.: The effects of deadlock avoidance on rail network capacity and performance. In: Hewitt, J. (ed.) MISG: Mathematics in Industry Study Group (2003)
9. Pachl, J.: Avoiding deadlocks in synchronous railway simulations. In: International Seminar on Railway Operations Modelling and Analysis, pp. 359–369 (2007)
10. Pachl, J.: Deadlock avoidance in railroad operations simulations. In: PROMET Traffic & Transportation. Number 11-0175, pp. 359–369 (2012)
11. Mittermayr, R., Blieberger, J., Schöbel, A.: Kronecker Algebra based Deadlock Analysis for Railway Systems. PROMET - Traffic & Transportation 24(5), 359–369 (2012)
12. Törnquist, J.: Computer-based decision support for railway traffic scheduling and dispatching: A review of models and algorithms. In: 5th Workshop on Algorithmic Methods and Models for Optimization of Railways, p. 659 (2006)

An Open Alternative for SMT-Based Verification
of SCADE Models

Henning Basold[1], Henning Günther[2], Michaela Huhn[3], and Stefan Milius[4]

[1] Radboud University Nijmegen and CWI Amsterdam, The Netherlands
h.basold@cs.ru.nl
[2] Institut für Informationssysteme, Technische Universität Wien, Austria
guenther@forsyte.at
[3] Department of Informatics, Clausthal University of Technology
Clausthal-Zellerfeld, Germany
Michaela.Huhn@tu-clausthal.de
[4] Lehrstuhl für Theoretische Informatik, FAU Erlangen-Nürnberg
Erlangen, Germany
mail@stefan-milius.eu

Abstract. SCADE is an industrial strength synchronous language and tool suite for the development of the software of safety-critical systems. It supports formal verification using the so-called Design Verifier. Here we start developing a freely available alternative to the Design Verifier intended to support the academic study of verification techniques tailored for SCADE programs. Inspired by work of Hagen and Tinelli on the SMT-based verification of LUSTRE programs, we develop an SMT-based verification method for SCADE programs. We introduce LAMA as an intermediate language into which SCADE programs can be translated and which easily can be transformed into SMT solver instances. We also present first experimental results of our approach using the SMT solver Z3.

1 Introduction

The software of safety-critical systems needs to fulfil strong requirements concerning its correctness. This is why great efforts are made to verify, validate and certify such software. A model-based development accompanied by formal verification is a well accepted means to frontload and complement quality assurance for software. In fact, formal methods, in particular formal verification techniques, are highly recommended by safety standards, such as DO-178B [11] for the avionics domain or EN50128 [8] for the railway domain, in a software process appropriate for the higher safety integrity levels.

For many safety-critical systems, synchronously clocked controllers are the preferred implementation method. SCADE[1] is an industrial strength modelling language and tool suite for the development of such controllers. Its language is based on the synchronous data flow language LUSTRE (Halbwachs et al. [17]) and was extended by various features, most importantly, by so-called safe state machines (André [2]). The tool suite

---

[1] SCADE is developed and distributed by Esterel Technologies, see
www.esterel-technologies.com

F. Lang and F. Flammini (Eds.): FMICS 2014, LNCS 8718, pp. 124–139, 2014.

includes, among other features, code generation, graphical modelling, test automation, and the SCADE Design Verifier (DV) for SAT-based verification[2].

However, while SCADE DV performs very well for certain verification tasks, it can fail badly for others due to complexity problems. In the latter case the user has little to no information guiding to the causes making verification infeasible. This makes it almost impossible to assess whether it may be most promising to take further measures to make the formal verification task at hand eventually feasible, to settle for a weaker verification result (e.g. using bounded model checking using the *debug strategy* of SCADE DV) or even abandon further formal verification attempts and rather invest more efforts in testing. This is a disadvantage both for practical application in industry and for research pertaining to formal verification with SCADE DV (see, e.g., the study [20] on formal safety analysis of two industrial SCADE models). It may also explain the industries' indecision towards adopting formal verification in productive processes.

The work we present here is intended as a first step to counteract the above disadvantage. It is inspired by Hagen and Tinelli's work [15,16] on the SMT-based verification of synchronous LUSTRE programs. We build on their ideas to make the first steps towards a new verification method for SCADE models. After recalling necessary preliminaries in Sec. 2, we introduce the language LAMA in Sec. 3. This language is intended as an intermediate language into which synchronous models such as SCADE models can be translated and that allows for an easy generation of SMT instances. In the ensuing Sec. 4 and 5 we then describe the translation of SCADE synchronous programs to LAMA and of LAMA programs to SMT instances. Further, in Sec. 6 we present a prototypical implementation of a verification tool based on these translations. As an SMT solver we use Z3 [26]. We also provide first experimental results comparing our verification tool with SCADE DV. While SCADE DV still outperforms our tool, our experiments provide an argument for the correctness of our translations. In addition, our verification tool is freely available online. Hence, the LAMA language and our implementation can serve as a platform for the further academic study of the verification of synchronous SCADE programs, in particular for trying out various optimization and abstraction techniques in future work.

Related work. This paper reports the results of the first authors master's thesis [5]. We already mentioned Hagen's and Tinelli's work [15,16] on the SMT-based verification of LUSTRE programs resulting in the model checker KIND (using Yices [12] as SMT solver). Recent progress on this using parallelization was reported by Kahsai and Tinelli [22]. The basic ideas for verifying synchronous models using a SAT solver and induction go back to Sheeran et al. [28], and were implemented in the LUCIFER tool [23], a precursor of SCADE DV. The basics and usage of SCADE DV were reported by Abdulla et al. [1].

There are several methods and tools available for the formal verification of LUSTRE programs. The Lesar tool comes with the LUSTRE distribution [19,27]. NBAC [21] is a verification tool that is founded on abstract interpretation. Luke is a verification tool written by Koen Claessen which is an inductive verifier using an eager encoding into a SAT solver. Rantanplan by Franzén [14] is an incremental SMT-based verification tool for the inductive verification of LUSTRE programs; Franzén compared his tool

---

[2] SCADE DV uses a SAT solver developed by Prover Technologies, see www.prover.com.

with NBAC and Luke. Champion et al. [9] proposed to enhance k-induction based verification for LUSTRE by automated lemma generation. In the STUFF tool they joined property-directed heuristics and the arbitrary combination of system variables to come up with invariants that allow to strenghten the property to be proven.

An alternative approach to the verificaton of SCADE programs was developed at Rockwell Collins (see Whalen at al. [29]). This approach makes use of a transformation from SCADE to LUSTRE that was provided by the SCADE code generator at the time. LUSTRE programs are then translated into SAL ("Symbolic Analysis Laboratory", see [25]), which also uses Yices as SMT solver. This translation is not freely available but was reimplemented by Hagen and Tinelli [16] to compare performace with KIND; the latter outperformed the SAL based verification in most cases. The SAL language comes quite close to LAMA but is missing automata; it does have quantifiers (over values), though, a feature not present in LAMA. Unfortunately, the translation from SCADE to LUSTRE is no longer provided by current SCADE versions.

2   Preliminaries

We begin with a very brief overview of the SCADE language and formal verification using SCADE DV in Sec. 2.1; for a detailed language description see [13].

In Sec. 2.2–2.4 we give a brief overview over the role of Satisfiability Modulo Theories (SMT), the SMT-logic and background theories we are using, and how we are encoding the semantics of synchronous systems using this logic and theories.

2.1   SCADE and SCADE DV

As we mentioned already, SCADE is a mixture of a LUSTRE-based synchronous dataflow languages and so-called safe state machines. The basic building blocks of a SCADE model are the *operators*, each of which declares its input, output and local (state) variables. The type system supports simple datatypes (**bool**, **int**, ...) as well as enumerations, arrays and records. The LUSTRE like dataflow part of the language allows to connect inputs to outputs using (among others) logical and arithmetic operations, case distinction ("if-then-else") and up to iterators (map and fold) on arrays. Information can be stored in local variables across clock cycles and, importantly, the delay operators fby ("followed by") and pre allow to access values of variables from previous clock cycles. The safe state machines allow to switch control between different dataflow diagrams. They support hierarchy, i.e., states can contain arbitrary dataflow or state machine models. Safe state machines and dataflow models are fully integrated. Figure 1 shows an example SCADE node (without the interface specification).

The behavior of a SCADE model is formally captured as a transition system on which SAT-based model checking of safety properties can be performed [1]. SCADE DV does not offer a temporal logic but properties have to be modeled as combination of an invariant and *synchronous observers* [18] in the SCADE modeling language. Such an observer for a given SCADE operator is itself a SCADE operator that receives the inputs and outputs of the operator to be observed and signals through a Boolean output whether the safety property it monitors holds. SCADE DV then verifies whether the Boolean output of the observer in parallel composition with the given SCADE operator is always **true**.

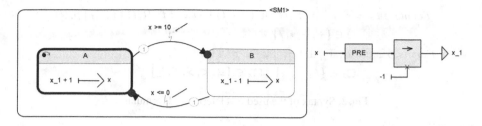

Fig. 1. Periodic counter in SCADE from [24]

2.2 Satisfiability Modulo Theories

In many cases performing model checking by fully exploring the state space of a system is infeasible at best, or even impossible. A lot of research has been devoted to tackle this problem. One possibility is to perform so-called *symbolic model checking* by encoding a system into logical formulas (usually in first-order logic). Most such descriptions use some so-called "background theory" $\mathcal{T}$ [3], which is independent of the system under consideration (e.g. integer arithmetic). It might be possible to encode such a theory $\mathcal{T}$ as "library" in first-order logic, but this can lead to performance problems. Usually, the required theories are nicely behaved, so a general purpose solver can be replaced by a specialized solver for $\mathcal{T}$. Using a fixed background theory $\mathcal{T}$, systems can often be described by quantifier free formulas. The validity of these formulas is then efficiently checked by combining a SAT-solver with a specialized solver for $\mathcal{T}$. This combination of SAT with specialized theories is called *Satisfiability Modulo Theories (SMT)*.

The SMT-solver that we are using in our implementation is Z3 [26]. To communicate with the solver we use the standardized text format SMT-LIBv2 [4].

2.3 Simplified SMT-Logic

In this paper we are using an instance of SMT with theories for arithmetic on the integers $\mathbb{Z}$, the rationals $\mathbb{Q}$ and the finite rings $\mathbb{Z}_n = \mathbb{Z}/n\mathbb{Z}$. Moreover, we need to be able to make inductive definitions on the naturals $\mathbb{N}$ and combine these basic types using a product type. Besides the usual arithmetic operators and relations among the basic types we will use λ-abstraction over variables of the basic types above. To ease readability we favor a specialized syntax over SMT-LIBv2, even though SMT-LIBv2 is used in the implementation. The syntax we use is displayed in Fig. 2. The used variables x range over a set Var of term variables, the special symbols ite and p_1, p_2 are functions having the expected meaning of if-then-else and product projections, respectively. The arithmetic operations and relations are overloaded for $\mathbb{Z}$, $\mathbb{Q}$ and $\mathbb{Z}_n$, and formulas can be used as terms of type $\mathbb{B}$ (Boolean).

Another feature we require is the ability to define uninterpreted symbols. We write $\Sigma = v_1 : A_1, \ldots, v_n : A_n$ for the uninterpreted signature with variables v_i of type A_i. If Γ is a set of formulas, then we say that a formula φ is *valid* in Σ and Γ, if φ holds for any assignment to variables in Σ under the assumption of Γ, denoted as $\Sigma; \Gamma \vDash \varphi$.

$$Terms \ni t ::= x \mid c \mid \varphi \mid t \,\Box\, t \mid \text{ite}(\varphi, t, t) \mid \lambda x.t \mid t \, t \mid (t, t) \mid p_1(t) \mid p_2(t)$$
$$\Box \in \{+, -, *, /\}$$
$$Forms \ni \varphi ::= x \mid \top \mid \bot \mid \neg\varphi \mid \varphi \,\Box_1\, \varphi \mid t \,\Box_2\, t$$
$$\Box_1 \in \{\wedge, \vee, \rightarrow\} \quad \Box_2 \in \{\equiv, <, >, \leq, \geq\}$$

Fig. 2. Syntax of the used SMT terms and formulas

2.4 Streams

One way of giving semantics to synchronous programs is by viewing them as stream transformations, i.e., functions taking streams of inputs to streams of outputs. A *stream* over a set X is a map $\sigma : \mathbb{N} \to X$. We denote the set of all streams over X by X^ω, hence a *stream transformation* is a map $X^\omega \to Y^\omega$.

The output of a synchronous program depends only on "what happened so far". More precisely, synchronous programs are in the class $\mathcal{C}(X, Y)$ of *causal* stream transformations, where $f : X^\omega \to Y^\omega$ is causal if for all $\sigma \in X^\omega$ and $n \in \mathbb{N}$ the value $f(\sigma)(n)$ only depends on $\sigma(0), \ldots, \sigma(n)$. The reason is that synchronous programs work stepwise, i.e., they are given by a map $c : S \times X \to S \times Y$ taking a state $s \in S$ and an input $x \in X$ to $c(s, x) = (s', y)$, a new state s' and an output y. Transition maps like c are known as *Mealy machines*, and inherently forbid "to look into the future".

We can represent streams over X directly in the SMT language from Sec. 2.2 as function symbols of type $\mathbb{N} \to X$. Assume we are given a transition map c, then the semantics of c for an input stream σ is given by the predicate

$$\text{Iter}(c, \sigma, \gamma, \tau, n) := (\gamma(n + 1) \equiv c_1(\gamma(n), \sigma(n))) \wedge (\tau(n) \equiv c_2(\gamma(n), \sigma(n))), \quad (1)$$

where $\gamma : S^\omega$ is the stream of internal states, $\tau : Y^\omega$ the stream of outputs and $c_i = p_i \circ c$, $i = 1, 2$. If σ, γ and τ are understood from the context, we just write $\widehat{c}_n = \text{Iter}(c, \sigma, \gamma, \tau, n)$. Given an *initial condition* $s_0 : S$, the formula $\Delta_n = (\gamma(0) \equiv s_0) \wedge \bigwedge_{i=0}^{n} \widehat{c}_i$ defines $\gamma(i)$ and $\tau(i)$, $i = 0, \ldots, n$ uniquely, i.e., it approximates the streams γ and τ up to the n-th position. Just using τ, we can thus approximate the corresponding causal $f \in \mathcal{C}(X, Y)$: $\Delta_n \vDash f(\sigma)(n) \equiv \tau(n)$.

This approximation is the basis for bounded model checking: given a predicate $P(x, s, y)$ on $X \times S \times Y$, we can check that P holds up to depth n by showing $\Sigma; \Delta_n \vDash \bigwedge_{i=0}^{n} P_i$. Here we simplify again notation by writing $P_i = P(\sigma(i), \gamma(i), \tau(i))$ and, moreover, we use $\Sigma = \sigma : X^\omega, \gamma : S^\omega, \tau : Y^\omega$.

On the other hand, if we want to prove that the predicate P holds for every $n \in \mathbb{N}$, we can show this by induction, i.e., by showing that $\Sigma; \Delta_0 \vDash P_0$ and $\Sigma; \widehat{c}_n, P_n, \widehat{c}_{n+1} \vDash P_{n+1}$ hold. Since this not possible for every c and P, one can try to strengthen the induction hypothesis by, for example, using k-induction [6,28].

3 The LAMA Language

We introduce the intermediate language LAMA (= *Low Abstraction & Mode Automata*) to bridge the gap between the numerous and complex concepts offered in the SCADE language and the encoding as a set of formulas that can be delivered to an SMT-solver.

LAMA supports a reduced set of language concepts only, but structured data types and automata are included as they are promising for optimizations when transferred to the SMT framework. In this sense, LAMA extends and varies from NBAC [21]: LAMA automata allow for hierarchical and parallel composition, local dataflow may be assigned to modes, i.e. automata states, at each level. LAMA automata are inspired by mode automata [24], but with the difference that the LAMA transitions semantics corresponds to strong transitions as used in safe state machines [2] in SCADE.

A LAMA program consists of a collection of declarations of types, constants, input, local, and state variables and nodes, a (global) dataflow, initializations, assertions and an invariant. A node is declared by its name and its input and output parameters. It may contain a set of subnodes $\mathcal{N}$, its own local and state variables V, a local flow F, initializations S_0, automata definitions $\mathcal{A}$, and an invariant Inv. A node is denoted by $N = (\textbf{node}\ x\ y\ \mathcal{N}\ V\ F\ S_0\ \mathcal{A}\ Inv)$ in what we call abstract syntax; the concrete syntax is shown in the example in Fig. 3. An automaton $A = (\textbf{automaton}\ L_A\ l_0\ E_A) \in \mathcal{A}$ consists of a collection L_A of modes (**location** in the concrete LAMA syntax) and an initial mode l_0. The body contains the transitions (**edge**) E_A between the modes.

In case a variable is not explicitly defined in each mode, the **default** block is used to define a default assignment. The usage of a node is denoted by $(\textbf{use}\ N\ t_1 \ldots t_k)$ in LAMA where t_i are the actual parameter terms.

A dataflow consists of local variable definitions and the initialization and transition definition for state variables.

The definition of the next state's value of a variable[3] is denoted by „ " (see line 6, Fig. 3). In order to deal with the SCADE operators fby and pre either a **transition** definition will be used, or an automata declaration is introduced (see Sec. 4 for details). LAMA expressions may use the usual logical, arithmetical and relational operators, projections (for product types), and pattern matching for user defined enumerations. Their use, as well as the full syntax of LAMA can be found in appendix A.1 in [5].

The scope of a variable is exactly the block in which it is declared (excluding inner blocks) with the exception of globally declared enumerations and constants.

The Type System. The syntax and semantics of LAMA types are shown in Fig. 4. The LAMA typing rules follow the Cardelli's ideas [7], the details are given in appendix A.2 in [5].

Causality Analysis. As for SCADE, LAMA programs have to be causal, meaning that the definition of a variable for the current time instant must not instantaneously depend on itself. In order to check causality, a dependency graph of the variables is constructed. If this yields a strict (evaluation) order on the variables, the program is causal. Our approach for LAMA is similar to the causality check in SCADE.

3.1 Dynamic Semantics

The internal state space of a LAMA program P is denoted $S = \prod_j \llbracket T_j^{int} \rrbracket$ where T_j^{int} is the type of a state variable v_j. The space of the input and output values is denoted $X =$

---

[3] i.e., the next value within the stream associated with x in the LAMA semantics.

```
1   nodes
2     node UpDown () returns (xo : int) let
3       local x1 : int;
4       state x : int;
5       definition xo = x1;
6       transition x' = x1;
7
8       automaton let
9         location A let definition x1 = (+ x 1); tel
10        location B let definition x1 = (- x 1); tel
11        initial A;
12        edge (A, B) : (= x 10);
13        edge (B, A) : (= x 0);
14        edge (A, A) : (not (= x 10));
15        edge (B, B) : (not (= x 0));
16      tel
17
18      initial x = (- 1);
19    tel
20  local x : int;
21  definition x = (use UpDown);
22
23  invariant
24    (and (>= x 0) (<= x 10));  — range: 0 to 10
```

Fig. 3. UpDown counter example adapted from [24]

$\prod_k \llbracket T_k^{in} \rrbracket$ and $Y = \prod_l \llbracket T_l^{out} \rrbracket$. As the definition of a variable may depend on the current modes of the automata, the semantics takes the modes into account: $Q = \prod_{A \in \mathcal{A}_P} L_A$.

The semantics of P is then given by a stream transformation $\llbracket P \rrbracket : X^\omega \to Y^\omega$ defined by a Mealy machine (Sec. 2.4) $c_P : S \times Q \times X \to S \times Q \times Y$ on the state space $S \times Q$. The mapping $\llbracket P \rrbracket$ is defined by the iteration of c_P: let x be an input stream, we put $(s_{n+1}, q_{n+1}, y_n) = c_P(s_n, q_n, x_n)$. This sequence starts at $(s_0, q_0) = (\llbracket S_0 \rrbracket, (l_0^A)_{A \in \mathcal{A}_P})$, the semantics of the initialization predicate, and initial modes of all automata. Using this iteration, we define $\llbracket P \rrbracket(x)(n) = y_n$. The LAMA semantics for the dataflow part coincides with the LUSTRE semantics.

For the sake of brevity, we discuss the automata semantics only informally: In LAMA a node N may contain a collection $\mathcal{A}$ of automata. If a flow refers to N in a **use**-construct, then N's automata are considered to run in parallel at the same hierarchical level. However, within a location l of any automaton $A \in \mathcal{A}$ a flow may use a subnode $N.M$ that again may contain a collection $M.\mathcal{B}$ of automata. The automata $B \in M.\mathcal{B}$ are the counterpart of subautomata residing within the state of a state machine in SCADE (see Sec. 4 for the translation).

For each automaton we distinguish between the *selected* mode at which the n-th step is assumed to start and the *active* mode that is executed at step n, $n \geq 0$. Let us assume node N is evaluated at step n. For each automaton $A \in \mathcal{A}$ the selected mode $m_{A,n}$ is considered and the most prior outgoing transition, whose guard evaluates to

$$\langle \textit{Type} \rangle ::= \langle \textit{BaseType} \rangle$$
$$| \quad \langle \textit{Identifier} \rangle$$
$$| \quad \langle \textit{BaseType} \rangle \,\hat{}\, n$$
$$| \quad (\, \# \, T_1 \dots T_n \,)$$
$$\langle \textit{BaseType} \rangle ::= \mathbf{bool}$$
$$| \quad \mathbf{int}$$
$$| \quad \mathbf{real}$$
$$| \quad \mathbf{sint} \, [n]$$
$$| \quad \mathbf{uint} \, [n]$$

$$[\![\mathbf{bool}]\!]\Sigma = \mathbb{B}$$
$$[\![\mathbf{int}]\!]\Sigma = \mathbb{Z}$$
$$[\![\mathbf{real}]\!]\Sigma = \mathbb{Q}$$
$$[\![\mathbf{sint}[n]]\!]\Sigma = \{-2^{n-1}, \dots, 2^{n-1} - 1\}$$
$$[\![\mathbf{uint}[n]]\!]\Sigma = \{0, \dots, 2^n - 1\}$$
$$[\![\mathbf{x}]\!]\Sigma = \Sigma(x)$$
$$[\![T^\wedge n]\!]\Sigma = [\![(\#\underbrace{T \dots T}_{n})]\!]\Sigma$$

$$[\![(\#T_1 \dots T_n)]\!]\Sigma = \prod_{i=0}^{n} ([\![T_i]\!]\Sigma)$$

Fig. 4. Syntax and semantics of LAMA types

true, is determined. If such a transition exists, it is executed and its target m'_A is said to be the *active* mode of A in step n. Otherwise the selected mode is set active, i.e. $m'_A = m_{A,n}$. This corresponds to strong transition semantics and giving outermost transitions priority as in SCADE. Now the flow definitions are evaluated for the active mode m'_A. In case the flow of m'_A makes **use** of a subnode with automata $B \in M.\mathcal{B}$, the selected modes m_B of all B are evaluated for outgoing transitions recursively until the innermost automata are reached. The result of the flow evaluation contributes to the next step's state variables s_{n+1}. Finally, the next step's *selected* mode $m_{A,n+1}$ is set to m'_A for all automata residing in N.

Comparison with SCADE. SCADE offers a lot more language concepts most of which are translated to LAMA as explained in Sec. 4. Some concepts are not handled yet, but left for a future extension of the translation: Among these are the basic type **char**, records, and type variables, sensors, signals, clocks, and probes. Functions, which can be translated to nodes easily, static input, and the **where** … **numeric** construct, which allows to declare polymorphic operators over numeric types, are missing. Within equations **guarantee**, **handle**, and **returns** are not handled yet, whereas in automata, dataflow cannot be assigned to transitions, **synchro**-transitions and **final** states are missing, as well as branching transitions. The sequential operators **when** and **merge** and clocked expressions are not supported. The use of higher order operators and clocked uses of operators are left out. Tuples, some array operations and structs can be easily handled.

Let us point out that even though the existing implementation cannot yet handle the full SCADE syntax, all missing language constructs can be reduced to the existing LAMA syntax in a straightforward way. Only for operator casts some primitive operators should be added to LAMA. Moreover, our translation does support a sufficiently large fragment of SCADE that allows to perform experiments on industrial relevant models such as the ones considered in Sec. 6.

4   Translating SCADE to LAMA

We are now going to describe the translation of a SCADE model to LAMA. Due to space constraints we can only sketch the general principles and indicate where the subtleties of the translation arise; a detailed description can be found in [5]. We also must assume that the reader is sufficiently familiar with the SCADE language (see [13]). Fig. 3 shows (a simplified) form of the translation result of the SCADE model from Fig. 1.

SCADE operators are translated to LAMA nodes. Note though that each instance of a SCADE operator has its own state memory. Thus, for every instance of a SCADE operator N a copy of the translation of N with a fresh name is generated in LAMA. Within a SCADE operator there are state independent (without any synchronous state machines) and state dependent dataflows, and these must be handled separately.

State independent dataflow. Logical and arithmetic base operations as well as variables, constants, array functions and if-then-else of SCADE have counterparts in LAMA, and are hence translated directly. Stream operators are handled as follows: each fby is replaced by a chain of pre and $\rightarrow$ (init) operators and then translated. For the translation of $\rightarrow$ and pre one has to distinguish several cases. In the first case of a SCADE statement $x = M \rightarrow$ pre N with $M = c$ a constant expression and N not containing $\rightarrow$ or pre, one translates this as a LAMA flow: **initial** x = c; **transition** x' = N; (the second case $x =$ pre M is handled by simply omitting the initialization of x – this is correct in LAMA if the original SCADE operator was correct). In the third case where M is not constant the **initial** statement is not allowed in LAMA and so the translation yields an automaton with three modes dummy$\xrightarrow{\text{true}}$init$\xrightarrow{\text{true}}$run where in init we have x = M; and in state run we have x = N. Finally, the remaining cases $x = M$ are treated by unrolling, i.e., M is rewritten so that one of the first three cases can be applied (see [5]).

State dependent dataflow. SCADE synchronous state machines are translated to LAMA state machines. Hierarchy of state machines in SCADE is handled by introducing LAMA nodes for subautomata. For example, let s be a state of a SCADE state machine containing another state machine M_s with states s_1, s_2 that read variables a, b, c and write to variable x. Then state s is translated to a state containing a statement $x = (\textbf{use } N_s \ a \ b \ c)$, where the LAMA node N_s contains the translation of state machine M_s.

Recall that SCADE knows several types of transitions between states of synchronous state machines. The *strong* transitions have the same semantics as transitions in LAMA and are translated directly, whereas *weak* transitions need a special treatment. In particular our translation needs to carefully handle several cases where a state has both types of transitions entering and/or leaving the state (see [5] for details). SCADE also distinguishes *restart* and *resume* transitions. The former leads to the initialization of all flows in the target state; they are translated by essentially transforming them into resume transitions, which have the same semantics in LAMA and can be translated directly.

We omit the description of the translation of default declarations as well as of pre and last within states. There are also some derived language constructs in SCADE that are translated by first replacing them by equivalent SCADE constructs whose translation we already explained; this concerns: the fby operator (mentioned previously), if-blocks (replaced by state machines), when-match-blocks (replaced by a case switch and an if-block) and the times operator.

Finally, let us mention two easy optimizations that are performed in this translation step: (1) pre operators are brought to the root of expressions as much as possible (e.g. by using the *distributive law* $f(\text{pre } M_1, \ldots, \text{pre } M_n) \equiv \text{pre } f(M_1, \ldots, M_n)$ that holds for every non stream operator f); (2) the elimination of auxiliary variables in textual SCADE code (especially when it is obtained from graphical models) by inlining. Both techniques reduce the number of state variables in the SMT instances obtained in the next transformation step and so lead to a smaller problem for the SMT solver at the end.

5 Translating LAMA to SMT

In this section we are going to translate a given LAMA program into a set of SMT-formulas that we can use to verify the invariant the program comes with. This is done by first translating the nodes (recursively) into Mealy machines, see Sec. 2.4, and then constructing another Mealy machine for the data flow of the program. The translation process yields one machine per variable and automaton, where a machine can use all inputs and the previous state of all machines in the current scope. More precisely, we are going to construct a signature Σ and formulas dependent on the step n, such that every symbol in Σ, except for input symbols, is defined by one formula. The symbols for each state variable and automaton have a stream type (over the type of the variable). One formula D_x then defines x at position $n + 1$, possibly using other symbols at position n. This translation is easier to implement and use than constructing one machine describing all state variables/automata at once.

5.1 SMT-Formulas from Nodes

Assume that we are given a LAMA node $N = (\textbf{node } x \ y \ \mathcal{N} \ V \ F \ S_0 \ \mathcal{A} \ P)$ of type $X \to Y$. We add symbols $x : [\![X]\!]^\omega$ and $y : [\![Y]\!]^\omega$ to the signature Σ, where one should note that X and Y may be product types if the node has several inputs or outputs. For every variable $(v : T) \in V$ of type T we add another symbol $v : [\![T]\!]^\omega$ to the signature Σ. Finally, for each $A = (\textbf{automaton } L_A \ l_0 \ E_A) \in \mathcal{A}$ we add two more symbols $act_A, sel_A : T(L_A)^\omega$ to Σ. Here we use a type $T(L_A)$ that encodes the modes of A, for example, using integers or bitvectors.

An equation $(v = M) \in F$ (where v can be an output y) gives rise to a formula $D_v := \lambda n. \ v(n) \equiv M(n)$, a state transition $s' = M \in F$ on the other hand defines $D_s := \lambda n. \ s(n + 1) \equiv M(n)$. The initial condition for s at 0 is given by the formula $I_s := (s(0) \equiv a)$ for $s = a \in S_0$. We describe the translation of LAMA terms M in Sec. 5.2.

The symbols $act_A, sel_A : T(L_A)^\omega$ for an automaton $A \in \mathcal{A}$ represent the active and the selected mode, respectively. Since we are using strong transition semantics, sel_A will always be defined by the formula $sel_A(n + 1) \equiv act_A(n)$ and the initial condition $I_A := (sel_A(0) \equiv l_0)$. The symbol act_A on the other hand is assigned the active mode of the automaton *in the current step*:

$$act_A(n) \equiv next(sel_A, E_A)(n),$$

where $next$ returns the active mode (see Sec. 3.1). Depending on the active mode we select the used computation for a variable v:

$$D_v := \lambda n. \ v(n) \equiv match(act_A, L_A, v)(n).$$

Here *match* selects the used flow for v, depending on the active mode:

$$match(act_A, L_A, v) := \lambda n. \text{ if } act_A(n) \equiv l_1 \text{ then } M_1(n)$$

$$\ldots$$

$$\text{else if } act_A(n) \equiv l_{n-1} \text{ then } M_{n-1}(n)$$
$$\text{else } M_n(n)$$

$$\text{for } (l_i, F_{l_i}) \in L_A \text{ and equations } (v = M_i) \in F_{l_i}.$$

Finally, we tie everything together by formulas describing the flow of N using an activation condition e_N ("enable N"):

$$D_N := \lambda n. \text{ if } e_N(n) \text{ then } \bigwedge_{v \in V} D_v(n) \text{ else } \bigwedge_{s \in state(V)} Id_s(n)$$

$$I_N := \bigwedge_{s \in state(V)} I_s$$

using the formula $Id_s(n) = (s(n+1) \equiv s(n))$ in case the dataflow of N is disabled.

The activation condition is only relevant in the case where a node is used inside a mode, since its dataflow is independently generated and shall only be active, if the mode in which the node is used is active. Let $l \in L_A$ be the mode in which a node N is used, then e_N is simply $e_N := \lambda n. act_A(n) \equiv l$.

Example 5.1. We translate here the node UpDown from Sec. 3. The resulting signature is $\Sigma = \{xo : \mathbb{N}^\omega, x1 : \mathbb{N}^\omega, x : \mathbb{N}^\omega, act_A, sel_A : T_A^\omega\}$ with $T_A = \{1, 2\}$. The state variables are defined by the formulas

$$D_{xo} \quad := \lambda n. \ xo(n) \equiv x1(n)$$
$$D_x \quad := \lambda n. \ x(n+1) \equiv x1(n)$$
$$D_{x1} \quad := \lambda n. \ x1(n) \equiv (\text{if } act_A(n) \equiv 1 \text{ then } x(n) + 1 \text{ else } x(n) - 1)$$

5.2 Translating Dataflow

There are two kinds of right-hand-sides one can have in the dataflow of LAMA: expressions or the use of a node. We will not describe the translation of LAMA expressions into SMT here, since this is just a point-wise application on streams. This leaves us with the case of (**use** N t) for a node identifier N and the argument t. Recall that we added symbols for input and output, say x, y, to the signature Σ of node N. The use of a node is driven by "connecting" x to t:

$$D_x := \lambda n. \ x(n) \equiv t(n).$$

The term (**use** N t) is translated to the symbol y, i.e., an equation $v = $ (**use** N t) is translated to $D_v := v(n) \equiv y(n)$ in Sec. 5.1.

5.3 SMT-Formulas from Programs

Finally, we translate the top level of a LAMA program. Such a program consists of node declarations and dataflow, which are handled as described in the previous subsections, and an invariant P. This P is immediately translated to an SMT-formula and hence we can check its validity according to Sec. 2.4, using the formulas D_N and D_v from the above translation in lieu of Iter from (1).

5.4 Correctness of the Translations

We briefly mention here a possible strategy for proving the correctness of the given translations. A scheme of the translation steps we have given is shown in the top row

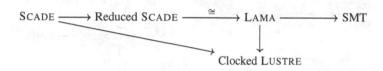

Fig. 5. Translation steps

of Fig. 5. In [10] Colaço et al. gave semantics to a fragment of SCADE, including safe state machines, by translating it into a variant of LUSTRE with clocks. Thus, a possible strategy would be to translate LAMA into this language as well and show that our translation yields equally behaving programs. If, moreover, we give semantics to LUSTRE with clocks in terms of Mealy machines, we can also prove our translation into SMT formulas correct.

However, this proof has not been carried out so far, and we leave it as future work. Instead, we have taken a more practical approach for the time being, in that we have compared our implementation to the SCADE Design Verifier, see Sec. 6.

6   Implementation and Experiments

In this section we describe a first implementation of the transformation of SCADE programs to SMT instances. We also present results of first experiments using our implementation on an industrial SCADE model. For this we reproduce verification results that were already obtained in [20] using SCADE DV, and we compare the running times.

Our implementation of the LAMA framework consists of the following components, all of which are written in the functional programming language *Haskell*:

- A library to parse, manipulate and render LAMA-programs: *language-lama*.
- A parser library for the SCADE (textual) language: *language-scade*.[4]
- An SMT interface abstraction which allows us to seamlessly use multiple different SMT solvers called *smtlib2*.[5]

---

[4] Available from https://github.com/hguenther/language-scade.
[5] Available from https://github.com/hguenther/smtlib2.

- A program to translate SCADE- into LAMA-programs: *scade2lama*.
- An interpreter for the LAMA language, which can be used to interactively run LAMA-programs: *lama-interpreter*.
- The verification component which verifies LAMA-programs by translating them into SMT: *lamasmt*.

All components are available under liberal free-software licenses.[6] The general work-flow and the interaction of the components can be seen in Fig. 6.

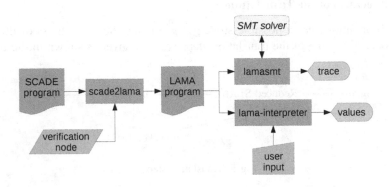

Fig. 6. Framework components and their interaction

SCADE programs are translated into the LAMA language using *scade2lama*. The user has to supply the name of the SCADE node whose properties shall be verified. The resulting LAMA program can then be formally verified using the *lamasmt* tool, which uses either bounded model checking or k-induction. It communicates with the SMT solver via the *smtlib2* library and produces a counterexample trace or states that the property holds for the node (this is only possible when using k-induction). If the k-induction is not able to prove the property within a specifiable depth, *lamasmt* can produce candidate-counterexamples from the induction step. These may be used later to generate lemmas, to strengthen the induction hypothesis, e.g. by adapting ideas from Champion et al. [9].

6.1   Benchmarks

We evaluated the performance of the *lamasmt* verification tool by applying it to a model of a level crossing system.[7] The details and the descriptions of hazards and the fault modes of this model can be found in [20].

We compared our tool with the SCADE DV, the proprietary verification tool bundled with SCADE. Like our tool, it can be used to verify the correctness of properties (called "proof strategy") or as a bounded model checker (called "debug strategy"). First, we compared SCADE DV's proof strategy against *lamasmt* with k-induction. We use the

---

[6] Available from https://github.com/hbasold/lama

[7] All benchmarks were performed on an Intel® Core™ Duo CPU P9600 @ 2.53 GHz with 4 GB of RAM.

Table 1. Comparing proof strategies

	SCADE DV		LAMA	
env. model	proven	time	proven	time
(1)	yes	12s	no (depth 27)	5h
(2)	no (depth 42)	205m	no (depth 46)	27h
(3)	yes	23h	no (depth 50)	68h

three environment models described in the study [20]: in model (1) a train is constantly occupying one of the two available tracks, while in model (2) a train can appear and disappear on track one at random, and in (3) a single train passes through track one for 40 cycles. The property to prove for all these environment models is that no train runs through an unprotected level crossing.

As Table 1 shows, the pure k-induction strategy does not work very well on the provided model. This confirms an observation made in [9] that without further heuristics k-induction does not scale up very well as a property may require a k that leads to a too large unfolding of the model, or it may not be k-inductive at all.

We also compared the BMC strategies of SCADE DV and LAMA on the five described fault modes of the model. Each fault mode was treated using environment model (1). The fault modes describe the following behaviours: a defect of a traffic light (*L1* and *L3*), a mis- or false-detection by a barrier sensor (*BS13* and *BS11* resp.), and a barrier that got stuck or is misbehaving (*B7* and *B9* resp.). We can see in Table 2 that both tools are able to find the three first fault modes and unable to find counter-examples for the last two. The found faults occurred at depth 27 in all cases.

Table 2. Comparing BMC strategies

	SCADE DV		LAMA	
bug	found	time	found	time
L1	yes	1s	yes	422s
BS13	yes	1s	yes	491s
B7 + BS11	yes	11s	yes	418s
B9	no (depth 35)	10s	no (depth 35)	24m
L3 + BS11	no (depth 50)	62s	no (depth 30)	13m

While the performance of *lamasmt* does not yet match that of the SCADE DV, the results nonetheless give us an indication that the implementation is indeed correct: There are no false errors being found, nor are any hazards undetected by our implementation. In the benchmarks, time and memory used by the intermediate translation steps are negligible, most of the time is taken by the SMT-solver.

7   Conclusion and Future Work

In this work, we developed an open experimentation platform for the verification of SCADE programs based on recent SMT technology. The verification process has been divided into several translation steps. First, SCADE programs are transformed into a small subset of SCADE that corresponds to programs in the intermediate language LAMA. LAMA keeps a few abstractions of SCADE, which are promising to facilitate optimization of the actual verification. After translating SCADE- into LAMA-programs, the resulting LAMA programs can almost directly be interpreted as sets of SMT formulas, describing transition steps. This step-wise description can then be used to find counterexample using bounded model checking or to prove predicates using k-induction.

These translation steps have been implemented as open source software. This software can already find the same counterexamples in a medium-sized design developed in industry as the proprietary SCADE Design Verifier, which comes with the SCADE suite. However, the verification procedure and performance are still lacking behind.

Since the developed software is meant to be an experimentation platform, future work obviously includes optimizing better verification techniques and the translations. This might effect the intermediate language LAMA itself.

References

1. Abdulla, P.A., Deneux, J., Stålmarck, G., Ågren, H., Åkerlund, O.: Designing safe, reliable systems using scade. In: Margaria, T., Steffen, B. (eds.) ISoLA 2004. LNCS, vol. 4313, pp. 115–129. Springer, Heidelberg (2006)
2. André, C.: Semantics of S.S.M (Safe State Machine). Tech. Rep. UMR 6070, I3S Laboratory, University of Nice-Sophia Antipolis (2003), http://rw4.cs.uni-saarland.de/teaching/esd07/papers/SSMsemantics.pdf
3. Barrett, C., Sebastiani, R., Seshia, S., Tinelli, C.: Satisfiability modulo theories. In: Biere, A., Heule, M.J.H., van Maaren, H., Walsh, T. (eds.) Handbook of Satisfiability, ch. 26, pp. 825–885. IOS Press (2009)
4. Barrett, C., Stump, A., Tinelli, C.: The SMT-LIB Standard: Version 2.0. In: Proc. 8th Intern. Workshop on Satisfiability Modulo Theories, Edinburgh, UK (2010)
5. Basold, H.: Transformationen von Scade-Modellen zur SMT-basierten Verifikation. Master's thesis, TU Braunschweig (2012), http://arxiv.org/abs/1403.2752
6. Bjesse, P., Claessen, K.: SAT-based verification without state space traversal. In: Hunt Jr., W.A., Johnson, S.D. (eds.) FMCAD 2000. LNCS, vol. 1954, pp. 372–389. Springer, Heidelberg (2000)
7. Cardelli, L.: Type systems. In: Tucker, A.B. (ed.) CRC Handbook of Computer Science and Engineering, ch. 97. Chapman and Hall (2004)
8. CENELEC: EN 50128 – Railway Applications – Software for Railway Control and Protection Systems. European Standard (2012)
9. Champion, A., Delmas, R., Dierkes, M.: Generating property-directed potential invariants by backward analysis. In: Proc. FTSCS. EPTCS, vol. 105, pp. 22–38 (2012)
10. Colaço, J.L., Pagano, B., Pouzet, M.: A conservative extension of synchronous data-flow with state machines. In: EMSOFT, pp. 173–182. ACM Press (2005)
11. DO-178B: Software considerations in airborne systems and equipment certification (December 2011)
12. Dutertre, B., de Moura, L.: The YICES SMT solver. Tech. rep., SRI Int. (2006)

13. Esterel: Scade language reference manual (2011)
14. Franzén, A.: Using satisfiability modulo theories for inductive verification of Lustre programs. Electr. Notes Theor. Comput. Sci. 144(1), 19–33 (2006)
15. Hagen, G.: Verifying safety properties of Lustre programs: an SMT-based approach. Ph.D. thesis, Department of Computer Science. The University of Iowa (2008)
16. Hagen, G., Tinelli, C.: Scaling up the formal verification of Lustre programs with SMT-based techniques. In: Proc. FMCAD, pp. 1–9 (2008)
17. Halbwachs, N., Caspi, P., Raymond, P., Pilaud, D.: The synchronous dataflow programming language LUSTRE. Proceedings of the IEEE 79(9), 1305–1320 (1991)
18. Halbwachs, N., Lagnier, F., Raymond, P.: Synchronous observers and the verification of reactive systems. In: Proc. of AMAST 1993. Workshops in Computing, pp. 83–96. Springer, London (1994)
19. Halbwachs, N., Raymond, P.: A turotial of Lustre (2002),
    http://www-verimag.imag.fr/~halbwach/lustre-tutorial.html (last accessed: March 13, 2014)
20. Huhn, M., Milius, S.: Observations on formal safety analysis in practice. Science of Computer Programming 80, Part A, 150–168 (2014)
21. Jeannet, B.: The NBAC verification/slicing tool, http://pop-art.inrialpes.fr/people/bjeannet/nbac/index.html (last accessed: February 17, 2014)
22. Kahsai, T., Tinelli, C.: PKind: A parallel k-induction based model checker. In: Barnat, J., Heljanko, K. (eds.) PDMC. EPTCS, vol. 72, pp. 55–62 (2011)
23. Ljung, M.: Formal modelling and automatic verification of Lustre programs using NP-Tools. Master's thesis, Prover Technology AB and Department of Teleinformatics, KTH, Stockholm (1999)
24. Maraninchi, F., Rémond, Y.: Mode-automata: About modes and states for reactive systems. In: Hankin, C. (ed.) ESOP 1998. LNCS, vol. 1381, pp. 185–199. Springer, Heidelberg (1998)
25. de Moura, L., Owre, S., Shankar, N.: The SAL language manual. Tech. rep., SRI International (2003), http://sal.csl.sri.com/doc/language-report.pdf (last accessed: March 12, 2014)
26. de Moura, L., Bjørner, N.: Z3: An efficient SMT solver. In: Ramakrishnan, C.R., Rehof, J. (eds.) TACAS 2008. LNCS, vol. 4963, pp. 337–340. Springer, Heidelberg (2008)
27. Pace, G., Halbwachs, N., Raymond, P.: Counter-example generation in symbolic abstract model-checking. Int. J. Software Tools and Technology Transfer 5(2), 158–164 (2004)
28. Sheeran, M., Singh, S., Stålmarck, G.: Checking safety properties using induction and a SAT-solver. In: Hunt Jr., W.A., Johnson, S.D. (eds.) FMCAD 2000. LNCS, vol. 1954, pp. 108–125. Springer, Heidelberg (2000)
29. Whalen, M., Cofer, D., Miller, S., Krogh, B.H., Storm, W.: Integration of formal analysis into a model-based software development process. In: Leue, S., Merino, P. (eds.) FMICS 2007. LNCS, vol. 4916, pp. 68–84. Springer, Heidelberg (2008)

Improving Static Analyses of C Programs with Conditional Predicates

Sandrine Blazy[1], David Bühler[2], and Boris Yakobowski[2]

[1] IRISA - University of Rennes, France
sandrine.blazy@irisa.fr
[2] CEA, LIST, Software Safety Lab, 91191 Gif-sur-Yvette, France
{david.buhler,boris.yakobowski}@cea.fr

Abstract. Static code analysis is increasingly used to guarantee the absence of undesirable behaviors in industrial programs. Designing sound analyses is a continuing trade-off between precision and complexity. Notably, dataflow analyses often perform overly wide approximations when two control-flow paths meet, by merging states from each path. This paper presents a generic abstract interpretation based framework to enhance the precision of such analyses on join points. It relies on *predicated* domains, that preserve and reuse information valid only inside some branches of the code. Our predicates are derived from conditionals statements, and postpone the loss of information. The work has been integrated into Frama-C, a C source code analysis platform. Experiments on real code show that our approach scales, and improves significantly the precision of the existing analyses of Frama-C.

1 Introduction

Formal program verification is an increasingly sought-after approach to guarantee the absence of undesirable behaviors in software. Static code analysis has already shown its industrial applicability to prove safety properties on critical or embedded code. Still, so as to remain tractable, these analyses involve sound but incomplete approximations of a program behavior. This may lead to false alarms, when some required properties cannot be proved statically even though they always hold at runtime. Abstract interpretation [5,6] is a well-known framework to over-approximate program executions through *abstractions* of the most precise mathematical characterization of the program. Designing such abstractions is a continuing trade-off between precision and efficiency.

Flow-sensitivity, which allows to infer static properties that depend on program points, is often considered as a prerequisite to obtain a precise program analysis. More agressive analyses are *path-sensitive*: the analysis of a program statement depends on the control-flow path followed to reach this statement. Nevertheless, most analyses sacrifice full path-sensitivity and perform approximations when two control-flow paths meet. Those approximations may lead to a significant loss of precision, and may preclude inferring some interesting properties of the program.

F. Lang and F. Flammini (Eds.): FMICS 2014, LNCS 8718, pp. 140–154, 2014.

```
                                          if (flag2)                        5
 1      if (flag1)                           { fd2 = open(path2);           6
 2         { fd1 = open(path1);               if (fd2==-1) {                7
 3            if (fd1==-1) exit(); }             if (flag1) close(fd1);     8
 4      [...] // code 1                          exit(); } }                9
                                          [...] // code 2                   10
                                          if (flag1) close(fd1);            11
                                          if (flag2) close(fd2);            12
```

Fig. 1. Example of interleaved conditionals

Consider as an example the code fragment of Fig. 1. Proving that the three calls to the `close` function are correct, i.e. that the corresponding `fd` variable has been properly created, heavily relies on the possible values for the `flag1` and `flag2` variables. An analysis that does not keep track of the relation between `flag1` and `fd1` on the one hand, and `flag2` and `fd2` on the other hand, will not be able to prove that the program is correct.

In this paper, we define an analysis in which information about the conditionals that have been encountered so far is retained using boolean predicates. These predicates guard the values inferred about the program. Our analysis is parameterized by a pre-existing analysis domain, which we use to derive a new *predicated* analysis. More precisely, we propagate two kinds of information that are not present in the original domain: a context and an implication map.

1. A *context* is a boolean predicate synthesized from the guards of the conditionals that have been reached so far, and that is guaranteed to hold at the current program point. In our example, at the beginning of line 8, the context would be $flag2 \land (fd2 = -1)$.
2. An *implication map* is a set of facts from the original analysis domain, guarded by boolean predicates. Each fact is guaranteed to hold when its guard holds. Implication maps postpone the loss of precision usually present at join points. In our example, assuming the existence of an analysis that verifies the validity of file descriptors, the implication map after line 6 would consist of the two following implications:

$$flag1 \mapsto valid\_fd(fd1) \qquad true \mapsto valid\_fd(fd2) \lor (fd2 = -1)$$

The first implication results from the analysis of the conditionals at lines 1-3; it precisely models the information we need between `flag1` and `fd1`. The second implication is simply the postcondition of the `open` function, which holds unconditionnaly: either `open` succeeds, or it fails with a return code of −1.

Our framework, based on abstract interpretation, is generic. We also integrated it into Frama-C, a modular platform dedicated to the analysis of C code [8]. Frama-C provides various sound analyses based on abstract interpretation, deductive verification or testing, implemented by a collection of plugins built around a common kernel. These plugins collaborate through logical properties expressed in ACSL, a C specification language [1,4]. Among them, the value analysis plugin [9,3] performs a forward dataflow analysis over intricate low-level abstract domains to compute an over-approximation of the possible values of variables at each program point. It aims at ensuring the absence of run-time errors in a given program. Our experiments show that predicated analyses over much simpler domains may significantly enhance and complement the results of the value analysis.

Related Work. Different approaches have been proposed in the litterature to solve instances of the problem we are addressing. *Trace-partitioning* [14] and *boolean partitioning* [7] would keep separate the different execution traces coming from the conditionals on `flag1` and `flag2` in Fig. 1. One downside is that `code 1` may need to be analyzed twice, and `code 2` up to four times. To avoid a blow-up in analysis time, the analyzer would need to reuse some parts of previous analyses. However, this requires a modular analysis and significant implementation efforts. Also, traces should be merged when it is no longer useful to keep them seperate. Syntactic criteria need to be used to detect such merge points. Conversely, trace partitioning can be used to unroll loop symbolically, something our approach does not handle. *Predicate abstraction* [11] would propagate a single fact along all execution paths, but this fact may be arbitrarily complex. In particular, the predicate is found incrementally, and refined until it is sufficient to guarantee the property under consideration. In our example, the predicate would likely link `flag1`, `fd1`, `flag2` and `fd2`. Using this approach, [10] shows how to transform any existing dataflow analysis into a predicated one, the predicates being found by successive refinement iterations. Still, finding the proper predicate may be abitrarily complex, resulting in hard to predict analysis times. Also, the refinement phase requires decidable theories and powerful decision procedures to find the counter-examples from which the predicate is deduced. We instead chose to limit ourselves to first-order predicates relating the conditionals present in the program.

The remainder of this paper is organized as follows. First, Sect. 2 introduces our language, simplified for the sake of illustration. Section 3 defines predicated domains and explains how to build a predicated analysis over a standard dataflow analysis, which we further improve in Sect. 4. Sect. 5 describes two domains that we used to validate our framework. Then, Sect. 6 presents the experimental evaluation of our practical implementation. Finally, Sect. 7 draws some conclusions.

2   A Generic Abstract Interpretation Based Framework

Our static analysis is based on abstract interpretation [5,6], and handles the whole C language. However, for the sake of brevity, we only present here a toy language. Abstract interpretation links a very precise, but generally undecidable, *concrete* semantics, to an *abstract* decidable one – the abstract semantics being a sound approximation of the concrete one. This section first defines the syntax of our toy language, then its concrete and abstract semantics.

Syntax. Figure 2 presents the syntax of our language. Programs operate over a fixed, finite set of variables $\mathcal{V}$ whose values belong to an unspecified set $\mathbb{V}$.

$$
\begin{aligned}
e \in \mathbf{exp} ::= \ & x & x \in \mathcal{V} & \qquad \mathtt{i} \in \mathbf{stmt} ::= x := e \\
| \ & v & v \in \mathbb{V} & \qquad \qquad \qquad \ | \ c \triangleleft \\
| \ & e \star e & & \\
c, p \in \mathbb{C} ::= \ & e \,|\, \neg c \,|\, c \wedge c \,|\, c \vee c & & \qquad P \in \mathbf{prog} \triangleq \mathcal{P}(\mathbb{N} \times \mathbf{stmt} \times \mathbb{N})
\end{aligned}
$$

Fig. 2. Syntax of our language

Expressions are either variables, constants, or the application of a binary operator $\star$ to expressions. We stratify expressions and conditionals, the truth value of an element of $\mathbb{V}$ being given by a mapping T from $\mathbb{V}$ to booleans. Statements are either assignments, or assume filters that halt execution when the condition does not hold. A program is represented by its control-flow graph where nodes are integer-numbered program points and edges are labelled by statements. By convention, the program starts at node 0. Encoding standard program constructs such as `if` or `for` in such graphs is immediate and not detailed in this paper. For clarity, we write our examples using a C-like syntax.

Concrete Semantics. A concrete state of the program at a node n of its control-flow graph is described by an environment $\rho \in \mathbb{V}^{\mathcal{V}}$ assigning a value to each variable. The semantics $[\![e]\!]_\rho$ (resp. $[\![c]\!]_\rho$) of an expression e (resp. a condition c) is its evaluation in the environment ρ, and implicitely depends on the evaluation of the operators $\star$.

Our concrete semantics maps each program node n to the set $\mathbb{S}(n)$ of all possible environments at this point; hence our semantics is a function in $\mathcal{P}\left(\mathbb{V}^{\mathcal{V}}\right)^{\mathbb{N}}$. The semantics $[\![\mathtt{i}]\!]$ of a statement $\mathtt{i}$ is a transfer function over a set of states, described in the first equalities of Fig. 3a. After an assignment on x, x is bound in the new states to the evaluation of the expression. Assume filters block evaluation, only allowing states in which the condition holds. The concrete semantics of the entire program P is then the smallest solution of the rightmost equations of Fig. 3a.

Abstract Semantics Abstract interpretation based analyses rely on an abstract domain $\mathcal{L}$, whose computable elements model a set of concrete states at a given program point. Such abstract domains must provide:

- a partial order $\sqsubseteq_{\mathcal{L}}$ according to the precision of abstract states,
- a monotone *concretization* function $\gamma_{\mathcal{L}}$ from $\mathcal{L}$ to $\mathcal{P}\left(\mathbb{V}^{\mathcal{V}}\right)$, linking the abstract states to the concrete ones,
- greatest and smallest elements $\top_{\mathcal{L}}$ and $\bot_{\mathcal{L}}$, such that $\gamma_{\mathcal{L}}(\top_{\mathcal{L}}) = \mathbb{V}^{\mathcal{V}}$ and $\gamma_{\mathcal{L}}(\bot_{\mathcal{L}}) = \emptyset$,
- sound approximations $\sqcup_{\mathcal{L}}$ and $\sqcap_{\mathcal{L}}$ of union and intersection of concrete states,
- sound abstract transfer functions $[\![\mathtt{i}]\!]_{\mathcal{L}}^{\sharp}$ from $\mathcal{L}$ to $\mathcal{L}$ that approximate the concrete semantics.

The correction theorems for the soundness of the abstract semantics are stated in the leftmost column of Fig. 3b. The abstract semantics is the least solution of the system of equations in the rightmost column. The soundness properties

(a) Concrete semantics

$$[\![x := e]\!]\,(S) \triangleq \{\rho\,[x \mapsto [\![e]\!]_\rho]\mid \rho \in S\}$$
$$[\![c \triangleleft]\!]\,(S) \triangleq \{\rho \mid \rho \in S \wedge \mathsf{T}\,([\![c]\!]_\rho) = \mathsf{true}\}$$

$$\mathbb{S}\,(0) \triangleq \mathbb{V}^\mathcal{V}$$
$$\mathbb{S}\,(n) \triangleq \bigcup_{(m,i,n)\in P} [\![i]\!]\,(\mathbb{S}\,(m))$$

(b) Abstract semantics

$$\gamma_\mathcal{L}(\top_\mathcal{L}) = \mathbb{V}^\mathcal{V}$$
$$\gamma_\mathcal{L}(l_1) \cup \gamma_\mathcal{L}(l_2) \subseteq \gamma_\mathcal{L}(l_1 \sqcup_\mathcal{L} l_2)$$
$$[\![i]\!]\,(\gamma_\mathcal{L}(l)) \subseteq \gamma_\mathcal{L}([\![i]\!]^\sharp_\mathcal{L}\,(l))$$

$$\mathbb{S}^\sharp_\mathcal{L}\,(0) \triangleq \top_\mathcal{L}$$
$$\mathbb{S}^\sharp_\mathcal{L}\,(n) \triangleq \bigsqcup_\mathcal{L} \left\{ [\![i]\!]^\sharp_\mathcal{L}\left(\mathbb{S}^\sharp_\mathcal{L}\,(m)\right) \mid (m,i,n) \in P \right\}$$

Fig. 3. Concrete and abstract semantics

ensure that any solution is a correct approximation of the concrete semantics. In practice, such systems are solved by iterative data-flow analysis [13,2].

Lemma 1. *All behaviors of the concrete semantics are captured by the abstract one. That is,* $\forall n \in P,\ \mathbb{S}\,(n) \subseteq \gamma_\mathcal{L}\left(\mathbb{S}^\sharp_\mathcal{L}\,(n)\right)$

We also define an operator called deps from expressions to sets of variables $\mathcal{P}(\mathcal{V})$, that will be useful when computing memory footprints. deps (e) is the set of variables on which the evaluation of e depends. On our toy language, this is the set of variables syntactically present in e. However, in a language with pointers, deps (e) usually depends on the current program point.

3   Predicated Analyses

This section presents our predicated analysis. We first define the domain that will represent its abstract states, then the transfer function on statements.

3.1   Predicated Domains

Our analysis derives a *predicated* analysis on top of an abstract domain $\mathcal{L}$. The additional information is two-fold. First, we add a boolean predicate $c \in \mathbb{C}$, called the *context*, standing for a set of facts that we know to hold at the current program point. Second, we add a mapping I from predicates in $\mathbb{C}$ to elements of $\mathcal{L}$, called a *map*. Maps stand for implications from guards to values; hence they contain information that are *conditional*: $I(p) = l$ implies that l is a correct approximation of the state as soon as p is verified. We use the syntax $\lambda p.l$ to denote maps, and write $\langle p \to l \rangle$ for a value l guarded by a predicate p.

We say that $\langle p \to l \rangle$ is *trivial* when $l = \top_\mathcal{L}$, as the value $\top_\mathcal{L}$ brings no information whatsoever. In order to have a decidable semantics, we restrict ourselves to maps in which all but a finite number of implications are trivial. To guarantee that our inclusion operator is antisymmetric, we only consider pairs of a context and a map in which implications that contradict the context or are redundant with another (stronger) implication are trivial. Formally, for any

$$\top_{\text{pred}} \triangleq (\text{true}, \lambda p. \top_{\mathcal{L}})$$

$$\bot_{\text{pred}} \triangleq (\text{false}, \lambda p. \top_{\mathcal{L}})$$

$$(c_1, I_1) \sqsubseteq_{\text{pred}} (c_2, I_2) \triangleq c_1 \Rightarrow c_2 \wedge \forall p \in \mathbb{C}, (c_1, I_1) \blacktriangleright \langle p \rightarrow I_2(p_2) \rangle$$

$$(c, I) \blacktriangleright \langle p \rightarrow l \rangle \triangleq \neg(c \wedge p) \vee (\exists p', p \Rightarrow p' \wedge I(p') \sqsubseteq_{\mathcal{L}} l)$$

$$(c_1, I_1) \sqcup_{\text{pred}} (c_2, I_2) \triangleq \text{canonize}(c_1 \vee c_2, \lambda p. (l_\cup(p) \sqcap_{\mathcal{L}} l_1(p) \sqcap_{\mathcal{L}} l_2(p)))$$

$$\text{where} \begin{cases} l_\cup(p) = \prod_{\mathcal{L}} \{I_1(p_1) \sqcup_{\mathcal{L}} I_2(p_2) \mid p \equiv p_1 \wedge p_2\} \\ l_1(p) = \prod_{\mathcal{L}} \{I_1(p_1) \mid p \equiv \neg c_2 \wedge p_1\} \\ l_2(p) = \prod_{\mathcal{L}} \{I_2(p_2) \mid p \equiv \neg c_1 \wedge p_2\} \end{cases}$$

$$\gamma_{\text{pred}}(c, I) \triangleq \{\rho \mid [\![c]\!]_\rho \wedge \forall p \in \mathbb{C}, [\![p]\!]_\rho \Rightarrow \rho \in \gamma_{\mathcal{L}}(I(p))\}$$

Fig. 4. Definition of $\mathcal{L}^{\text{pred}}$, the predicated domain over $\mathcal{L}$

$p \in \mathbb{C}$, a pair (c, I) must verify respectively $\neg(p \wedge c) \Rightarrow (I(p) = \top_{\mathcal{L}})$ and $\forall p' \not\equiv p, (p \Rightarrow p' \wedge I(p') \sqsubseteq_{\mathcal{L}} I(p)) \Rightarrow (I(p) = \top_{\mathcal{L}})$. A context and a map that do not verify these last two properties can always be canonized into a pair that does, by mapping the contradictory or redundant implications of I to $\top_{\mathcal{L}}$. We write canonize this operation. We call *context-implication-map pair*, ranged over by Φ and abbreviated as *CI-pair*, a context and a map that verify all these properties. CI-pairs will represent the abstract state of our predicated analysis.

We define $\mathcal{L}^{\text{pred}}$, the *predicated domain over* $\mathcal{L}$, as the set of CI-pairs equipped with the operations of Fig. 4. $\top_{\text{pred}}$ (resp. $\bot_{\text{pred}}$) denotes the most general (resp. most restrictive) context. Both $\top_{\text{pred}}$ and $\bot_{\text{pred}}$ are made up of trivial implications only. CI-pairs are ordered by the relation $\sqsubseteq_{\text{pred}}$: (c_1, I_1) is more precise than (c_2, I_2) when c_1 is stronger than c_2, and when (c_1, I_1) implies all the implications of I_2. This last property is defined using an auxiliary relation $\blacktriangleright$ stating that a CI-pair *verifies* an implication. The relation $(c, I) \blacktriangleright \langle p \rightarrow l \rangle$ holds when either p contradicts c, or there exists an implication of I stronger than $\langle p \rightarrow l \rangle$.

Example 1. Consider the example of Fig. 5, where $\mathcal{L}$ is a basic interval domain. The notation $[i]$ stands for the singleton interval $[i; i]$. We write Φ_i for the state at the end of line i, its context and non-trivial implications being shown in the two rightmost columns. For instance, Φ_3 maps the three variables assigned at lines 1-3 to their respective values, under the **true** guard. The relation $\Phi_7 \sqsubseteq_{\text{pred}} \Phi_8$, that relates the state at the end of the else branch and after the first conditional, holds. First, the implications guarded by **true** and $\neg c$ in Φ_8 are implied by the **true**-guarded implication of Φ_7. Then, the implication guarded by c contradicts the context of Φ_7. Finally, all trivial implications of Φ_8 are implied by the corresponding one in Φ_7.

Let $\Phi_1 = (c_1, I_1)$ and $\Phi_2 = (c_2, I_2)$ be two CI-pairs. The join $\sqcup_{\text{pred}}$ between them is the smallest CI-pair whose context is implied by c_1 and c_2, and whose implications are verified by both Φ_1 and Φ_2. Its context is simply $c_1 \vee c_2$. Within the implication map, the operator $l_\cup$ combines implications of the two previous

```
1    x = 0;
2    y = 0;
3    v = 1;
4    if (c) {
5        x = v;
6    } else {
7        y = v;
8    }
9    w = 0;
10   if (c) {
11       c = 2;
12   }
```

line	Φ_{line}: state after the statement	
	context	implications
3	true	$true \mapsto v \in [1], x \in [0], y \in [0]$
5	c	$true \mapsto v \in [1], x \in [1], y \in [0]$
7	$\neg c$	$true \mapsto v \in [1], x \in [0], y \in [1]$
8	$c \vee \neg c \equiv$ true	$true \mapsto v \in [1], x \in [0,1], y \in [0,1]$ $c \mapsto v \in [1], x \in [1], y \in [0]$ $\neg c \mapsto v \in [1], x \in [0], y \in [1]$
9	true	$true \mapsto v \in [1], w \in [0], x \in [0,1], y \in [0,1]$ $c \mapsto v \in [1], w \in [0], x \in [1], y \in [0]$ $\neg c \mapsto v \in [1], w \in [0], x \in [0], y \in [1]$
10	c	$true \mapsto v \in [1], w \in [0], x \in [1], y \in [0]$
11	true	$true \mapsto v \in [1], w \in [0], x \in [1], y \in [0], c \in [2]$
12	true	$true \mapsto v \in [1], w \in [0], x \in [0,1], y \in [0,1]$ $c \mapsto v \in [1], w \in [0], x \in [1], y \in [0], c \in [2]$

Fig. 5. Example of an analysis using a predicated interval analysis

maps: the $\mathcal{L}$-join of values present under guards p_1 and p_2 respectively of Φ_1 and Φ_2 is kept under the new guard $p_1 \wedge p_2$. Conversely, the operators l_1 and l_2 preserve the values only present in Φ_1 or Φ_2 respectively. A value valid in Φ_1 under a guard p_1 may be present in the join provided that the new guard negates c_2 (so that Φ_2 also verifies the implication) – resulting in the guard $\neg c_2 \wedge p_1$. Values present in Φ_2 are likewise present under guards that negate c_1. Note that this additional information from Φ_i is thrown away if all guards $p \wedge \neg c_j$ contradict the new context, i.e. whenever $c_i \Rightarrow c_j$.

Example 2. Consider again Fig. 5. We have $\Phi_8 = \Phi_5 \sqcup_{pred} \Phi_7$. The value implied by true in Φ_8 comes from the operator $l_\cup$, and is equal to $I_5(true) \sqcup_\mathcal{L} I_7(true)$. Conversely, the value implied by c comes from the operator l_1, which negates the context of Φ_7; furthemore, the value is exactly $\Phi_5(true)$. Note that the intervals inferred in Φ_5 and Φ_7 are entirely retained, guarded by the negations of the converse contexts; no information is actually lost.

Finally, the concretization $\gamma_{pred}(c, I)$ of an element of the predicated domain is the set of states wherein c is true and all implications of I are valid.

3.2   Abstract Transfer Functions

We now define in Fig. 6 our abstract semantics for statements in $\mathcal{L}^{pred}$. The gist of the analysis is to apply the transfer functions of $\mathcal{L}$ to each of its elements in the map, which is carried out by the lift function, while new implications will be created by $\sqcup_{pred}$ for values that are present in only one branch at a junction point. However, to remain sound, we also need to invalidate predicates (either in the context or in a guard) whose truth values are possibly modified by a statement. Following standard dataflow terminology, we define a kill operator,

$$\text{lift}\,(\mathtt{i}, (c, I)) \triangleq \left(c, \lambda p.\; [\![\mathtt{i}]\!]^{\sharp}_{\mathcal{L}}\,(I\,(p)) \right)$$

$$\text{kill}\,(x, (c, I)) \triangleq \left(\begin{cases} c & \text{if } x \notin \text{deps}\,(c) \\ \mathbf{true} & \text{otherwise} \end{cases} \\ \lambda p. \begin{cases} I\,(p) & \text{if } x \notin \text{deps}\,(p) \\ \top_{\mathcal{L}} & \text{otherwise} \end{cases} \right)$$

$$\text{refine}\,(h, (c, I)) \triangleq \text{canonize}\left(c \wedge h, \lambda p. {\textstyle\prod}_{\mathcal{L}} \left\{ I\,(p') \mid h \wedge p \Rightarrow p' \right\} \right)$$

$$[\![x := e]\!]^{\sharp}_{\text{pred}}\,(\varPhi) \triangleq \text{lift}\,(x := e, \text{kill}\,(x, \varPhi))$$

$$[\![c \triangleleft]\!]^{\sharp}_{\text{pred}}\,(\varPhi) \triangleq \text{lift}\,(c \triangleleft, \text{refine}\,(c, \varPhi))$$

Fig. 6. Definition of the abstract semantics $[\![.]\!]^{\sharp}_{\text{pred}}$

that removes contexts and implications depending on a certain variable x. This operator is used after an assignment $x := e$, as it modifies the value of x.

While kill and lift used in conjunction are sufficient to define a sound abstract semantics for $\mathcal{L}^{\text{pred}}$, they never use the existing implications or enrich the context. Yet, the join operation retains specific information of each branch only when they have different non-**true** contexts. Thus, we define an operator refine that enriches the context by a new predicate $h \in \mathbb{C}$, supposed to be verified. This operator also learns information by simplifying the map according to h. More precisely, the valid value under a guard p is the $\mathcal{L}$-meet of the elements implied by any guard weaker than $p \wedge h$.

Within our abstract semantics $[\![.]\!]^{\sharp}_{\text{pred}}$, there are two natural places where refine may be used. First, after an assume statement $c \triangleleft$, the predicate c holds by definition. Second, after a statement $x := e$, the equality $x = e$ holds (provided the value of e does not depend on x). In practice, this second rule rapidly leads to the creation of intractable contexts. Hence, we only enrich our states on assume statements. Let us stress that any application of refine($h, \cdot$) is sound, provided h actually holds. Refining more or less aggressively results in a trade-off between precision and complexity.

Example 3. At line 4 in Fig. 5, in the branches of the conditional, the operator refine enriches the context according to the condition. After the conditional, the context reverts to **true** due to the join between $\varPhi_5$ and $\varPhi_7$. Note that despite the canonization, the join and the lift function duplicate the value of variables v and w at line 8 and 9 respectively. At line 10, on a conditional with the same condition c, the refine operator maps the **true** guard to $I_9(\mathbf{true}) \sqcap_{\mathcal{L}} I_9(c)$, as both **true** and c are implied by the new context c. We have re-learnt the information known about x and y at line 5. Meanwhile, the c guard becomes redundant with the **true** one, while $\neg c$ contradicts the context. Both implications are changed to trivial ones by the canonize operator. On line 11, c is overwritten. Hence, the context c is reset to **true** by the kill operator. Finally, upon exiting the conditional, we lose the information coming from the else branch, as negating the context **true** would result in a trivial implication, that would never hold.

But the information coming from the then branch is preserved under the guard $\neg\neg c \equiv c$.

Lemma 2. *Our predicated analysis over $\mathcal{L}^{\mathrm{pred}}$ is sound.*

$$\gamma_{\mathrm{pred}}\left(\varPhi_1\right) \cup \gamma_{\mathrm{pred}}\left(\varPhi_2\right) \subseteq \gamma_{\mathrm{pred}}\left(\varPhi_1 \sqcup_{\mathrm{pred}} \varPhi_2\right)$$

$$[\![\mathtt{i}]\!]\left(\gamma_{\mathrm{pred}}\left(\varPhi\right)\right) \subseteq \gamma_{\mathrm{pred}}\left([\![\mathtt{i}]\!]_{\mathrm{pred}}^{\sharp}\left(\varPhi\right)\right)$$

Moreover, we can state a stronger result, that links, at a program point n, the abstract semantics of $\mathbb{S}_{\mathcal{L}}^{\sharp}$ with its equivalent $\mathbb{S}_{\mathrm{pred}}^{\sharp}$ for $\mathcal{L}_{\mathrm{pred}}$.

Theorem 1. *Our predicated analysis is as precise as the non-predicated one.*

$$\forall n \in P,\ given\ (c_n, I_n) = \mathbb{S}_{\mathrm{pred}}^{\sharp}\left(n\right),\ then\ I_n(\mathtt{true}) \sqsubseteq_{\mathcal{L}} \mathbb{S}_{\mathcal{L}}^{\sharp}\left(n\right)$$

Of course, the predicated analysis can be more precise. As an example, on line 10 of the program of Fig. 5, the non-predicated analysis would have inferred the value $I_9(\mathtt{true})$. Our own result – namely $I_{10}(\mathtt{true})$ – is much more precise.

4   Improving the Analysis

This section explains how to avoid computing guarded values that are needlessly redundant, and details some strategies to decrease the complexity of our analysis.

4.1   Avoiding Redundant Values

As previously remarked in example 3, our analysis keeps within implications more information than needed. Even though we avoid redundant implications in the map, some values of $\mathcal{L}$ may encode information partially present under weaker guards. Furthermore, the transfer function of the underlying domain may be costly and it is applied to every element of $\mathcal{L}$ in the map. In order to decrease the practical complexity of the predicated analysis, we require two additional features from the underlying domain $\mathcal{L}$.

1. A more lightweight transfer function $[\![\mathtt{i}, p]\!]_{\mathcal{L} \times \mathbb{C}}^{\sharp}$ over statements $\mathtt{i}$, parameterized by the predicate p that guards the processed value. This way, the analysis can be more precise on the $\mathtt{true}$ guard only and avoids the duplication of new information. Thus, $[\![\mathtt{i}, \mathtt{true}]\!]_{\mathcal{L} \times \mathbb{C}}^{\sharp}$ may be defined as $[\![\mathtt{i}]\!]_{\mathcal{L}}^{\sharp}$, while $[\![\mathtt{i}, \cdot]\!]_{\mathcal{L} \times \mathbb{C}}^{\sharp}$ applied to a non-$\mathtt{true}$ guard should be defined as a very imprecise operation, that only guarantees the soundness of the analysis on $\mathcal{L}$. Formally, we only require $[\![\mathtt{i}, \cdot]\!]_{\mathcal{L} \times \mathbb{C}}^{\sharp}$ to be an over-approximation of $[\![\mathtt{i}]\!]_{\mathcal{L}}^{\sharp}$. The lift operator is then redefined as

$$\mathrm{lift}\left(\mathtt{i}, (c, I)\right) \triangleq \left(c, \lambda p.\ [\![\mathtt{i}, p]\!]_{\mathcal{L} \times \mathbb{C}}^{\sharp}\left(I\left(p\right)\right)\right)$$

line	context	implications after the statement
3 ...		
4 if (c) {		true $\mapsto v \in [1]; x \in [0,1]; y \in [0,1]$
5 x = v;	8 $\quad c \vee \neg c \equiv$ $\quad\quad$ true	$c \mapsto x \in [1]; y \in [0]$
6 } else {		$\neg c \mapsto x \in [0]; y \in [1]$
7 y = v;		true $\mapsto v \in [1]; w \in [0]; x \in [0,1]; y \in [0,1]$
8 }	9 $\quad$ true	$c \mapsto x \in [1]; y \in [0]$
9 w = 0;		$\neg c \mapsto x \in [0]; y \in [1]$
10 ...		

Fig. 7. Analysis of Fig. 5 with factorization

2. A difference operation $\setminus_{\mathcal{L}}$ that discards information already contained in another element of $\mathcal{L}$, that we use to simplify implication maps. Ideally, $a \setminus_{\mathcal{L}} b$ should be as large as possible, while retaining all the information of a not already present in b. To be sound, we require $a \sqsubseteq_{\mathcal{L}} a \setminus_{\mathcal{L}} b$. We define an operator reduce, that simplifies each implication by all the values mapped to weaker guards, and we use it whenever we need to canonize a map (i.e. after a join or a refinement).

$$\mathsf{reduce}\,(I) \triangleq \lambda p.\, I\,(p) \setminus_{\mathcal{L}} \left(\prod_{\mathcal{L}} \{I\,(q) \mid p \Rightarrow q, p \not\equiv q\} \right)$$

$$\mathsf{canonize'}\,(\varPhi) \triangleq \mathsf{reduce}\,(\mathsf{canonize}\,(\varPhi))$$

These two operators may lose a lot of information; ideally, they would just keep the values that the non-predicated analysis fails to compute.

Example 4. Let us come back to the example of Fig. 5, improved in Fig. 7. When joining the values coming from lines 5 and 7, the reduce operator removes under the guards c and $\neg c$ the information about v, which is already present under the weaker guard true. In parallel, after line 9, the modified lift operator does not apply the full interval analysis to the values guarded by c and $\neg c$. Instead, we use a simpler abstraction, that only removes information about variables that are overwritten. This way, the information about w is no longer duplicated.

4.2   Convergence of the Analysis and Practical Complexity

Throughout the analysis of a given program, all guards of non trivial implications present in a map are derived from the conditionals of the program, so their number remains finite. In practice, this number can be high; we discuss a possible way of limiting it in Sect. 6. The predicated analysis essentially amounts to performing the underlying analysis over the values under each guard (except for the refine operations, which allow us to be more precise). Thus, if the underlying domain provides (or requires) a widening operator to effectively compute the fixpoint, then it can (and should) be lifted as well. Finally, if the underlying transfer functions are monotonic, so are the predicated ones, which ensures the termination of our analysis.

Some operators of the abstract semantics may seem costly to compute, but efficient implementations or simpler operators can mitigate this. For instance, at a junction point of the control-flow graph, $\Phi_1 \sqcup_{\mathsf{pred}} \Phi_2$ creates fresh implications through the operators l_1, l_2 and $l_\cup$ (Fig. 4). Both l_1 and l_2 only traverse one map once. On the other hand, $l_\cup$ requires $|\Phi_1| \times |\Phi_2|$ operations, where $|\Phi|$ is the number of non trivial implications in Φ. However, any implication $\langle p \to l \rangle$ that held before the control-flow split (and that has not been invalidated since) still exists in Φ_1 and Φ_2, and will exist in the join. Then, any implication of the form $\langle p \wedge p' \to l \sqcup_{\mathcal{L}} l' \rangle$ is redundant with $\langle p \to l \rangle$ and does not need to be considered. An optimized implementation should thus consider only the subparts of the maps that are distinct. In order to further speed up the analysis, we can also use a more approximate join, that keeps only implications $\langle p \to l_1 \sqcup_{\mathcal{L}} l_2 \rangle$ such that $\langle p \to l_1 \rangle \in \Phi_1$ and $\langle p \to l_2 \rangle \in \Phi_2$.

The refine and reduce operators alter the values guarded in the implications, w.r.t. the context (for refine) and weaker guards (for reduce). Nevertheless, the value under the true guard is quite special, as it is the broadest one. We can define easier to compute versions of these operators, at the expense of precision. They only refine the value under true, and reduce other values accordingly:

$$\mathsf{reduce}\,(I) \triangleq \lambda p.\, I\,(p) \setminus_{\mathcal{L}} I\,(\mathsf{true})$$

$$\mathsf{refine}\,(h, (c, I)) \triangleq \mathsf{canonize}'\left(c \wedge h, I\left[\mathsf{true} \mapsto \bigsqcap_{\mathcal{L}} \{I\,(p) \mid h \Rightarrow p\}\right]\right)$$

5   Applications

This section describes the two abstract domains on which we have instanciated a predicated analysis in the Frama-C platform. Note that our framework could also be applied to other domains, e.g. intervals or the "valid file descriptors" domain used for Fig. 1.

5.1   A First Abstract Domain: Initialized Variables

A first simple domain retains at each progam point the set of variables that were properly initialized. Our experiments on a generated C code, where initialization of variables happens far before their uses, showed that this domain is very useful. In the abstract semantics of this domain, we introduce a new default value $\varnothing$ in $\mathbb{V}$, to which all variables are equal at program entry (i.e. $\mathbb{S}\,(0) \triangleq \{\lambda x.\varnothing\}$).

$$\gamma_{\mathsf{init}}\,(V) = \{\rho \mid \forall x \in V, \rho\,(x) \neq \varnothing\}$$

$$[\![x := e]\!]^\sharp_{\mathsf{init}}\,(V) = \begin{cases} V \cup \{x\} & \text{if } \mathsf{deps}\,(e) \subseteq V \\ V \setminus \{x\} & \text{otherwise} \end{cases} \qquad \begin{aligned} \mathsf{deps}\,(x := e) &\triangleq \mathsf{deps}\,(e) \\ \mathsf{deps}\,(c \lhd) &\triangleq \mathsf{deps}\,(c) \end{aligned}$$

$$[\![c \lhd]\!]^\sharp_{\mathsf{init}}\,(V) = V$$

The execution of a statement is correct when all the involved variables are initialized. We extend deps to instuctions: $\mathsf{deps}\,(\mathtt{i})$ denotes the set of variables the statement $\mathtt{i}$ depends on. Then, a program P is correct according to this initialized semantics when $\forall\,(n, \mathtt{i}, m) \in P, \mathsf{deps}\,(\mathtt{i}) \subseteq \mathbb{S}^\sharp_{\mathsf{init}}\,(n)$.

$$\llbracket c \vartriangleleft, p \rrbracket^{\sharp}_{\mathsf{eq} \times C} (E) \triangleq \begin{cases} E \sqcup \{e_1 - e_2\} & \text{if } p \sqsupseteq \textbf{true} \text{ and } c - (e_1 - e_2) \\ E & \text{otherwise} \end{cases}$$

$$\llbracket x := e, p \rrbracket^{\sharp}_{\mathsf{eq} \times C} (E) \triangleq \begin{cases} \mathsf{kill}_{\mathsf{eq}} (x, E) \cup \{x = e\} & \text{if } p \equiv \textbf{true} \text{ and } x \notin \mathsf{deps}\,(e) \\ \mathsf{kill}_{\mathsf{eq}} (x, E) & \text{otherwise} \end{cases}$$

$$\mathsf{kill}_{\mathsf{eq}} (v, E) \triangleq \{(a = b) \in E \mid v \notin \mathsf{deps}\,(a) \wedge v \notin \mathsf{deps}\,(b)\}$$

$$E \setminus_{\mathsf{eq}} F \triangleq \{(a = b) \in E \mid (a = b) \notin F\}$$

$$\gamma_{\mathsf{eq}} (E) \triangleq \{\rho \mid (a = b) \in E \Rightarrow \llbracket a \rrbracket_{\rho} = \llbracket b \rrbracket_{\rho}\}$$

Fig. 8. Abstract semantics for the equality domain

5.2   A Second Abstract Domain: Equalities

Our experiments also relied on a symbolic domain tracking equalities between C expressions. It aims at enhancing the precision of Frama-C's existing value analysis plugin, whose abstract domains are non-relational. Our intents are also somewhat similar to those of Miné [12], in particular abstracting over temporary variables resulting from code normalization. Our equality domain boils down to retaining equalities stemming from assignments or equality conditions. Its formal definition is presented in Fig. 8, where the set E of equalities increases on equality assume statements, and on assignments that do not refer to the variable being modified. To be sound, the transfer function on assignments must also remove equalities that involve the overwritten variable, through the $\mathsf{kill}_{\mathsf{eq}}$ operator. Following Sect. 4.1, we present simplified transfer functions, for which only the **true** guard is enriched, and in which the operator $\setminus_{\mathsf{eq}}$ can be used to remove redundant equalities.

This domain lends itself to a natural extension of our analysis, namely the strengthening of the context by backward-propagating information from $\mathcal{L}$ when modifying the context. For example, the equalities can be used to quotient the context by equal expressions. Furthermore, during the weakening of a context – when the truth value of one of its litterals is modified – we may substitute the litteral by an expression equal to it, instead of resetting the context.

Moreover, we were faced with code patterns similar to the one presented in Fig. 9, in which the condition of a branch is defined within a previous one – resulting in an implicit dependency between the two conditions h and p. To handle this pattern, we extend refine so that, when computing $\mathsf{refine}\,(h, (c, I))$ with I containing $\langle p \to (h = 0) \rangle$, then we also add $\neg p$ to the new context.

```
if(p) {
    ...
    h = e;
} else {
    h = 0;
}
if (h)
    ...
```

Fig. 9. Code pattern

Thus, imprecision in the refinement of contexts can be reduced by crossing information between underlying and predicated domains.

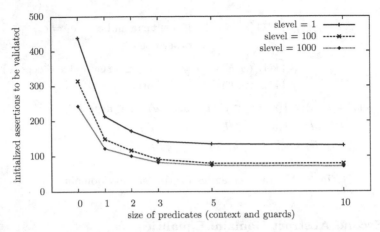

slevel	assertions to be validated	initialization assertions	validated assertions/clevel					
			1	2	3	5	10	
1	632	439	225	267	296	305	308	6.4s
10	600	409	199	241	270	279	282	9.8s
100	504	315	166	198	223	235	236	38s
1000	430	243	121	142	160	169	172	502s
			6s	9s	15s	24s	116s	time

Fig. 10. Experimental results

6   Experimental Results

We have integrated our predicated analyses framework as a new plugin of the Frama-C platform. This plugin runs above the value analysis plugin (abbreviated as VA), which we mainly use to get aliasing information on pointers. This information is needed to ensure the soundness of the deps operator.

Perimeter of our Analysis. At each program point where it cannot guarantee the absence of run-time error, VA emits as an alarm an ACSL assertion that excludes the failure case. These alarms may correspond to real bugs, if the statement can give rise to an error at execution time, or may be due to a lack of precision. To limit imprecisions caused by junctions in the control-flow graph, VA implements an instance of trace partitionning, and propagates separately multiple abstract states coming from different branches. As dissociating every feasible execution path leads to untractable analyses, the number of parallel states maintained by VA is limited but configurable by the slevel parameter. Still, high slevel values may lead to high analysis time.

Using a predicated analysis over a simple domain to prove some of the ACSL assertions emitted by VA can avoid this blow up. By construction, we mainly improve VA's results on successive assume statements with identical conditions[1]. Although such pattern is relatively unusual in idiomatic C code, it is much more frequent in generated programs, for which our method is well adapted.

Some generated programs can include a very large number of nested conditional branchs and loops, leading to overly wide contexts in our own analysis. To avoid a complexity explosion, we limit the number of litterals in the predicates used in contexts and guards (thereby decreasing the precision of our results), according to a parameter clevel. Conversely, our prototype implements a precise version of the abstract semantics operators presented in Sect. 3, without the relaxations proposed in Sect. 4.2.

Results. We tested our plugin on a C program of 5000 lines generated by the industrial environment SCADE, devoted to real-time software. As often with such codes, multiple conditionals are heavily used – typically to test automata states or clocks. Our results are presented in Fig. 10. We first applied VA, which emitted various assertions to further validate (column 2). As expected, a higher slevel results in fewer alarms. Between 55% and 70% of those are assertions requiring variables to be properly initialized (column 3), which are those our underlying domain understands. We then ran our predicated analysis, instantiated by the domain presented in Sect. 5.1, with different limits for the size of predicates (columns "validated assertions"). The last column indicates the analysis time of VA, while that of the predicated analysis is given in the last line.

While VA produces significantly less alarms with a higher slevel, its analysis time also increases drastically. This is unsurprising, as fully partitioning for k successive conditionals may require as much as 2^k distinct states. On the other hand, our plugin is effective to quickly validate numerous assertions left unproven by VA, even with strongly limited predicates. The precision of our analysis increases rapidly with the clevel parameter, while the analysis times remains reasonable. More generally, it turns out that small contexts are sufficient to retain most of the relevant information: less assertions remain to be validated with clevel = 1 and slevel = 1 than with clevel = 0 and slevel = 1000. Intuitively, even inside deeply nested conditionals (which generate complex contexts), only the more recent guards are useful. In general, our results show that it is much more cost efficient to increase the clevel parameter than the slevel parameter.

7   Conclusion

This work provides a generic framework to enhance the precision of standard dataflow analyses. This framework constructs a derived predicated analysis able to mitigate information loss at junction points of the control-flow graph, by retaining the conditional values about each branch. Our analysis strives to minimize redundant information processing due to these disjunctions. Experimental tests led through the static analysis platform Frama-C on generated C code showed that a predicated analysis over simple domains can significanlty improve the results of prior analyses.

---

[1] Modulo conjunction, disjunction and negation, but only over uninterpreted expressions; in particular, $x < y$ and $y > x$ are not considered as being equivalent guards.

The litterals of our predicates are expressions that we currently consider as opaque. In order to improve our analysis, we intend to give some meaning to the operators in these expressions and to extend the logical implication between guards accordingly. In particular, we will handle successive conditions on distinct but related expressions, such as $(x \geq 0) \lhd$ and $(x \geq 2) \lhd$. Moreover, prior syntactic analyses or heuristics could help to select relevant predicates for the contexts, which would no longer be extended at each assume statement. This would avoid maintaining implication guards that will never be useful again later in the program. Finally, it would be worthwhile to apply our predicated analysis over more complex abstract domains.

References

1. Baudin, P., Cuoq, P., Filliâtre, J.C., Marché, C., Monate, B., Moy, Y., Prevosto, V.: ACSL: ANSI/ISO C Specification Language, Version 1.8 (2014), http://frama-c.com/download/acsl-implementation-Neon-20140301.pdf
2. Bourdoncle, F.: Efficient chaotic iteration strategies with widenings. In: Pottosin, I.V., Bjorner, D., Broy, M. (eds.) FMP&TA 1993. LNCS, vol. 735, pp. 128–141. Springer, Heidelberg (1993)
3. Chebaro, O., Cuoq, P., Kosmatov, N., Marre, B., Pacalet, A., Williams, N., Yakobowski, B.: Behind the scenes in sante: a combination of static and dynamic analyses. Autom. Softw. Eng. 21(1), 107–143 (2014)
4. Correnson, L., Signoles, J.: Combining analyses for C program verification. In: Stoelinga, M., Pinger, R. (eds.) FMICS 2012. LNCS, vol. 7437, pp. 108–130. Springer, Heidelberg (2012)
5. Cousot, P., Cousot, R.: Abstract interpretation: A unified lattice model for static analysis of programs by construction or approximation of fixpoints. In: POPL, pp. 238–252. ACM (1977)
6. Cousot, P., Cousot, R.: Abstract interpretation frameworks. J. Log. Comput. 2(4), 511–547 (1992)
7. Cousot, P., Cousot, R., Feret, J., Mauborgne, L., Miné, A., Monniaux, D., Rival, X.: Combination of abstractions in the ASTRÉE static analyzer. In: Okada, M., Satoh, I. (eds.) ASIAN 2006. LNCS, vol. 4435, pp. 272–300. Springer, Heidelberg (2007)
8. Cuoq, P., Kirchner, F., Kosmatov, N., Prevosto, V., Signoles, J., Yakobowski, B.: Frama-C - A software analysis perspective. In: Eleftherakis, G., Hinchey, M., Holcombe, M. (eds.) SEFM 2012. LNCS, vol. 7504, pp. 233–247. Springer, Heidelberg (2012)
9. Cuoq, P., Prevosto, V., Yakobowski, B.: Frama-C's value analysis plug-in, http://frama-c.com/download/value-analysis-Neon-20140301.pdf
10. Fischer, J., Jhala, R., Majumdar, R.: Joining dataflow with predicates. In: Wermelinger, M., Gall, H. (eds.) ESEC/SIGSOFT FSE, pp. 227–236. ACM (2005)
11. Graf, S., Saïdi, H.: Verifying invariants using theorem proving. In: Alur, R., Henzinger, T.A. (eds.) CAV 1996. LNCS, vol. 1102, pp. 196–207. Springer, Heidelberg (1996)
12. Miné, A.: Symbolic methods to enhance the precision of numerical abstract domains. In: Emerson, E.A., Namjoshi, K.S. (eds.) VMCAI 2006. LNCS, vol. 3855, pp. 348–363. Springer, Heidelberg (2006)
13. Nielson, F., Nielson, H.R., Hankin, C.: Principles of program analysis. Springer (2005)
14. Rival, X., Mauborgne, L.: The trace partitioning abstract domain. ACM Trans. Program. Lang. Syst. 29(5) (2007)

Detecting Consistencies and Inconsistencies of Pattern-Based Functional Requirements

Christian Ellen[1], Sven Sieverding[1], and Hardi Hungar[2]

[1] OFFIS - Institute for Information Technology
Escherweg 2,26121 Oldenburg, Germany
<ellen,sieverding>@offis.de
[2] German Aerospace Center - Institute of Transportation Systems
Lilienthalplatz 7, 38108 Braunschweig, Germany
hardi.hungar@dlr.de

Abstract. The formal specification of functional requirements can often lead to inconsistency as well as unintended specification, especially in the early stages within the development process. In this paper, we present a formal model checking approach which tackles both of these problems and is also applicable during the requirements elicitation phase, in which no component model is available. The presented notion of consistency ensures the existence of at least one possible run of the system, which satisfies all requirements. To avoid trivial execution traces, the "intended" functional behavior of the requirements is triggered. The analysis is performed using model checking. More specifically, to reduce the overall analysis effort, we apply a bounded model checking scheme. If the set of requirements is inconsistent the method also identifies a maximal sub-set of consistent requirements. Alternatively, a minimal inconsistent sub-set can be computed. The approach is demonstrated on a railway crossing example using the BTC Embedded Specifier and the iSAT model checker.

Keywords: Formal Methods, Contract-based Design, Verification, Consistency Analysis, Requirements Engineering.

1 Introduction and Related Work

The elicitation and formalization of requirements are very important steps in today's development processes of safety relevant embedded systems, especially if they have to follow industrial standards like ISO26262[7]. In the early stages of the development process, feedback on the consistency of the current set of requirements can help to avoid (often costly) problems in later stages.

On the one hand, tools like the BTC Embedded Specifier [1] or the Requirements Quality Suite [2] can be used to support requirement engineers in the early requirements elicitation phase, but do not offer a formal consistency analysis.

---

[1] www.btc-es.de/index.php?idcatside=52
[2] www.reusecompany.com/requirements-quality-suite

F. Lang and F. Flammini (Eds.): FMICS 2014, LNCS 8718, pp. 155–169, 2014.
© Springer International Publishing Switzerland 2014

On the other hand, several different notions of consistency for requirements have been formally defined (*e.g.*, [6,4,1]). These often require explicit knowledge of the system architecture (component model) or can only be applied by specialists in formal methods.

Within this paper, we are bridging this gap by: Defining a sound general notion of the consistency of functional requirements, namely *existential consistency*, instantiating this notion with the semantics of the BTC Pattern language [3], and fully integrate the analysis within the Embedded Specifier. Our goal is to provide the consistency information directly accessible to the requirement engineer, without the need of special training. In addition, the analysis avoids trivial consistency results by taking into account the "intended" behavior of the patterns.

Since our analysis is a formal analysis method, scalability is a important factor for its applicability. This is addressed by using a bounded model checking (BMC) procedure based on the state-of-the-art constraint solver iSAT [5]. The presence of *false-inconsistency* results (esp. in large numbers) due to the incompleteness of the BMC approach may lead to a lower industrial acceptance of the approach. Therefore, we address this issue by defining a automated procedure to detect guaranteed *maximal consistent* sets of requirements as well as a second procedure to detect a guaranteed *minimal inconsistent* set of requirements.

In this paper, we use parts of the railroad crossing system, developed by Leveson [8], as a running example throughout the paper to demonstrate our approach. This example is usually used to demonstrate real time analysis or correctness checks. The idea behind this the scenario is as follows:

As soon as a train approaches the crossing, the gate has to close. If the gate is closed, the train is allowed to enter the crossing. When the train finally leaves the crossing area, the gate has to open again. The main safety goal for this scenario is: Whenever a train is in the crossing area, the gate has to be closed.

For this paper, we use only the basic version of the crossing with only one rail track and one gate. We will define formal functional requirements for this scenario and perform the proposed consistency analysis on this system. It is worth mentioning that we are only checking the consistency of the requirements and not the correctness of the specification.

The article is structured as follows: Section 2 introduces the semantics of the BTC Pattern language, Section 3 defines the formal basis on which the different notions of consistency, see Section 4, are defined. Section 5 describes how the analysis is integrated into the Embedded Specifier. The paper concludes with Section 6.

2   BTC Patterns

We choose to use the commercial tool BTC Embedded Specifier to demonstrate our approach. The Embedded Specifier provides its own requirement language, to which we will refer as the "BTC patterns" throughout this paper. First, we give an overview of the semantics of the BTC pattern, before we formally introduce them in Section 3. These BTC patterns [3] are structured templates of the following strcuture:

<Activation mode>_<Base Pattern>_<Start-up Phase>

2.1   Base Pattern

The base patterns are structured text blocks which have a formal semantic, but are close to natural language. They usually have a trigger and reaction structure *e.g.*, P_implies_Q_during_next_X_steps. This base pattern specifies that a property Q has to hold for the next X steps after a property P is satisfied.

The parameters P and Q of the pattern have to be instantiated using boolean expressions ($\neg, \vee, \wedge, \Rightarrow, \Leftrightarrow$) over integer arithmetic literals ($+, -, *, /, <, \leq, =, \geq$, $>$) and variables (called macros). By convention, a name of a macro starts with a Dollar sign ($). In addition, a positive, non-zero integer value has to be assigned to the parameter X.

The complete list of all patterns can be found in the documentation of the tool [3]. The documentation also includes, for each pattern, an observer automaton defining its semantics.

2.2   Start-up Phase

The start-up phase allows to model a delay after the start of a system. This can be used to avoid side effects resulting from a not yet properly initialized system state.

_immediate The requirement must hold directly after the start of the system.
_after_N_steps The requirement must hold after waiting exactly N steps.
_after_reaching_R The requirement must hold one step after R occurs, but R may not occur at all.

2.3   Activation Modes

The activation mode defines how a pattern is activated after the start-up phase of the system.

init__ The requirements must hold for the first step of the system (after start-up).
first__ The requirements must hold for the first occurrence of the trigger property (usually P) if there is any occurrence.
cyclic__ The requirements must hold for multiple iterations of the pattern after initialization. If the pattern is not active, it will be activated every time its activation condition is valid. This explicitly excludes an activation of the pattern if the last instance is not completed (iterative semantics).

2.4   Example

For the railroad crossing system, we can use the base pattern, already mentioned in Section 2.1, to model the procedure to close the gate. Whenever a train enters the crossing and the gate is in an upright position (P = $TrainEnters $\land$ $GateIsUp), the gate shall move down (Q = $GateMovesDown) for the next five ($X = 5$) steps. We use the `cyclic_` activation mode, because the gate shall close every time a train enters. We do not have a start-up phase in the system, we use `_immediate`. The requirement for closing the gate again is of the same structure. Both instantiated BTC pattern are shown in Table 1 with the ID P1 and P2 respectively.

Table 1. Railroad crossing pattern instantiations

ID	BTC pattern
P1	*cyclic_P_implies_Q_during_next_X_steps_immediate* P: $TrainEnters $\land$ $GateIsUp Q: $GateMovesDown X: 5
P2	*cyclic_P_implies_Q_during_next_X_steps_immediate* P: $TrainExit $\land$ $GateIsDown Q: $GateMovesUp X: 5
P3	*cyclic_Q_only_after_P_immediate* Q: $TrainEnters P: $TrainExit
P4	*cyclic_Q_only_after_P_immediate* Q: $TrainExit P: $TrainEnters

We also need two additional requirements to model the constraint, that only one train at the time is allowed to be within the crossing area. Therefore, we choose to use the BTC pattern *cyclic_Q_only_after_P_immediate*, which restricts the ordering of occurrences of events. Requirement P3 in the Table 1 specifies that a new train is only allowed to enter, if the previous train has left. P4 models, that a train can only exit after it enters the crossing before.

The predefined observer automaton in Figure 1 reflects the semantics of one BTC pattern used for P1 and P2 in the example. It is based on a counter automaton (similar to a Büchi state machine) and it accepts an input string, if the error state is never reached. In case of this example pattern, as long as no P occurs, the automaton is accepting the input within its initial state. If P occurs, during the next max_X steps Q has to hold and the parameter P is ignored. In case, Q does not hold while in state 1 of the observer automaton, the failure state – state 2 – is entered. Failure states are always sinks, which means, whatever values P and Q will assume in the future, the automaton cannot reach the fair state again.

cyclic_P_implies_Q_during_next_X_steps_immediate

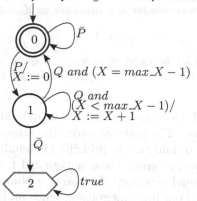

Fig. 1. Example of the BTC pattern modeling the process to close the gate after a train approaches. The parameter of the pattern are as follows:

- P : \$TrainEnters $\wedge$ \$GateIsUp
- Q : \$GateMovesDown
- max_X : 5

3   Trace and Pattern Semantics

Within this section, we formally define the semantics of functional requirements by means of counter automatons and traces. A set of traces is grouped to a specification for which the semantic is extended to address the intended behavior of a requirement.

These general definition of the terms allows us to define the notions of consistency and inconsistency (Section 4) independent of the semantics of the used pattern language.

3.1   Traces and Formulas

In [4,6] the authors specify the semantic foundation of requirement contracts. We restate the main definitions and assumptions.

Definition 1 (Variable, Requirement, Value, Time, Evolution)

1. $\mathbb{X}$ is a set of variables, $X \in \mathbb{X}$, each with an associated type $\textbf{type}(X)$. For each $\textbf{type}$ we assume a set of values $\mathcal{V}_{type}$
2. $\mathcal{R}(\mathbb{X})$ is a set of requirements over the variables among $\mathbb{X}$
3. $\mathbb{N}_0$ is the domain of time, with $i \in \mathbb{N}_0$
4. An evolution ε_X of variable X is a function in $\varepsilon_{type(X)} \subseteq [\mathbb{N}_0 \rightarrow \mathcal{V}_{type(X)}]$ which associates to each point in time a value $x \in \mathcal{V}_{type(X)}$. A prefix of an evolution $\varepsilon_{type(X)}|_u$ is a restriction of an evolution ε_x to points in time $i \leq u$.

We use x_i as a shorthand notation for the value $x \in \mathcal{V}_{type(X)}$ at time $i \in \mathbb{N}_0$ of a variable $X \in \mathbb{X}$ according to an evolution ε_X.

In the following w.l.o.g., we assume $\textbf{type}$ to be either *Boolean* (0/1-*Integer*) for the macros used in the patterns or positive *Integer* for time bound parameters. A correct typing of the variables, with respect to the parameters of the pattern at hand, is also assumed.

Definition 2 (Trace). *Given a set of variables* $\mathbb{X}$, *the set* $\mathcal{S}(\mathbb{X})$ *of traces (or sequences) for* $\mathbb{X}$, *is the set of combined evolutions for the variables in* $\mathbb{X}$, *s.t.:*

$$\mathcal{S}(\mathbb{X}) =_{def} \{(X \mapsto \varepsilon_X)_{X \in \mathbb{X}} | \varepsilon_X \in \varepsilon_{type(X)}\}$$

A prefix *(intial segment) of a trace* $\sigma \in \mathcal{S}(\mathbb{X})$ *is given by a bound* $k \in \mathbb{N}_0$ *and consists of all the prefixes* $\varepsilon_X|_k$ *with* $X \in \mathbb{X}$. *The set of prefixes of length* k *of traces over* $\mathbb{X}$ *is denoted by* $\mathcal{P}_k(\mathbb{X})$.

A trace $\sigma \in \mathcal{S}(\mathbb{X})$ represents an execution of a system modeled by the individual evolutions of the system variables over time. The systems under investigation are assumed to start at a point in time ($i = 0$) and run (in principle) indefinitely long. Dependend on the selected verification procedure these unbounded traces can be handled differently (*e.g.*, by LTL model checking). In case of a bounded model checking procedure, as it is applied in our implementation, finite prefixes of these traces enter the picture. In our implementation the general concept of requirements $\mathcal{R}$ is instantiated by means of BTC Patterns.

3.2   Pattern Semantics

As illustrated in the example in Sec. 2.4, the semantics of a pattern is given by an automaton. In the following definitions, the propositional parameters of the patterns are not instantiated, while the step parameters are already given by natural numbers. The full instantiation is done afterwards by replacing all parameters with boolean conditions over $\mathbb{X}$.

Definition 3 (Counter Automaton)

1. A *counter automaton* $A(\mathbb{Q}) = (S, \mathbb{Q}, \mathbb{W}, T, I, F)$ *over a set of parameters* $\mathbb{Q}$ *consists of finite sets of* states S, *boolean parameters* $\mathbb{Q}$, *counters* $\mathbb{W}$, *and* transitions T. *Each* $t \in T$ *is labeled by a boolean condition* $cond(t)$ *on parameters and counters and disjoint sets of counters to be* incremented *($inc(t)$) and* resetted *($reset(t)$). The counter conditions are of the form* $W \sim n$ *with* $W \in \mathbb{W}$, $n \in \mathbb{N}_0$ *and* $\sim \in \{<, =\}$. *The state* $I \in S$ *is the initial state, and* $F \in S$ *is a failure state. The* size *$|A|$ of A is the number of states, $|S|$.*
2. *A counter automaton is* complete *and* deterministic *if the conditions at the set of transitions leaving a state are exhaustive and pairwise exclusive, and the failure state has no transition leading to another state.*
3. *A* run *of a counter automaton is a trace* $\sigma \in \mathcal{S}(\{s\} \cup \mathbb{Q} \cup \mathbb{W})$ *with* $s_0 = I$, $W_0 = 0$ *for every* $W \in \mathbb{W}$, *and for* $i \in \mathbb{N}$:

$$\exists t \in T. s_i \rightarrow_t s_{i+1} \wedge \sigma_i \models cond(t) \wedge W_{i+1} = \begin{cases} W_i + 1 & c \in inc(t) \\ 0 & c \in reset(t) \\ W_i & else \end{cases}$$

4. *A run is* accepting *if* $\forall i \in \mathbb{N}: s_i \neq F$. *The semantics* $\mathcal{S}(A(\mathbb{Q}))$ *of a counter automaton* $A(\mathbb{Q})$ *is the set of its accepting runs, restricted to the evolutions of elements of* $\mathbb{Q}$.
5. *If* $\mathbb{W} = \emptyset$, *the counter automaton is said to be* propositional.

The approach presented in the rest of the paper rests on the fact that counter automata capture the semantics of patterns.

Proposition 1. *The semantics of a pattern* $P(\mathbb{Q})$ *is given by a complete and deterministic counter automaton* $\mathcal{A}(P(\mathbb{Q}))$. *A trace* σ *over* $\mathbb{Q}' \supseteq \mathbb{Q}$ *satisfies* $P(\mathbb{Q})$, *denoted by* $\sigma \models P(\mathbb{Q})$, *if* $\sigma|_{\mathbb{Q}} \in \mathcal{S}(\mathcal{A}(P(\mathbb{Q})))$.

Fig.1 shows an example automaton. Though the semantics of patterns is given in terms of counter automata, counters can be eliminated. There is an equivalent propositional automaton with 5 copies of the state "1" (the counter runs from 0 to 4.). This fact will be used later in completeness argumentations.

Proposition 2. *Every counter automaton* A *is equivalent to a propositional automaton* A'. *I.e., there is a propositional automaton* A' *s.t.* $\mathcal{S}(A) = \mathcal{S}(A')$, *with*

$$|A'| \leq |A| \times \underset{W \in \mathbb{W}}{\bigtimes} (|W| + 2)$$

, *where* $|W|$ *is the maximal value* $n \in \mathbb{N}_0$ *occurring in counter conditions over* W.

Proof. Since counter values enter conditions only by comparisons to constants, there is a maximal relevant value for each counter: The highest constant to which it is compared. Therefore, only finitely many counter valuations (including $W = 0$ and an artificial additional value for all values higher than the highest constant) are relevant. These can be flattened out in the state set.

3.3   Specifications and Their Standard Semantics

In this article, specifications consisting of sets of patterns are considered.

Definition 4 (Specification). *A specification* $C(\mathbb{X})$ *consists of a set of instantiated patterns* $\{P_1(\mathbb{X}_1), \ldots P_m(\mathbb{X}_m)\}$ *with* $\mathbb{X}_i \subseteq \mathbb{X}$. *The instantiation replaces the boolean parameters of a pattern by boolean conditions over the variables. The semantics of a specification is the intersection of the sets of accepting traces of the automata defining the semantics of the patterns in the specification. A trace* $\sigma(\mathbb{X})$ *satisfies a specification, denoted by* $\sigma \models C(\mathbb{X})$, *if the trace satisfies all patterns modulo the instantiation.*

Thus, a system complies to the specification if it satisfies all patterns, *i.e.*, if its traces are a subset of the intersection of all trace sets of the patterns. This can be reflected on the level of automata by the usual synchronous product of automaton.

Proposition 3 (Synchronous Product). [3] *Let* $\{A_i | i = 1 \ldots n\}$ *be a set of counter automata. Then*

$$\mathcal{S}\left(\underset{i=1}{\overset{n}{\bigtimes}} A_i\right) = \bigcap_{i=1}^{n} \mathcal{S}(A_i), \quad and \quad \left|\underset{i=1}{\overset{n}{\bigtimes}} A_i\right| = \underset{i=1}{\overset{n}{\bigtimes}} |A_i|,$$

where $\times$ *denotes the synchronous product of the automaton after renaming parameters and counters of the* A_i *to avoid name clashes.*

---

[3] Technical details of the construction are deferred to a more complete presentation.

3.4   Intended Specification Semantics

For practical purposes, the pure logical view of the previous section will be extended. If one looks at the example pattern (Fig. 1), the requirements engineer will most likely intend the final system to have a trace where a train approaches the crossing ("train enters" becomes true) while the gate is up. If this trace is ruled out by some other patterns in the specification, this will most probably be an error.

This observation gives rise to a definition of the *intended* semantics of the patterns of a specification. Semantically, this relies on a labeling of automaton states. Given a pattern and the automaton $A(\mathbb{Q}) = (S, \mathbb{Q}, \mathbb{W}, T, I, F)$ defining its semantics, the activation of a trigger in the pattern corresponds to a subset $R \subset S$, s.t. reaching a state in R corresponds to activating the relevant trigger. In the example, one expects that there will be traces of the system where P is triggered, so that the state labeled "1" is reached by some legal trace of the system. In general, trigger activation might correspond to reach one of a set of states, and if several triggers are to be activated, there are correspondingly several state sets.

Definition 5 (Intended Semantics). *Let a pattern with labeled triggers and the correspondingly annotated counter automaton $A, \mathbb{R}$ with $\mathbb{R} = \{R_1, \ldots, R_m\}$ be given. Then the* intended *semantics of the annotated pattern is the set of traces of A originating in runs of A which meet each set in $\mathbb{R}$ at least once. I.e.:*

$$\mathcal{S}_I(A, \mathbb{R}) := \{\sigma \in \mathcal{S}(A) | \forall i \in \{1, \ldots, m\}. \exists j. \sigma(s)_j \in R_i\}$$

The synchronous product from Prop. 3 can be lifted to annotated counter automatons in an obvious way.

The reader may note that asking for activation of triggers changes the nature of the game. Patterns by themselves define only safety properties in the technical meaning of this term in temporal logic. A safety property is characterized by the fact that it is true for trace if and only if it is true for all its finite prefixes. Activation of triggers adds an element of liveness to that. Thus, activation of triggers cannot be captured by the automaton of Def. 3, and we need the additional concept of reaching states. An equivalent technical alternative consists in specifying the required activations by additional (fair) automata. This is possible since the pattern automata are deterministic. Fig. 2 shows an example of a simple trigger automaton.

Such trigger automaton could also model more complex behavior, *i.e.,* some pattern require P to hold for more than one step. For every pattern in the BTC library a trigger automaton was defined, reflecting the "intention" of the specific pattern.

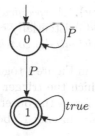

Fig. 2. Trigger automaton for the pattern of Figure 1. The trigger requires P : $GateOpen$ && $TrainEnters$ to be evaluated to true for at least one step. This will force the requirement to execute its intended behavior, *i.e.*, to close the gate, at least once.

Definition 6 (Trigger Requirements). *A specification may have associated additional trigger requirements. For specifications by BTC patterns* $C(\mathbb{X})$*, there is a standard set of trigger requirements* $C{\uparrow}(\mathbb{X})$*.*

4   Consistency

In the context of requirements engineering and contracts, many different notions of consistency are defined. Consistency can be analyzed for the relationship of a contract to the interface of a component (*e.g.,* [9]), to possible environments ([2]), or purely between a set contracts (*e.g.,* [1]). Our notion of consistency analysis addresses the latter and is specialized for functional requirements. It checks if for a given specification $C(\mathbb{X})$ at least one trace over $\mathbb{X}$ exists. Within this section, we define notions of such existential consistency.

4.1   Existential Consistency

For infinite traces the existence of at least one possible execution of a system which fulfills all requirements of the specification C is defined as follows:

Definition 7 (Existential Consistency). *A specification* $C(\mathbb{X})$ *is existentially consistent, denoted by* $cons(C(\mathbb{X}))$*, iff there exists at least one trace* $\sigma \in \mathcal{S}(\mathbb{X})$ *s.t.* $\sigma \models C(\mathbb{X})$

This definition is weaker compared to other definitions of contract consistency (*e.g.,* [2,1]) in which C must hold for all possible traces over the input variables in $\mathbb{X}$. In contrast to these approaches, our method does not assume any underlying component model of the system. It is applicable in an earlier design state in which no component or architecture definition is available. Especially, neither a definition of the components input and output variables, nor the interconnection of components has to be defined. Our so called *existential consistency* is purely based on observations of traces of different variables and the requirements defined so far.

For the railroad crossing requirement in Figure 1, *existential consistency* is given by a trace on which P never holds. On this trace the automaton will always stay in the initial state. As already mentioned in the previous section, this trivial solution does not reflect the "intended" behavior of the requirement. Thus, we extend the notion of consistency to *triggered existential consistency*.

Definition 8 (Triggered Existential Consistency). *A specification* $\mathcal{C}(\mathbb{X})$ *with associated trigger requirements* $\mathcal{C}{\uparrow}(\mathbb{X})$ *is triggered existentially consistent, denoted by* $cons{\uparrow}(\mathcal{C}(\mathbb{X}))$, *iff the set* $\mathcal{C}(\mathbb{X}) \cup \mathcal{C}{\uparrow}(\mathbb{X})$ *is existentially consistent.*

Applying this definition to the example requirement in Figure 1 together with the trigger in Figure 2 yields a consistent trace on which the trigger condition $\$TrainEnters \wedge \$GateIsUp$ holds at least once. This forces the observer of the requirement to leave the initial state and observe the "intended" behavior of $GateMovesDown$ for 5 steps.

4.2   Bounded Consistency

Some model checking techniques can deal with the verification of properties on full (infinite) traces (*e.g.,* Linear Temporal Logic (LTL) model checking). For scalability reasons often techniques like bounded model checking (BMC) are used, which consider only finite prefixes of traces. These methods are a priori incomplete because of the boundedness of the prefixes. Applied to the existential consistency problem, they might fail to discover inconsistencies due to their limited search horizon.

Therefore, when using bounded existential consistency one has to determine whether a finite witness prefix for bounded consistency ensures the existence of a witness for general consistency. This holds, if the bounded prefix contains a loop to a previously visited state (including counters) within the prefix.

Definition 9 (Loop). *If* $\mathcal{C}(\mathbb{X})$ *is defined by BTC patterns, a prefix* π *of length* k *of a trace* σ *is called a loop for* $\mathcal{C}(\mathbb{X})$ *iff there exists an* $i \in \mathbb{N}_0$ *with* $i < k$ *s.t.* $\forall \mathcal{A}(\mathrm{P}(\mathbb{Q})) \in \mathcal{C}(\mathbb{X}) : s_i = s_k \wedge \mathbb{W}_i = \mathbb{W}_k \wedge \mathbb{Q}_i = \mathbb{Q}_k.$

The idea is that, as far as the patterns are considered, the state of the system at time k is indistinguishable from the one at the beginning of the loop at time i. Such a loop can then always be extended to a infinite run by iteratively appending the evolution between i and k. Since the semantics is given by counter automatons, this means that all counters and variables at time i must have the same value as at time k and that the active states must be the same.

Based on this definition the notion of bounded existential consistency can be defined.

Definition 10 (Bounded Existential Consistency). *A specification* $\mathcal{C}(\mathbb{X})$ *is bounded existentially consistent for a depth bound* k, *denoted by* $cons_k(\mathcal{C}(\mathbb{X}))$, *iff there exists at least one prefix* $\pi \in \mathcal{P}_k(\mathbb{X})$ *s.t.* $\forall c \in \mathcal{C}(\mathbb{X}) : \pi \models c$ *and* π *is a loop for* $\mathcal{C}(\mathbb{X})$.

Proposition 4. *Bounded existential consistency implies existential consistency:*

$$cons_k(\mathcal{C}(\mathbb{X})) \implies cons(\mathcal{C}(\mathbb{X}))$$

Proof. Let $cons_k(\mathcal{C}(\mathbb{X}))$ with $\pi^0 \models \mathcal{C}(\mathbb{X})$ and $i \in \mathbb{N}_0$ be the lower point in time of the loop. Then, starting with $j = 0$, π^j can be extended to a prefix π^{j+1}

by extension of π^j with the partial evolutions $\varepsilon_X|_{[i,k]}$ within π^0 of all variables $X \in \mathbb{X}$. By construction, π^{j+1} is a loop for $\mathcal{C}(\mathbb{X})$ and therefore $cons_{|\pi^j|}(\mathcal{C}(\mathbb{X})) \Rightarrow cons_{|\pi^{j+1}|}(\mathcal{C}(\mathbb{X}))$. From Def. 9 follows $|\pi^j| < |\pi^{j+1}|$ and therefore successive application of the extension constructs a trace σ s.t. $\sigma \models \mathcal{C}(\mathbb{X})$. From Def. 7 follows $cons(\mathcal{C}(\mathbb{X}))$ for the trace σ.

To generalize this for the "intended" semantics, the definition of a loop has to be extended to include the occurrence of fair states within the loop. Then, the definition of bounded triggered consistency is straightforward.

Definition 11 (Bounded Triggered Consistency). *A set of functional requirements $\mathcal{C}(\mathbb{X})$ with associated set of trigger requirements $\mathcal{C}{\uparrow}(\mathbb{X})$ is bounded trigger consistent for a depth bound k, denoted by $cons_k{\uparrow}(\mathcal{C}(\mathbb{X}))$, iff the set $\mathcal{C}(\mathbb{X}) \cup \mathcal{C}{\uparrow}(\mathbb{X})$ is k-bounded existential triggered consistent.*

Also in the case of triggered consistency, bounded consistency implies consistency.

Proposition 5. *Bounded triggered consistency implies existential consistency:*

$$cons_k(\mathcal{C}(\mathbb{X}) \cup \mathcal{C}{\uparrow}(\mathbb{X})) \implies cons(\mathcal{C}(\mathbb{X}) \cup \mathcal{C}{\uparrow}(\mathbb{X}))$$

Proof. This property relies on the fact that, in most general case, Büchi trigger conditions for BTC patterns require triggers to be activated infinitely often. If this happens on the cycle of the finite prefix, it will happen infinitely often on the infinite trace constructed from that.

Since bounded (existential) consistency for a given depth bound k relies on the runs of the counter automata on a finite set of parameter evolutions, this is decidable.

Proposition 6. *For a set of functional requirements $\mathcal{C}(\mathbb{X})$ with associated set of trigger requirements $\mathcal{C}{\uparrow}(\mathbb{X})$ and an arbitrarily given depth bound k, it is decidable whether $cons_k{\uparrow}(\mathcal{C}(\mathbb{X}))$ does hold.*

The following theorem states that a depth bound can be computed which is sufficient large so that bounded existential (triggered) consistency is guaranteed to hold if the unbounded does so.

Theorem 1. *Let $\mathcal{C}(\mathbb{X})$ be a set of functional requirements defined by BTC patterns. Then bounds k_1 and k_2 can be computed s.t.*

$$cons(\mathcal{C}(\mathbb{X})) \Rightarrow cons_{k_1}(\mathcal{C}(\mathbb{X})), \text{ and}$$
$$cons{\uparrow}(\mathcal{C}(\mathbb{X})) \Rightarrow cons_{k_2}{\uparrow}(\mathcal{C}(\mathbb{X}))$$

The proof of the theorem relies on the fact the BTC patterns can be defined by propositional automata (Proposition 2). Essentially, one has to find a loop in the product automaton combining all properties. Estimations on the size of the bounds can be derived from studying the resulting graphs—states are vertices, transitions are edges. The following proposition illustrates the principles which can be applied here.

Proposition 7. *Given a directed graph with a distinguished initial vertex consisting of n vertices, for any set V of vertices, which can be covered by one path starting in the initial vertex, there is such a path of length at most n^2.*

Proof. The path covering V moves through the strongly connected components (SCCs) of the graph. In an SCC of size m, to reach a particular vertex, there is a path moving through a set of intermediate vertices (at most $m - 1$) and ending in that vertex. At most $m - 1$ such paths are needed, to reach all states except the initial one. These path can be combined into one path of length less than $m - 1$ (number of paths) times $m - 1$ (number of nodes to be reached) plus one (initial vertex)[4]. The paths covering the single SCCs are then connected by pieces of length at most $m - 1$. This establishes n^2 as a (not tight) bound.

Theorem 1 and the opposite implications from Proposition 4 and 5 imply decidability of (triggered) existential consistency. As a further consequence, BMC is indeed complete for checking (triggered) consistency of specifications given by BTC patterns.

This theoretical result serves as a foundation of the practical method which is developed in the subsequent section. Though a bound derived from Proposition 7 will be too large to be of much practical relevance, there is hope for tighter bounds resulting from arguments which take the specific form of the pattern automata into account. And also, one may look for approximation procedures whith internal completeness checks.

The practical approach is intended to deal with specifications which will be, at least in the beginning, inconsistent. If a set of requirements is consistent, an analysis procedure can provide the prefix as witness trace of the consistency. In case of an inconsistency result, such a witness does not exist. Therefore, it is of interest for a practical application, which requirements form a maximal consistent subset and which requirements are causes for the inconsistencies.

Definition 12 (Maximal Consistent Subset). *A subset of functional requirements $\mathcal{D}(\mathbb{X}) \subseteq \mathcal{C}(\mathbb{X})$ is called maximal consistent subset w.r.t. a notion of consistency $CONS \in \{cons(\cdot), cons_k(\cdot), cons\uparrow(\cdot), cons_k\uparrow(\cdot)\}$, iff $CONS(\mathcal{D}(\mathbb{X}))$ and $\forall c \in \mathcal{C}(\mathbb{X}) \setminus \mathcal{D}(\mathbb{X}) : \neg CONS(\mathcal{D}(\mathbb{X}) \cup \{c\})$*

An analysis may check iteratively if there are subsets of sizes $|\mathcal{C}(\mathbb{X})| - i$ for increasing $i \in \mathbb{N}$ if the analysis concluded that the full set of requirements is inconsistent. In the context of early validation of requirements, the presence of a high number of false inconsistency results due to the incompleteness of the bounded consistency analysis is a problem. These can be reduced by further increasing k up to K_{max}. If this procedure is applied to the example requirements of Table 1, the presented set of requirements is indeed inconsistent for $i = 0$ and $cons_k\uparrow(\cdot)$. Setting $i = 1$ generates a maximal consistent subset $\{P1, P2, P3\}$ together with an witness trace which violates the requirement $P4$. It is easy to see, that in this trivial example the requirements $P3$ and $P4$ are causing the

---

[4] It is not hard to see that this bound can be tightened to $\lceil m/2 \rceil \times (\lfloor m/2 \rfloor + 1)$.

inconsistency. Triggering $P3$ by observation of a $TrainEnters$ signal will violate $P4$ (which expects an $TrainExit$ signal first) and vice versa. For large numbers of requirements the root causes of the inconsistencies may be hard to detect, especially if a interaction of multiple requirements is required. Therefore, we define the notation of bounded existential inconsistency separately which tries to identify minimal inconsistent subsets.

Definition 13 (Minimal Inconsistent Subset). *A subset of functional requirements* $\mathcal{D}(\mathbb{X}) \subseteq \mathcal{C}(\mathbb{X})$ *is called minimal inconsistent subset w.r.t. a notion of consistency* $CONS \in \{cons(\cdot), cons_{K_{max}}(\cdot), cons\uparrow(\cdot), cons_{K_{max}}\uparrow(\cdot)\}$, *iff* $\neg CONS(\mathcal{D}(\mathbb{X}))$ *and* $\forall c \in \mathcal{D}(\mathbb{X}) : CONS(\mathcal{D}(\mathbb{X}) \setminus \{c\})$

Using this definition, the consistency analysis may be performed iteratively for all subsets of increasing size and even a bounded analysis can detect inconsistencies without the occurrence of false negative results. In our example, the algorithm first concludes that all sets of size 1 are consistent, which corresponds to the fact that each single requirement is consistent on its own. When analyzing the sets of size 2, the algorithm identifies the set $\{P3, P4\}$ to be minimal inconsistent.

Both, the analysis for maximal consistent subsets and the analysis for minimal inconsistent subsets may complement each other. An analysis for a feasible k can compute a maximal consistent subset $\mathcal{D}(\mathbb{X}) \subseteq \mathcal{C}(\mathbb{X})$. If not $\mathcal{D}(\mathbb{X}) = \mathcal{C}(\mathbb{X})$, a minimal inconsistent subset can be computed starting with the sets containing one of the inconsistent requirements not in the maximal consistent subset.

Alternatively, if a minimal consistent subset of size i is computed first, a subsequent consistency analysis with parameter $i - 1$ may be used to generate a witness trace which violates a requirement and fulfills all other requirements. For example, the identified inconsistent set $\{P3, P4\}$ can be used in a consistency analysis with $i = 1$. This will generate a witness trace which fullfills the intended semantics of $P3$ and violates $P4$ or vice versa.

5 Tool Integration

To evaluate our approach, we prototypically implemented the bounded triggered consistency analysis (Def. 11) using the satisfiability modulo theories (SMT) solver iSAT [5,10] and integrated the analysis directly into the user interface of the BTC Embedded Specifier. This enables the analysis to be used directly during the requirements elicitation phase. After entering new requirements, the analysis can be used for two purposes. First, it can check if the newly entered requirement is consistent on its own (*e.g.*, the parameters are instantiated correctly) or if it conflicts with already existing requirements. Second, the provided witness trace for the new specification can be used for debugging purposes. Figure 3 shows a part of such an witness trace for one of our analysis runs on the railroad crossing example. As discussed in the previous sections, the requirements $P3$ and $P4$ are conflicting. The partial witness trace shows that by observing $\$TrainExit$ in step 1 before $TrainEnters$ in step 9 will violate $P4$. The red marker at the end of the trace indicates that the model checker did not investigate more than 15 steps.

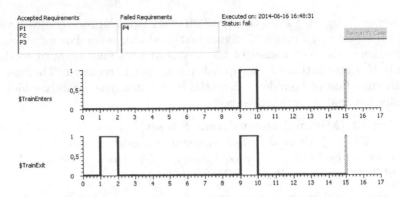

Fig. 3. Screenshot of the analysis results in the BTC Embedded Specifier. The maximal consistent sub-set of requirements, the inconsistent requirements, as well as a part of the witness trace are shown.

6 Conclusion and Future Work

Within this paper, we introduced the formal semantics for different notions of consistency. These are based on general functional requirements which we defined semantically as observable contracts over infinite traces and finite prefixes. As an instance of such requirements, we demonstrated how the definitions can be used to perform an existential bounded consistency analysis using the BTC Pattern language. This analysis, as well as a procedure to compute maximal consistent subsets has been implemented using the bounded model checker iSAT as a backend and has been fully integrated into the Embedded Specifier tool s.t. it may support the users directly during the specification of a requirement. In general, the analysis is applicable in early phases of the development process without explicit knowledge of any system model apart form the available variables.

For future extensions, the consistency analysis could be lifted to a general consistency analysis, in cases where more structural information of the system at hand is available (*e.g.,* components and their interfaces).

In addition, we plan to perform an evaluation of the applicability and the performance of the procedures in larger industrial use cases.

Acknowledgments. The research leading to these results has received funding from the ARTEMIS Joint Undertaking under Grant Agreement N°332830 (CRYSTAL) and German national funding from BMBF N°01IS13001A.

References

1. Aichernig, B.K., Lorber, F., Ničković, D., Tiran, S.: Require, test and trace it. Tech. Rep. IST-MBT-2014-03, TU Graz (2014), https://online.tugraz.at/tug_online/voe_main2.getVollText?pDocumentNr=637834&pCurrPk=77579 (visited on: March 06, 2014)

2. Benveniste, A., Caillaud, B., Nickovic, D., Passerone, R., Baptiste Raclet, J., Reinkemeier, P., Sangiovanni-vincentelli, A., Damm, W., Henzinger, T., Larsen, K.: Contracts for systems design. Tech. rep., Research Centre Rennes – Bretagne Atlantique (2012)

3. BTC Embedded Systems AG: BTC Embedded Validator Pattern Library, Release 3.6 (2012)

4. Damm, W., Hungar, H., Henkler, S., Stierand, I., Josko, B., Oertel, M., Reinkemeier, P., Baumgart, A., Büker, M., Gezgin, T., Ehmen, G., Weber, R.: SPES 2020 Architecture Modeling. Tech. rep., OFFIS e.V. (2011)

5. Eggers, A., Kalinnik, N., Kupferschmid, S., Teige, T.: Challenges in constraint-based analysis of hybrid systems. In: Oddi, A., Fages, F., Rossi, F. (eds.) CSCLP 2008. LNCS, vol. 5655, pp. 51–65. Springer, Heidelberg (2009)

6. Hungar, H.: Compositionality with strong assumptions. In: Nordic Workshop on Programming Theory, pp. 11–13. Mälardalen Real–Time Research Center (November 2011)

7. International Standard Organization: Road Vehicles - Functional Safety (November 2011)

8. Leveson, N.G., Stolzy, J.L.: Safety analysis using petri nets. IEEE Transactions on Software Engineering 13(3), 386–397 (1987)

9. Rajan, A., Wahl, T. (eds.): CESAR - Cost-efficient Methods and Processes for Safety-relevant Embedded Systems. Springer (2013) No. 978-3709113868

10. Teige, T., Eggers, A., Fränzle, M.: Constraint-based analysis of concurrent probabilistic hybrid systems: An application to networked automation systems. Nonlinear Analysis: Hybrid Systems 5(2), 343–366 (2011)

Test Specification Patterns
for Automatic Generation of Test Sequences

Ugo Gentile[1], Stefano Marrone[2], Gianluca Mele[1],
Roberto Nardone[1], and Adriano Peron[1]

[1] Università di Napoli "Federico II", DIETI, Italy
{ugo.gentile,roberto.nardone,adrperon}@unina.it,
gianluca.mele@studenti.unina.it
[2] Seconda Università di Napoli, Dip. di Matematica e Fisica, Italy
stefano.marrone@unina2.it

Abstract. Model Based Testing (MBT) enables automatic generation of test cases using models to specify the system behavior and requirements. Key features of MBT approaches are the automation level and the complexity of non-automated steps. Usually, test case generation is supported by some automatic technique whereas modeling is manually performed. UML statecharts or other extended finite state machine formalisms are widely used to build behavior models. To ease their development, as well as the extraction of test cases from them, is an important aspect to be addressed in order to perform testing activities with lower skill, cost and effort. This paper aims at providing a contribution to both the issues. Test Specification Patterns (TSPs) are proposed and expressed by means of UML annotated statecharts as a mean to aid the construction of models and build specifications on the base of well known recurring problems and their solutions (patterns). In order to improve usability and increase the automation level, a transformational approach is defined which derives Promela code from specifications built by TSPs composition and applies model checking to obtain test sequences by using the SPIN model checker. The usage of TSPs and the test case generation process is illustrated on a test scenario from the Radio Block Centre, the vital core of the modern railway control systems.

Keywords: Test Specification Patterns, Test Case Generation, Model Checking, Model Transformations, ERTMS/ETCS.

1 Introduction

As the complexity and the criticality of control systems increased, automatic generation of test sequences became more and more relevant in achieving reduction of cost and development time, as well as a general improvement of product quality. Testing generation approaches are mainly based on the use of model-based techniques [10,14] and formal methods [4,27] which require high skilled personnel in both modelling the system under test and defining test case specifications. As an example, model checking is exploited for test case generation [9]

F. Lang and F. Flammini (Eds.): FMICS 2014, LNCS 8718, pp. 170–184, 2014.

relying on the idea that counterexamples may be interpreted as test sequences. Indeed, model checking is a well assessed approach for test sequence generation in the context of Model Based Testing (MBT). In the last decade, Model Driven Engineering has emerged as a leading methodology not only in the development of software artifacts [26] and evaluation of quantitative system properties [21,3] but also in supporting testing activities [20,13]. Scientific works mainly address the definition of languages and methodologies for model development and test case generation algorithms: at the best of our knowledge, few works focus on test specification methods with the objective of reducing the complexity of the modelling activity. The paper aims to fill this gap by defining a model-based approach to aid the test engineer in modelling test specifications. The work is part of a wider research project addressing test case automatic generation through model checking techniques. Specifically, Test Specification Patterns (TSPs) are proposed as a way to build complex specifications relying on a well-known recurring problems and their related solutions (patterns).

In order to increase the automation level of the test case generation process, a transformational approach that derives Promela *never claims* from the specifications built by TSPs composition, is defined. A *never claim* is used to specify a behavior that should never happen. It consists of propositions or boolean expression on the state of system and may be used to match either finite or infinite behaviors. In the proposed approach SPIN model checker [12] is used to generate counterexamples from never claims if the defined behavior (i.e. the specification) is true. The steps of the generated counterexample represent the steps of a test sequences.

In order to improve usability, the approach is empowered by model-driven techniques: (1) the usage of the Verification & Validation (V&V) UML profile allows for capturing both system and requirement features by a high level model; (2) the usage of a model transformation chain enables the automatic generation of Promela code from UML state machines annotated with V&V UML Profile stereotypes. This work also extends the V&V UML profile and the transformation chain to support TSPs [7]. The usage of TSPs and the test case generation process is illustrated on a test scenario from the Radio Block Centre (RBC), the vital core of modern railway control systems.

The remainder of this paper is organized as follows. Section 2 sketches the scientific and research background of our work. Section 3 introduces the Test Specification Patterns and their representation by the V&V UML profile. Section 4 describes how the Promela code is generated from TSPs. Section 5 contains a brief description of the RBC system and illustrates the application of the test sequence generation approach to this case study. Finally, Section 6 closes the paper and provides some hints about future directions.

2   Background

In this Section, we provide some pointers to the context in which TSPs have been developed. Moreover, a brief review of the related work is reported.

2.1   The CRYSTAL Project

The ARTEMIS Joint Undertaking project CRYSTAL (CRitical sYSTem engineering AcceLeration) [1] takes up the challenge to establish and push forward an Interoperability Specification (IOS) and a Reference Technology Platform (RTP) as a European standard for safety-critical systems. CRYSTAL is strongly industry-oriented and will provide ready-to-use integrated *tool chains* having a mature technology-readiness level. To achieve technical innovation, CRYSTAL developed a user-driven approach based on four pillars [23], the first of them is to apply engineering methods to industrially relevant Use Cases from the automotive, aerospace, rail and health sectors and *increase the maturity of existing concepts* developed in previous projects on European and national level, like CESAR [2] and MBAT [3]. The work described in this paper was born in the rail domain and specifically from the needs expressed by Ansaldo STS (ASTS), an international transportation leader (Railway/Mass Transit). The overall objectives of the work are: reduce validation and test effort, in particular the time needed for the definition of *system level* tests. Previous steps addresses the definition of both a model driven methodology and of a language for the specification of high level formal models of critical systems. This paper focuses on the definition of modeling guidelines to support the modeler in representing system aspects/requirements, in particular by the introduction of the concept of Test Specification Patterns (TSPs). TSPs are a way to easily create test specifications to be used to automate the generation of test sequences.

2.2   V&V UML Profile and Test Sequence Generation

Previous work has been published in [7] and extended in [17]. This preliminary work focuses on the development of a UML profile and a chain of model transformations. The V&V UML profile is used to annotate UML state machine based models which represent both the system behaviour and the test specification. The V&V UML profile is organized into a set of packages, as shown in Figure 1(a).

Figure 1(b) exemplifies the usage of the V&V UML profile on the model of a simplified car controller (CC) taken from [8]. The CC has two Boolean inputs that represent the decision to accelerate or brake. Upon acceleration, the car starts moving, with either slow or fast velocity. Upon braking the car immediately stops. Figure 1(c) shows a test specification representing the requirement "When brakes are pressed a car must stop". Since the V&V UML profile aims at providing a unifying modelling framework for Verification & Validation (both analysis and testing), it is built upon existing UML profiles, specifically the UML Testing Profile (UTP) [22] and the MARTE-DAM profile[4] [2]. The V&V UML Profile stereotypes used throughout the paper are reported in Table 1.

---

[1] http://www.crystal-artemis.eu/

[2] http://www.cesarproject.eu/

[3] http://www.mbat-artemis.eu/

[4] MARTE-DAM stands for Modeling and Analysis of Real-Time and Embedded Systems - Dependability Analysis and Modelling.

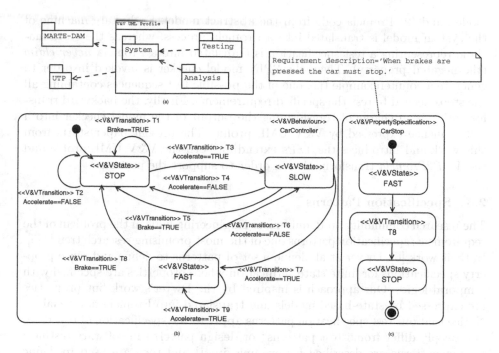

Fig. 1. Overview of V&V UML Profile: top-level packages (V&V UML Profile) (a), model of a car controller (b), property specification (c)

Table 1. Used stereotypes in the V&V UML Profile

Stereotype	Inherits / Extends	Tags: type
V&VBehaviour	- / StateMachine	requirements: V&VRequirement[*]
V&VTestSpecification	V&VPropertySpecification StateMachine	verifies: V&VRequirement[*]
V&VState	BehavioralItem / Vertex	
V&VTransition	BehavioralItem / Transition	
V&VTestCase	V&VBehavior / StateMachine	covers: V&VRequirement[*]

V&VBehaviour is used to represent the behaviour of a system; by means of the tag *requirements*, it may provide the description of one or more requirements expressed by natural language. *V&VTestSpecification* is used to specify the requirement covered by the test sequence that must be generated. This information is provided by the tag *verifies*. *V&VState* is used to represent a state of the system under test inside a state machine annotated with the *V&VBehaviour* stereotype; transitions between states are tagged with the *V&VTransition* stereotype. *V&VTestCase* is used to represent the test sequence generated by applying the model transformation chain. It is also modeled by a state machine. The tag *covers* specifies the requirement covered by the test sequence. The transformation chain can be split into forward and backward transformation sub-chains. They both consist of a model-to-model transformation and a model-to-text transformation. The forward transformation (*VVP2Promela*) generates: (1) a Promela abstract model, and (2) Promela code from the abstract model. Each state machine of the system model is translated into a Promela process, whereas the state machine representing a test specification is translated into a Promela *never claim* (the negated property). Then, the SPIN model checker is invoked in order to generate a counterexample (i.e. one of the possible test sequences containing all the steps needed to test the specified requirement). Finally, the backward transformation is in charge of transforming the output of the model checker into a test sequence expressed by V&V UML profile. The present paper starts from this work and introduces the TSPs extending both the V&V UML profile and the *VVP2Promela* transformation in order to support the patterns.

2.3   Specification Patterns

The research community on Requirement Engineering finds in the problem of the requirement/specification patterns one of the most promising research trends [5]. In their work [6], Dwyer at al. define a set of patterns to define and reuse property specifications for finite state verification where properties are specified with temporal logics. Our approach is inspired by the Dwyer's work but properties are expressed by state-based models and translated into Promela never claims. Notice that our test specification patterns apply to the specification of test cases and deeply differ from "test patterns" or design patterns in software testing : testing patterns are described for example in [1] and they are used to define testing strategies; the work in [25] defines a set of testing patterns from classical design patterns in order to find "recurring" errors.

    Back to property specification patterns, some attempts to extend the work of Dwyer at al. have been done: in [16] an extension to the specification of real-time properties is introduced, while an extension to probabilistic properties is described in [11]. Other meaningful approaches based on specification patterns are introduced in [28] where Validation Patterns are defined for the verification of embedded systems, and in [19] where specification patterns are used for a run-time monitoring of the system behavior. Further research effort has been spent in facilitating the application of specification patterns by the support of software tools: SPIDER [15], PROPEL [24] and Prospec [18] are some examples. With respect to the specification patterns, TSPs are oriented to a testing-based form of verification. This feature is the main semantic difference between TSPs and the specification patterns in [6].

3   TSPs Definition and Implementation

TSPs are a way to gather the previous and consolidated experiences in testing and provide a set of guidelines for test specification. The sources considered for the identification of the TSPs set proposed in this paper are: (1) requirement specifications of critical systems[5]; (2) scientific literature (e.g., [6,29]). The set

---

[5] In this phase of the work and due to the nature of the industrial use case, only the ERTMS/ETCS specification has been considered, counting tens of functional requirements.

of TSP that we are presenting below does not want to be exhaustive since they are part of a work in progress.

TSPs have been divided into two categories and are listed in Table 2: (1) *Control Patterns* address properties related to the evolution of the system Related concerns are parallelism, sequence and/or loops; (2) *Data Patterns* refer to the management of data within the property to verify (e.g., set and evaluation of variables inside the test specification).

In the following we intend for model elements both transitions and states and for covering a model element respectively the passage through a transition and the reaching of a state.

Table 2. List of Test Specification Patterns

Name	Pattern
Control Patterns	
Sequence	It specifies an ordered sequence of steps of the test specification. A test sequence generated according to this pattern must fulfill the step of the test specification in the specified order.
Cover	It specifies that a model element is covered at least once within a specific point of the test specification.
NotCover	It specifies that a model element is not reached before the fulfillment of the following step of the test specification (within a specified Sequence).
Next	It specifies that two model elements are reached in a close succession.
And	It checks that two or more sub-steps are accomplished regardless of their order.
DetChoice	It allows to choose between two alternative sub-steps with respect to a condition.
Memory	It takes into account some alternative steps that, according to which step is fulfilled, address the future steps of the test specification to fulfill.
Loop	It specifies that a model element is reached for a defined number of times.
Any	It allows to verify that at least one of the model elements specified within this pattern is reached at least once.
Data Patterns	
Test	It tests the value of a variable (of the model of the systems or of the test specification) to address a choice in the specification future behaviour.
Set	It allows to assign the value of an internal variable of test specification.
Assert	It waits until a variable assumes a specified value.

Extensions to the V&V domain model: Figure 2 shows the *Testing* and the *System* packages of the V&V domain model. The package *Testing* contains the subpackage *Specification* and the package *System* contains the subpackages *Structure* and *Behavior*[6]. With the respect to the previous version of the domain model, the modifications due to the introduction of the TSPs are::

---

[6] For sake of space, some edges in the Figure 2 (i.e. cover/not cover, assert/set) represent couples of distinct associations of the domain model.

- the introduction of the *Property* metaclass in the *Behaviour* subpackage: by means of this class it is possible to associate an *ExternalVariable* of our domain model to a *BehaviouralItem*;
- the substitution of the *Partial* and *Full VerificationContext*s into the *PropertySpecification* and *TestCase* classes. *PropertySpecification* models the test specification state machine (i.e., the input to the automatic generation process); *TestCase* models the output of the process (i.e., the state machine representing the test sequence);
- the introduction of *TestStep* and *TestTransition* as the model elements constituting the *TestSpecification*;
- the definition of *TestType* enumeration, listing some kinds of *TestStep*s (AND, ANY, LOOP, etc.);
- the *cover* and *not cover* associations between *TestStep* and a *BehaviouralItem* (system state and/or transition);
- the *assert* and *set* associations between *TestStep* and a *Property*;
- the *test* association between *TestTransition* and *Property*.

In this context, a Test Specification Pattern can be specified as a *TestSpecification* "template". The composition relation between *TestStep* and *TestSpecificationItem* enables the construction of a *TestSpecification* by means of composition of patterns. The formal definition of composition rules is a work in progress.

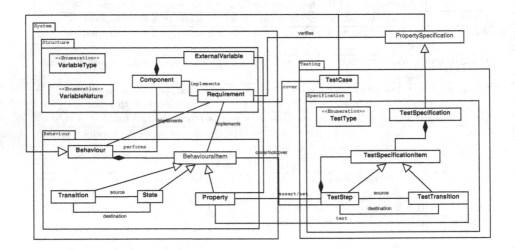

Fig. 2. Extended V&V domain model

Extensions to the V&V UML profile: the constructs defined in the domain model have been implemented as UML stereotypes and DataTypes in the V&V UML profile. Table 3 describes the stereotypes newly added or modified by the introduction of the TSPs.

There are three main stereotypes and two datatypes. The V&VTestSpecification stereotype is used to annotate a UML State Machine as a test specification.

Table 3. New stereotypes in V&V UML profile

Stereotype	Inherits / Extends	Tags: type
V&VTestSpecification	PropertySpecification / StateMachine	
V&VTestStep	TestSpecificationItem / Vertex	Kind: TestType[1]
		Assert: V&VExpression[0..1]
		Set: V&VExpression[0..1]
		Cover: BehavioralItem[0..1]
		NotCover:BehavioralItem[0..1]
		LoopCounter: Integer[0..1]
V&VTestTransition	TestSpecificationItem / Transition	Test: V&VExpression[0..1]

It can contain both V&VTestSteps and V&VTestTransitions. The first are used to annotate the UML States representing the single steps of the specification. A V&VTestStep can be tagged with: 1) *Kind* specifies the kind of the step[7]; 2) *Assert* contains the expression to evaluate in case of Assert pattern (null, otherwise); 3) *Set* points to the expression to execute; 4) *Cover*, used in the cover patterns, points to the BehavioralItem that the test case must reach; 5) *NotCover* points to the BehavioralItem BehavioralItem that the test case must not reach; 6) *LoopCounter* defines the number of the iterations to verify of the elements enclosed in a Loop pattern. The two datatypes are: TestType, already discussed, and V&VExpression that represents the string of the property to set/verify.

The concrete representation of the TSPs relies on the UML State Machine diagram. Some of them are described in this Section on a simply example and in Section 5.1 on the Railway case study. Some of the TSPs summarized in Table 2, as the *Memory* one, are not showed since they are a compact representation of the other TSPs. Figure 3, 4 and 5 represent the test specification models of three TSPs : the Next Pattern in Figure 3, the And Pattern in Figure 4 and the Any Pattern in Figure 5. The test specifications described in this Section are built on the base of the state machine of the CC in Figure 1(b). Figure 3 shows the case in which we want to create a test specification that is used to verify the presence of direct edge between *FAST* and *STOP* states after the passage through the transition *braking*. Figure 4 considers the case in which we are interested in reaching the states *STOP* and *FAST* in a unordered sequence starting from the *SLOW* state. In this case the And TSP has been used. The example in Figure 5 shows the application of the Any, Set and Test TSPs. With the Any TSP we verify that one of the two possible behavior of brakes is covered. More specifically we check by using a Set TSP on a local variable if a brake has been pressed ($a == TRUE$) or not ($a==FALSE$). Hence, with the sequence of steps we want to verify that if the reached state is *SLOW* and the previous was *FAST*, the next state will be *STOP*. To control what was the previous state we check the value of the local variable a by using a Test TSP (TestTransition *stopping* within the Figure 5).

---

[7] According to its type it may assume one of the following values: AND, ANY, NONE, DETCHOICE, LOOP, MEMORY, TEST, NEXT. NONE is a value assumed when no specific pattern is implemented by the TestStep.

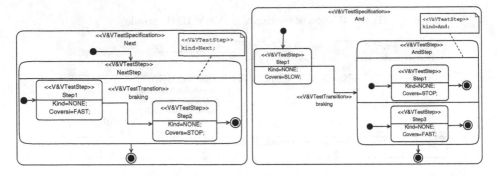

Fig. 3. Car Controller : TSP *Next*   **Fig. 4.** Car Controller : TSP *And*

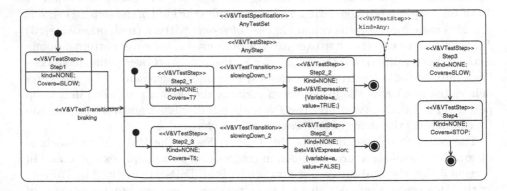

Fig. 5. Car Controller : TSPs *Any*, *Test* and *Set*

4   Promela Code Generation

Figure 6 depicts the process as described in Subsection 2.2 and extended in order to automate the support to TSPs.

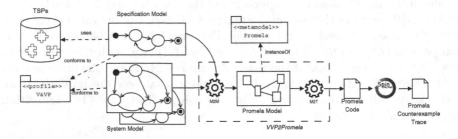

Fig. 6. Extended model-driven approach for TSPs support

Here some hints about the generation of Promela code from TSPs are given. By means of the *VVP2Promela* transformation chain, as stated in Section 1, each test specification generates a Promela never claim that is used to specify a behaviour that should never happen in the state space of the Promela model of the system. Listing 1.1 shows the translation in Promela of the example in Figure 3; Listing 1.2 shows the translation in Promela of the *AndStep* state implementing the AND pattern as for the example in Figure 4.

Listing 1.1. Sequence never claim

```
never {
  Step1:
  if
  :: (state == FAST) -> goto
     Step2
  :: else -> goto Step1
  fi;
  Step2:
  if
  :: (state==STOP) -> goto
     endStep
  :: else -> goto Step2
  fi;
  endStep:
  skip

}
```

Listing 1.2. Any never claim

```
never {
  test_S1:
  if
  :: (state == SLOW) -> goto \
     NOTE{AndStep}
  :: else -> goto Step1
  fi;
  AnyStep:
  if
  :: (transition == T4) -> goto
     endStep
  :: (transition == T7) -> goto
     endStep
  :: else -> goto AndStep
  fi;
  endStep:
  skip
}
```

5   The Radio Block Centre Use Case

Radio Block Centre (RBC) is a computer-based system in charge of controlling the movements of the trains on the track area that is under its supervision, in order to guarantee a safe inter-train distance. RBC is integrated within the European Rail Traffic Management System/European Train Control System (ERTM-S/ETCS), a standard for the interoperability of the European railway signaling systems. ERTMS/ETCS ensures both technological compatibility among the European railway networks and the integration of the new signaling system with the existing national train interlocking systems. RBC continuously monitors the train movements; it receives the exact position of the train from EVC (European Vital Computer) and information about the train detection and the route status from the Interlocking and Automatic Block System. The main objective of the train control system is to timely transmit to each train on-board system (i.e., the EVC) its up-to-date Movement Authority (MA) and the related speed profile. Communication is performed via GSM-R. The MA contains information about the distance a train may safely cover, depending on the status of the forward track; in addition, MA may contain the Temporary Speed Restriction (TSR) message that contains speed restrictions on a specific part of the track: normally a TSR is sent in case of planned works on the tracks. When a TSR is activated,

RBC sends a TSR message to the EVC that must reply by sending an ACK message. If the ACK message is received from the EVC, the message is correctly delivered, otherwise RBC re-sends the message: after the three attempts, the RBC shall send a braking command by means of an Unconditionally Emergency Stop (UES).

5.1   Application to RBC

In this Subsection, an application of the proposed approach is shown by applying it to the management functionalities of the TSR and Unconditionally Emergency Stop (UES) messages of the RBC. The test specifications are realised with the TSPs and consider the following requirements: *(REQ1)* RBC shall send a UES message to EVC if the acknowledgement to a TSR message does not arrive after three attempts; *(REQ2)* after two attempts to send a TSR message, RBC may accomplish the management of the TSR without sending a UES message.

Figure 7 and Figure 8 show the behaviour of the RBC by means of two UML State Machines respectively modelling the management of the TSR and of the UES messages. In Figure 7, the *TSR_START* state represents the first state of the TSR management: it initialises the *count* and the *timer_state* respectively representing the number of the attempts of sending the TSR message and the Boolean value used to indicate if the state is timed up or not. The transition *T01* imposes the transmission of the TSR message (first attempt) setting the *count* to 1. The state *TIMER_ON* is a waiting state after which the RBC may: (1) increase the *count* if the acknowledgement to the TSR message does not arrive, (2) end the procedure if an ack is received by the train, (3) go to the *Aborting* state after three attempts. This last condition frees the evolution of the second state machine (Figure 8) that, after the initial state, sends a UES message to the train. The synchronisation of the two state machines is achieved by the *UES_status* variable.

Test specification of REQ1: Figure 9(a) shows the application of the TSPs to the modelling of a proper test specification for *REQ1*. To realise the test specification, three different patterns have been composed: a *NotCover*, used to avoid the receive of an ack (T04 transition); an *Assert*, that controls that the RBC sends a UES message; and a *Sequence*, used to combine the first two patterns.

Test specification of REQ2: the test specification described in Figure 9(b) shows the case in which the acknowledgement to a TSR message arrives after two attempts. The test specification is realised by a *Sequence* of a *Loop* pattern and a *Cover* pattern. The *Loop* pattern (Step1) checks that another Sequence of two steps occurs twice in the test case. These steps are: Step1_1 and Step1_2, modelled by two *Cover* patterns, respectively covering the *TIMER_ON* state and the *T02* transition. Therefore, when the acknowledgement arrives on the third attempt, Step2 (modelled by a *Cover* pattern) controls that the *T04* transition is covered and that the machine ends without sending a UES message. In this case, the Promela never claim generated by the *VVP2Promela* transformation

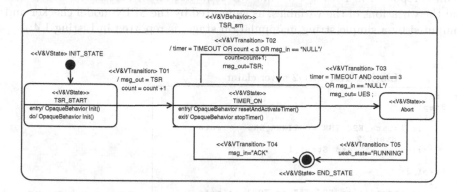

Fig. 7. TSR management

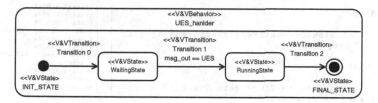

Fig. 8. UES management

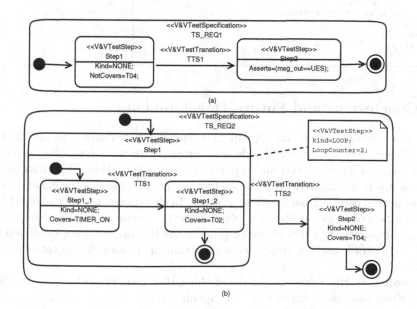

Fig. 9. Test specifications of REQ1 (a) and of REQ2 (b)

chain is reported in Listing 1.3 while the sequence of the states, the transitions and the variations of the variables, as generated by the SPIN model checker and computed by a simple string manipulation stage, is reported in Listing 1.4.

Listing 1.3. REQ2 never claim

```
never{
  Step1_1:
    if
      :: (state_EBC_TSR == TIMER_ON) -> goto
         Step1_2
      :: else -> goto Step1_1
    fi;
  Step1_2:
    if
      :: (transition_EBC_TSR == T02) -> goto
         Loop1Step
      :: else -> goto Step1_2
    fi;
  Loop1Step:
    if
      :: 1 -> atomic{countLoop1=countLoop1+1; goto
         Loop1Check;}
    fi;
  Loop1Check:
    if
      :: (countLoop1 == 2) -> goto Step2
      :: else -> goto Step1_1
    fi;
  Step2:
    if
      :: (transition_EBC_TSR == T04) -> goto
         endStep
      :: else -> goto Step2
    fi;
  endStep:
    skip;
}
```

Listing 1.4. REQ2 test sequence

```
state=TSR_START
transition=T01
state=TIMER_ON
input=(msg_in = NULL)
transition=T02
state=TIMER_ON
input=(timer = TIMEOUT)
transition=T02
state=TIMER_ON
input=(msg_in = ACK)
transtion=T04
```

6   Conclusions and Future Developments

This paper introduces the concept of Test Specification Pattern as an effective and efficient way to specify the desired property to test according to state-based model of a critical system. In particular, we believe that TSPs may play a relevant role in automated model based testing processes where the generation of test sequences can be a hard task to address. In this paper, we have showed how the definition of proper patterns applicable to the specification of test sequences may be supported by a model driven process. At this aim we have extended the V&V UML profile and set up proper model transformations to generate Promela code.

According to the research agenda of the CRYSTAL project, research effort will address the migration of the Test Specification Patterns to other domain-specific languages. In addition, we will investigate the definition and the usage of System Specification Patterns to aid the development of state-based models for critical and embedded systems.

Acknowledgments. This paper is partially supported by research project CRYS-TAL (Critical System Engineering Acceleration), funded from the ARTEMIS Joint Undertaking under grant agreement n. 332830 and from ARTEMIS member states Austria, Belgium, Czech Republic, France, Germany, Italy, Netherlands, Spain, Sweden, United Kingdom.

References

1. Common test patterns and reuse of test designs, http://msdn.microsoft.com/en-us/library/cc514239.aspx
2. Bernardi, S., Merseguer, J., Petriu, D.C.: A dependability profile within MARTE. Journal of Software and Systems Modeling (2011)
3. Bernardi, S., et al.: Enabling the usage of UML in the verification of railway systems: The DAM-rail approach. Reliability Engineering & System Safety 120, 112–126 (2013)
4. Bosik, B.S., Ümit Uyar, M.: Finite state machine based formal methods in protocol conformance testing: from theory to implementation. Computer Networks and ISDN Systems 22(1), 7–33 (1991)
5. Cheng, B.H.C., Atlee, J.M.: Research directions in requirements engineering. In: Future of Software Engineering, pp. 285–303. IEEE CS (2007)
6. Dwyer, M.B., Avrunin, G.-S., Corbett, J.C.: Patterns in property specifications for finite-state verification. In: Proc. of the ICSE 1999, pp. 411–420. ACM (1999)
7. Flammini, F., Marrone, S., Mazzocca, N., Nardone, R., Vittorini, V.: Model-driven V&V processes for computer based control systems: A unifying perspective. In: Margaria, T., Steffen, B. (eds.) ISoLA 2012, Part II. LNCS, vol. 7610, pp. 190–204. Springer, Heidelberg (2012)
8. Fraser, G., Wotawa, F., Ammann, P.E.: Testing with model checkers: A survey. Softw. Test. Verif. Reliab. 19(3), 215–261 (2009)
9. Gargantini, A., Heitmeyer, C.: Using model checking to generate tests from requirements specifications. SIGSOFT Softw. Eng. Notes 24(6), 146–162 (1999)
10. Gargantini, A., Riccobene, E.: Asm-based testing: Coverage criteria and automatic test sequence generation. Journal of Universal Computer Science 7(11), 1050–1067 (2001)
11. Grunske, L.: Specification patterns for probabilistic quality properties. In: Proc. of ICSE 2008, pp. 31–40. ACM, New York (2008)
12. Holzmann, G.: Spin Model Checker, the: Primer and Reference Manual, 1st edn. Addison-Wesley Professional (2003)
13. Javed, A.Z., Strooper, P.A., Watson, G.N.: Automated generation of test cases using model-driven architecture. In: Second International Workshop on Automation of Software Test (2007)
14. Kitamura, T., Do, N.T.B., Ohsaki, H., Fang, L., Yatabe, S.: Test-case design by feature trees. In: Margaria, T., Steffen, B. (eds.) ISoLA 2012, Part I. LNCS, vol. 7609, pp. 458–473. Springer, Heidelberg (2012)
15. Konrad, S., Cheng, B.H.C.: Facilitating the construction of specification pattern-based properties. In: Proc. of Requirements Engineering, pp. 329–338 (August 2005)
16. Konrad, S., Cheng, B.H.C.: Real-time specification patterns. In: Proc. of ICSE 2005, pp. 372–381 (May 2005)

17. Marrone, S., Flammini, F., Mazzocca, N., Nardone, R., Vittorini, V.: Towards model-driven v&v assessment of railway control systems. International Journal on Software Tools for Technology Transfer (2014)
18. Mondragon, O., Gates, A.Q., Roach, S.: Prospec: Support for elicitation and formal specification of software properties. Electr. Notes Theor. Comput. Sci. 89(2), 67–88 (2003)
19. Mondragon, O., Gates, A.Q., Roach, S., Mendoza, H., Sokolsky, O.: Generating properties for runtime monitoring from software specification patterns. Int. Journal of Software Engineering and Knowledge Engineering 17(1), 107–126 (2007)
20. Mussa, M., Ouchani, S., Al Sammane, W., Hamou-Lhadj, A.: A survey of model-driven testing techniques. In: Proceedings of QSIC 2009, pp. 167–172 (August 2009)
21. Mustafiz, S., Sun, X., Kienzle, J., Vangheluwe, H.: Model-driven assessment of system dependability. Software & Systems Modeling 7(4), 487–502 (2008)
22. UML testing profile, Version 1.1, OMG document (2012)
23. Pflügl, H., El-Salloum, C., Kundner, I.: Crystal, critical system engineering acceleration, a truly European dimension. ARTEMIS Magazine 14, 12–15 (2013)
24. Smith, R.L., Avrunin, G.S., Clarke, L.A., Osterweil, L.J.: PROPEL: an approach supporting property elucidation. In: Proc. of ICSE 2002, pp. 11–21 (May 2002)
25. Soundarajan, N., Hallstrom, J.O., Shu, G., Delibas, A.: Patterns: from system design to software testing. Innovations in Systems and Software Engineering 4(1), 71–85 (2008)
26. Terrier, F., Gérard, S.: MDE benefits for distributed, real time and embedded systems. In: Kleinjohann, B., Kleinjohann, L., Machado, R., Pereira, C., Thiagarajan, R.S. (eds.) From Model-Driven Design to Resource Management for Distributed Embedded Systems. IFIP, vol. 225, pp. 15–24. Springer, Boston (2006)
27. Tretmans, J.: A formal approach to conformance testing. In: Proc. of the IFIP TC6/WG6.1 Workshop on Protocol Test Systems VI, pp. 257–276. North-Holland Publishing Co., Amsterdam (1994)
28. Tsai, W.-T., Yu, L., Zhu, F., Paul, R.: Rapid embedded system testing using verification patterns. IEEE Software 22(4), 68–75 (2005)
29. Van der Aalst, W.M.P., Ter Hofstede, A.H.M., Kiepuszewski, B., Barros, A.P.: Workflow patterns. Distributed and Parallel Databases 14(1), 5–51 (2003)

Randomised Testing of a Microprocessor Model Using SMT-Solver State Generation

Brian Campbell and Ian Stark

LFCS, School of Informatics, University of Edinburgh, UK
{Brian.Campbell,Ian.Stark}@ed.ac.uk

Abstract. We validate a HOL4 model of the ARM Cortex-M0 micro-controller core by testing the model's behaviour on randomly chosen instructions against a real chip.

The model and our intended application involve precise timing information about instruction execution, but the implementations are pipelined, so checking the behaviour of single instructions would not give us sufficient confidence in the model. Thus we test the model using sequences of randomly chosen instructions.

The main challenge is to meet the constraints on the initial and intermediate execution states: we must ensure that memory accesses are in range and that we respect restrictions on the instructions. By careful transformation of these constraints an off-the-shelf SMT solver can be used to find suitable states for executing test sequences.

Keywords: Randomised testing, microprocessor models, HOL, SMT.

Mechanised formal models of instruction set architectures provide a basis for low-level verification of software. Obtaining accurate models can be difficult; most architectures are described in large reference manuals consisting primarily of prose backed up by semi-formal pseudo-code. Once a model is produced it is common to test individual instructions against hardware to gain confidence in the model (for example, [7]), but some effects may require a sequence of several instructions to appear.

This is relevant for the intended application of our model. We wish to extend existing low-level verification work using Myreen's decompilation [9] to include timing properties. We want to use a realistic processor with a relatively simple cost model, because our technique is largely orthogonal to the low-level timing analysis and we do not wish to spend resources recreating a complex worst-case execution time analysis (such as those surveyed in [13]).

While the ARM Cortex-M0 has a simple cost model, even this design has a non-trivial microarchitecture in the form of a three stage pipeline (fetch, decode and execute). Hence to build confidence in our model, and in particular the timing information contained in the model, we wish to test sequences of instructions in order to exercise the pipeline.

However, finding a processor state in which an arbitrary sequence of instructions can be executed without faulting is not always easy. Consider the sequence

F. Lang and F. Flammini (Eds.): FMICS 2014, LNCS 8718, pp. 185–199, 2014.
© Springer International Publishing Switzerland 2014

```
ldrsh    r0, [r1, r2]   ;  load r0 from r1+r2 (16 bits, sign-extended)
lsls     r0, r0, r2     ;  shift r0 left by r2
bcs      +#12           ;  branch if carry set
add      r0, r0, r2     ;  add r2 to r0
ldr      r3, [r0, #0]   ;  load r3 from r0
```

Fig. 1. An example test sequence of M0 code

in Figure 1. The final instruction reads a word from memory at an address stored in the r0 register. We must ensure that this address is a valid location in memory, which makes up a tiny fraction of the processor's address space.

Moreover, r0's contents is a result of several operations: a half-word load, sign-extension, shift and bitvector addition, where r2's value is used in several different ways. Finding solutions to such constraints is a natural application for an SMT (Satisfiability Modulo Theories) solver with good bitvector support.

The solutions provided by the solver will specify parts of the registers and memory, including the placement of instructions. For example, if the bcs branch is taken then the next instruction must be placed 12 bytes later. Whether the processor takes the branch is also decided by a non-trivial calculation due to the shift instruction; again, we leave this to the SMT solver.

Note that the constraints come from two sources; some, such as instruction alignment, come directly from the model in the form of hypotheses to a theorem. However, the model is not intended to be comprehensive, especially where details about particular implementations are concerned. Thus we need to add additional constraints to capture these details, such as the size and layout of memory.

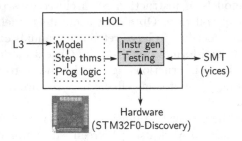

Fig. 2. Outline of the testing system

The testing system is outlined in Figure 2. The model is written in the L3 specification language, and the generated HOL version is accompanied by tool libraries, shown in the dashed box. Instruction generation is separated from the main testing code, and can be overridden manually. An SMT solver is invoked to help find a pre-state using an adaption of the HolSmtLib library [12], and the hardware is invoked over a USB link. Our software is available online[1].

---

[1] https://bitbucket.org/bacam/m0-validation

Our contributions are to demonstrate that symbolic evaluation with SMT constraint solving is an effective way to test a formalised microprocessor model, and that the ability to add additional constraints is useful for bridging the gap between a model and an implementation, and for checking hypotheses about deviations from the model.

Section 1 briefly describes the M0 model and accompanying tools, then the description of the testing system begins with the generation of instructions in Section 2 and continues in Section 3 with the construction of pre-states which satisfy the restrictions on successful execution. Section 4 discusses the practicalities of running the tests on the hardware, and Section 5 presents the outcomes of testing. We consider the results and variations of the system in Section 6, then consider related work before concluding.

1   The Processor Model

The ARM Cortex-M0 model we use was developed by Anthony Fox in his L3 domain specific language [6]. It is a greatly simplified adaption of his ARMv7 model, with the addition of instruction cycle timings from the ARMv6-M reference manual [1]. L3 provides a specification language with imperative features that allows models to closely follow the pseudo-code typically found in such manuals.

An automatic translation produces a version for the HOL4 proof assistant [8], together with Standard ML versions of the instruction decoder and encoder. The main interface to the model itself is a step function,

$$\text{NextStateM0} : m0\_state \rightarrow m0\_state \ option,$$

where the type $m0\_state$ is a record containing register values, memory content, flags, and other miscellaneous information about the processor state. The memory is represented as a HOL function from 32-bit words representing addresses to 8-bit contents.

```
[Aligned (s.REG RName_PC,2),        s.MEM (s.REG RName_PC) = 3w,
 Aligned (s.REG RName_0 + 0w,4), s.MEM (s.REG RName_PC + 1w) = 104w,
 ¬s.AIRCR.ENDIANNESS, ¬s.CONTROL.SPSEL, s.exception = NoException]
⊢ NextStateM0 s = SOME (s with
        <|REG := (RName_PC =+ s.REG RName_PC + 2w)
            ((RName_3 =+ s.MEM (s.REG RName_0 + 0w + 3w) @@
                        s.MEM (s.REG RName_0 + 0w + 2w) @@
                        s.MEM (s.REG RName_0 + 0w + 1w) @@
                        s.MEM (s.REG RName_0 + 0w)) s.REG);
        count := s.count + 2; pcinc := 2w|>)
```

Fig. 3. Example step theorem for ldr r3,[r0,#0]

Additional tools are provided in two HOL libraries. The first, stepLib, provides symbolic evaluation of the step function for individual instructions. An

example is shown in Figure 3. The hypotheses assert that the program counter
and source address are correctly aligned, that the instruction is present in memory and that certain control flags are set correctly. The conclusion states that
the model's step function will succeed with an updated state, where the program
counter is moved forward, the result of the load is present and two ticks of the
processor's clock have passed. (The HOL term $(k$ =+ $v)$ m denotes a map which
returns v at k and is m everywhere else.) For branches, which are the only conditional instructions in the ARMv6-M architecture, two theorems are returned:
one for when the branch is taken, and one for when it is not.

The second library provides separation-logic-like specifications for instructions. The principal intended use for the model is to provide low-level verification
using Myreen's decompilation technique [9], and these specifications provide the
interface between the model and the decompilation library.

We could test the model directly, or test one of these two libraries. In order
to determine what constraints on the state are necessary for successful execution we need to perform symbolic evaluation of the instructions. If we used the
separation-logic specifications we would have to make memory aliasing decisions
before we can obtain the preconditions. Thus by testing stepLib we obtain the
symbolic evaluation and can leave the aliasing decisions to the SMT solver.

The model does not currently support interrupts and exceptions, which are
not necessary for the verification work we intend to do in the near future. Hence
we leave these for further work, briefly discussing them in Section 6.

2   Instruction Sequence Generation

We produce instruction sequences by randomly picking instructions that are
supported by the model. The M0's subset of the Thumb instruction set is fairly
small; the reference manual lists 77 instructions [1, §A6.7] of which the model
only supports the user-level instructions. Thus we take the opportunity to provide a fresh list of the instruction formats for cross checking against the model.
In Section 6 we will consider alternative approaches.

Figure 4 gives a datatype for fragments of M0 instruction formats and a few
sample formats. While the datatype has a few generic constructors for literal and
immediate bit strings, the rest are specialised for targeting the M0. Registers

```
datatype instr_format =  Lit of int list    | Imm of int
       | Reg3             | Reg4NotPC        | Reg4NotPCPair
       | CmpRegs          | RegList of bool (* inc PC/LR *)
       | STMRegs          | Cond             | BLdispl

val instrs = [
( 1,([Lit [0,0,0,1,1,0,0], Reg3, Reg3, Reg3],          "ADD (reg) T1")),
(14,([Lit [1,1,0,1], Cond, Imm 8],                     "B T1")),
( 1,([Lit [0,1,0,0,0,1,1,1,0], Reg4NotPC, Lit [0,0,0]], "BX")),
( 1,([Lit [1,1,1,1,0], BLdispl],                       "BL")),
...
```

Fig. 4. Language for instruction formats and sample formats

come in three-bit and four-bit representations[2], with several further variants for pairs of registers and specific instructions.

Each format consists of a list of fragments. For example, the ADD instruction format in Figure 4 has a constant prefix, the destination register and two source registers. The integer before the format is a weighting, which is used here to make the conditional branches appear more often than other instructions. A name is given to each format for debugging and logging purposes.

The Branch with Link instruction format BL is the most unusual. It is the only 32-bit instruction supported by the model (the rest are system instructions) and the offsets for the jump are very large (up to 16MB) compared to the amount of memory available (kilobytes). Thus almost all BL instructions are unusable, and untestable. To produce useful instructions the BLdispl fragment picks and encodes branch displacements with magnitude bounded by the size of SRAM.

2.1 Sanity Checks

We perform several automated tests of our generator. The first is an internal consistency check which ensures that every format is either 16 or 32 bits long.

To cross check the generator against the model, we split the list of instruction formats into the instructions that we expect the model to support, and those that we believe the model does not. We then ask the model for theorems about several instances of each format, ensuring that they are present for all supported instructions and absent for all other instructions. We also check that only the conditional branches generate multiple theorems.

Following the discovery of an extra instruction in the model, we ensured that no further extra instructions were present by performing a manual check of the format list against stepLib. It may be possible to devise automated checks of this, but the small instruction set makes a manual comparison the most effective use of time. More details, and the other testing results, can be found in Section 5.

3 Generating Pre-states for Testing

Having chosen a sequence of instructions we can obtain theorems describing the behaviour of each one from stepLib and combine them into a single result by taking the theorem for the final instruction and repeatedly instantiating the start state with the step theorem for the previous instruction, simplifying at each step to keep the symbolic state a reasonable size. Also, to keep this process manageable we randomly pick whether to take each branch so that we only have one step theorem for each instruction.

Recall the example sequence in Figure 1. We saw the step theorem for an ldr instruction in Figure 3. After combining the step theorems the conditions become more complex due to the symbolic execution. For example, the requirement from the ldr instruction that the address for the load in r0 is aligned is now expressed in terms of the initial state, reflecting how r0 is calculated:

---

[2] Many instruction formats only use r0 to r7 to keep the instructions compact.

```
Aligned (s.REG RName_2 +
          sw2sw (s.MEM (s.REG RName_1 + s.REG RName_2 + 1w) @@
                 s.MEM (s.REG RName_1 + s.REG RName_2))
        <<~ w2w ((7 >< 0) (s.REG RName_2)), 4)
```

where (7 >< 0) selects the low byte of r2 and <<~ performs the shift.

These hypotheses make up the bulk of the constraints the pre-state must satisfy, but we must also meet additional requirements that are imposed by the hardware, and translate the constraints into a form suitable for the solver.

3.1   Additional Requirements

For successful execution on the device, the state must satisfy requirements about areas where the model is deliberately incomplete (often because they vary between implementations):

- self-modifying code must be forbidden;
- the memory map and its restrictions must be respected;
- a test harness is required to stop execution cleanly; and
- the model's implicit invariant that stack pointers are always aligned must be enforced.

The last point is the result of starting execution from a state loaded by the debugger; the model (and the manual's pseudo-code) establish the alignment of the stack pointers on reset and maintain it throughout execution. We must respect that invariant in our states, or the debug interface will reject them.

To implement the restrictions on self-modification and the memory map we need to know the symbolic positions of every instruction and memory access. Recovering this information after combining the step theorems would be difficult at best. For example, if we throw away the result of a load,

```
ldr r0, [r1, #0]
ldr r0, [r2, #0]
```

then the use of the address in r1 will disappear in the combined theorem. Instead, we record the symbolic addresses in each step theorem by adding free variables for the set of instruction locations and accessed memory locations, and hypotheses to give symbolic values to them. The symbolic value for the instruction is given by the program counter, and we can find all memory accesses by finding the terms which consult the memory field of the state, s.MEM.

For example, for the final instruction in the example, we add a hypothesis for the instruction location, two for the memory access for the instruction, and another four for the word that is loaded:

```
instr_start 4 = s.REG RName_PC,
memory_address 4 = s.REG RName_PC,
memory_address 5 = s.REG RName_PC + 1w,
memory_address 0 = s.REG RName_0,
memory_address 1 = s.REG RName_0 + 1w,
memory_address 2 = s.REG RName_0 + 2w,
memory_address 3 = s.REG RName_0 + 3w,
```

Combining the extended step theorems as before performs symbolic evaluation of the earlier instructions, restating these addresses in terms of the initial state:

```
instr_start 4 = s.REG RName_PC + 8w,
memory_address 4 = s.REG RName_PC + 8w,
memory_address 5 = s.REG RName_PC + 9w,
memory_address 0 = s.REG RName_2 +
                   sw2sw (s.MEM (s.REG RName_1 + s.REG RName_2 + 1w) @@
                          s.MEM (s.REG RName_1 + s.REG RName_2))
                   <<~ w2w ((7 >< 0) (s.REG RName_2)),
...
```

The remaining addresses are similar. We can then add constraints requiring all accesses to be in the range of the target device's SRAM. For self-modification we can discover the symbolic locations written to by examining the memory field of the post-state record, then constrain them to be disjoint from the instructions.

By extracting the expression for the post-state program counter we can synthesise locations for the harness instructions, and so add constraints requiring them to be present and unmodified by execution. In most of our tests the harness consists of a single software breakpoint instruction[3].

3.2   Practical HOL

The technique outlined above of combining step theorems by instantiation and simplification is intended to keep the symbolic state manageable. However, there are two further issues we need to address to achieve this.

The main problem was that when a memory update is distributed to the uses of memory by evaluation, subsequent memory lookups will be partially evaluated into aliasing checks. These grow quickly, especially when load-multiple and store-multiple instructions are involved; every address written to is compared against every address read. We could attempt to avoid exposing these aliasing checks by curtailing evaluation, but we chose the more compact solution of introducing free variables for the intermediate memory states. The updates from store instructions are moved to hypotheses which constrain the free variable to be exactly the intermediate memory state.

For example, storing a single byte with strb r0, [r1,#0] updates the memory field of the state record,

```
s with <|MEM := (s.REG RName_1 =+ (7 >< 0) (s.REG RName_0)) s.MEM;
        REG := (RName_PC =+ s.REG RName_PC + 2w) s.REG;
        count := s.count + 2; pcinc := 2w|>
```

so we add the new hypothesis

```
Abbrev (mem_step_0 = (s.REG RName_1 =+ (7 >< 0) (s.REG RName_0)) s.MEM)
```

using HOL's Abbrev mechanism to prevent the definition being used during simplification, and put the variable in the state record:

---

[3] Hardware breakpoints would also work, but are slightly harder to use on our main target device.

```
s with <|MEM := mem_step_0;
          REG := (RName_PC =+ s.REG RName_PC + 2w) s.REG;
          count := s.count + 2; pcinc := 2w|>
```

The second problem is that unconstrained evaluation will reveal implementation details about the model and HOL libraries, which it is important to avoid for the SMT translation described in the next section, and to keep the size of terms reasonable. Restricting the computation rules used during evaluation prevents this, along with careful choices of simplification and rewrite rules.

3.3   Preparing for SMT Solving

The constraints we obtain consist largely of bitvector operations, first-order logic and a little natural number arithmetic, which suits the abilities of a number of SMT solvers. HOL4 already comes with the HolSmtLib package for interfacing with Yices 1 and Z3 [12]; we used Yices because HolSmtLib's translation for Yices supports a greater range of HOL types and terms. We do not expect that using another solver would pose any major problems.

Normally, HolSmtLib proves goals where the free variables are universally quantified. To use an SMT solver in this way the library must negate the goal and check that that is *unsatisfiable*. We thus have to adapt the library, because we wish to check that the constraints are *satisfiable*, treating the free variables as *existentially* quantified and using the satisfying assignment returned for them to construct the pre-state for testing. Hence we adapted the library to remove the negation and parse the satisfying assignments.

However, the subset of HOL supported by the translation to Yices' input language is still rather small, and the definitions used in the model do not always fit within it. For example, the Aligned predicate is defined by

```
Aligned (w, n) = (w = n2w (n * (w2n w DIV n)))
```

which is not well supported as it switches between bitvectors and natural numbers using n2w and w2n. Thus during the process of combining the step theorems above we are careful not to unfold definitions like Aligned. Instead, we use HOL theorems about them to rewrite them into the supported subset. For example, the model already provides the result

```
(∀a : word32. Aligned (a, 1)) ∧
(∀a : word32. Aligned (a, 2) = ~word_lsb a) ∧
(∀a : word32. Aligned (a, 4) = ((1 >< 0) a = 0w:word2)) ∧
(∀a : word8.  Aligned (a, 4) = ((1 >< 0) a = 0w:word2))
```

which provides a bitvector interpretation for all of the necessary cases. We prove simple results to ensure that bit selection, shifts and addition are also in the expected form, and slightly more complex ones to obtain the overflow and carry bits for addition.

By using HOL theorems we know that the transformations are *sound*; the worst case for an error is that we end up with constraints that the SMT solver cannot handle. We also extended the transformation itself for a few terms that are awkward to deal with in HOL: right rotation, map updates, 8-bit bitvector to natural conversion, and variable bit indexing. The latter two are defined in a brute-force fashion by large if-then-else trees, but perform well in practice. These do not benefit from any soundness guarantees, but are not critical to the soundness of the testing procedure because we check in HOL that the generated assignments satisfy the hypotheses from the model when we use them.

To find the above set of rewrites that are required to target the SMT-friendly subset of HOL we performed a survey of the step theorems produced by the model. For a randomly chosen set of instructions from each format we attempted to translate the step theorem into Yices' input language. As each unsupported definition was discovered, we added a new rewrite, until no more were found.

One example of this is the carry bit from the lsls instruction in the example, where it decides whether the branch is taken. The step theorem from the model calculates it from the registers,

```
if w2n ((7 >< 0) (s.REG RName_2)) = 0 then s.PSR.C else testbit 32
    (shiftl (w2v (s.REG RName_0)) (w2n ((7 >< 0) (s.REG RName_2))))
```

saying that the old value is used if no shift is done, otherwise the correct bit is extracted from r0. However, the shift and test are done using *bitstrings* rather than bitvectors, a different but related HOL4 type which is not supported by the SMT translation. This was discovered during the survey of instruction formats described above. Thus we proved a small theorem,

$$\forall x : \text{word32. testbit 32 (shiftl (w2v } x\text{) } n\text{) =}$$
$$\text{if } (n > 0) \wedge (n <= 32) \text{ then } x \text{ ' } (32 - n) \text{ else F}$$

that expresses the shift and test as a bit selection, and added it to the set of rewrites applied to the step theorems. The resulting theorems still need some of our extensions to the Yices translation. Note that these transformations can be sensitive to changes in the model; in particular, if more step theorems exposed bitstring operations like this, then we may need to perform more rewriting.

Once all of the constraints have been translated, Yices is invoked and if successful returns a satisfying partial assignment. We can form a partial pre-state from this; for our example this is (eliding some irrelevant details):

```
<| MEM :=
    (0x20000000w =+ 136w) ((0x20000001w =+ 94w) ((0x20000002w =+ 144w)
    ((0x20000003w =+ 64w)  ((0x20000004w =+ 4w)  ((0x20000005w =+ 210w)
    ((0x20000006w =+ 16w)  ((0x20000007w =+ 68w) ((0x20000008w =+ 3w)
    ((0x20000009w =+ 104w) ((0x2000000Aw =+ 0w)  ((0x2000000Bw =+ 190w)
    ((0x200002F0w =+ 7w)   ((0x200002F1w =+ 0w)  rand_mem)))))))))))));
    PSR := rand_flags with C := F;
    REG := (RName_PC =+ 0x20000000w) ((RName_1 =+ 0xFFFFE9F8w)
            ((RName_2  =+ 0x200018F8w) rand_regs));
    count := 0 |>
```

Instantiating the *rand_* free variables with random data provides a full pre-state.

4   Test Execution and Comparison

We can now instantiate the combined theorem that describes the behaviour of the instructions with the pre-state we have discovered, and hence obtain a concrete post-state to compare against the device. This step is complicated slightly by the abstraction of the intermediate memory values (Section 3.2) and the size of the term describing the whole memory. For the former we progressively instantiate each variable using the definition we recorded in the hypothesis, then use evaluation to make the next memory value concrete. For the latter we split up the state record before supplying the concrete values; this prevents duplication of the large memory term in several places where it is projected away.

At the end of this process we should obtain a theorem with no hypotheses giving the model's concrete prediction of the behaviour of the device. By checking that the hypotheses have been discharged we do not have to trust the SMT translation and solver.

To perform the test we used the OpenOCD debugging tool [10] to write the pre-state to the microcontroller on the development board and start execution. To encode the processor flags into the binary Application Processor Status Register (APSR) we use the HOL function provided by the model. If the test is successful, the device will halt at the breakpoint instruction in the test harness. The same tool is used to read the post-state back from the board.

Precise cycle timings are obtained by directly setting up and reading back the device's SysTick counter timer from the debugger. This timer only ticks while the processor is running, so it stops once the breakpoint is reached. We then have to correct for the time spent in the harness. However, the reference manual does not provide a cycle count for breakpoints, but experimentally we measured a consistent overhead of 3 cycles. (This matches the reasonable hypothesis that there will be 2 cycles overhead to fill the pipeline at the start, and one more at the end to execute the breakpoint.)

The post-state retrieved from the board is then compared to the model's prediction, checking the register contents (adjusting the PC for the extra instructions in the test harness), the SRAM, the APSR and the cycle count.

Some failed tests might not reach the breakpoint instruction; for example, a branch might not be taken when it is expected to, or a memory access may fault. In these cases the comparison will fail because the program counter will be incorrect, and usually other parts of the state too.

4.1   Scaling Up Testing

To perform large test runs, and to debug the testing code, we designed logging with several features in mind:

- Ease of rerunning tests, if necessary with the same random background data for memory, flags and registers.
- Classification into successes and failures (impossible combination of instructions, SMT solver returned 'unknown', exception due to bug in model or test code, or genuine mismatch).
- Data about the differences between the post-state and the model.
- Text that can be read manually.

This is implemented in a straightforward manner, where there is one file per classification with one line per test. Each line contains a numerical identifier, the instruction sequence, branch choices, the test harness used, and details about the failure, if any. The random data used in each test case is stored in a file named using the identifier, so that it can be reproduced precisely when necessary. Instruction placement and profiling of the testing code were added to the logs later to provide more detail.

5 Outcomes from Testing

First, the consistency tests for Section 2's instruction generation revealed a missing instruction pattern for ldrsb in stepLib, with the result that ldrsb instructions were present in the model but code using them could not be verified. A few minor bugs when generating step theorems were also found.

Recall that these consistency tests do not detect *extra* instructions in the model. Our manual check for these was prompted by Fox discovering one such instruction. Fortunately, as we can bypass the instruction generation we could immediately test for this instruction and confirm its absence from the device.

Similarly, there are alternative forms of the bx and blx instructions which the reference manual marks as UNPREDICTABLE, i.e., they might work but should not be used. L3 already features the syntax for indicating this, but doesn't act upon it, so the variants are present in the model. Again, if we bypass the instruction generator we can test these variants, finding that a few of these instructions behave normally on the hardware we have.

Moving on to the results from the randomised testing, we tried sequences of 5 to 10 instructions long. Test failures with bx and blx instructions uncovered a bug where the check on the Thumb mode bit was reversed. The lack of support for self-modifying code can be seen if we turn off the additional constraints to prevent it, as can the invariant about the alignment of the stack pointer.

Finally, we encountered anomalies with the timing model where some test sequences would take one cycle longer than predicted. Several test cases which produced these anomalies were examined, revealing that in each case the SMT solver had chosen to place instructions in the last word of SRAM. This was reinforced by testing manually chosen sequences with extra constraints which forced instructions to be placed in or around the last word. More intensive evidence was provided by adding constraints to require or forbid an instruction placed in the final word for a full test run.

This explanation fits with the processor's pipeline design: executing an instruction from the last word implies attempting to fetch the next word, but this does not exist. Presumably it is handling this corner case that consumes an extra processor cycle.

5.1 Performance

To give a general indication of the performance of the system, we performed a test run of 1000 sequences of 5 instructions for this paper. Of the 1000, 105 had no possible pre-state, 882 matched the model's prediction, and 13 did not match; each instruction format was used in at least 34 viable tests. All of the non-matching cases differed only in execution time, and had an instruction in the last word. None of the successful tests did.

To compare the effects of increasing the sequence length, n, we present the per-test rate of impossible cases and mean time in seconds for each stage:

n	Impossible	Generation	Combination	Pre-state	SMT	Instantiation	Testing
5	0.105	0.037	0.769	2.418	0.313	4.795	3.272
7	0.145	0.053	1.585	5.909	1.101	8.662	3.437
9	0.320	0.038	2.917	11.239	5.114	12.956	3.516

The rate of impossible combinations increases as the probability of incompatible instructions and branch choices increases. The main time costs are the stages involving the full 8kB of memory; it may be possible to reduce this by restricting the memory to the test's footprint.

These were measured on a dual-core 8GB Intel Core i5-3320M using a development version of HOL4 from March 2014 running on PolyML 5.5.1. The generated HOL and SML for the M0 model and tools is present in the HOL4 distribution[4]. An STM32F0-Discovery board was used as the target.

6 Discussion

For a simple microprocessor like the Cortex-M0 we can ask whether testing sequences of instructions rather than individual instructions is worth the extra effort. Indeed, the mistakes in the model and tools could have been detected by single instructions, and even the timing anomaly could be detected despite appearing to be the result of the processor's pipeline.

However, it is only through testing sequences that we know this. Moreover, by adjusting the additional constraints that we add we can also witness the lack of support for self-modifying code, and if we wanted to extend the model to support that, or to support timing when executing from slower memory (such as the flash memory on the STM32F0), only sequences of instructions would explore the relevant behaviour.

The form of the generated code. We generate the sequences of instructions to be executed by picking each instruction individually. We do not expect this code to reflect real application code, but one feature that is worth considering in detail is the likelihood of generating loops. First, note that the execution cannot stop inside a loop because a breakpoint is used to halt execution. More importantly, we must generate the same instructions several times with an appropriate branch. For example, we manually tested the following sequence to show that the extra timing penalty for placing instructions in the last word of memory could build up over time, only taking the bcs branch to the breakpoint at the end:

---

[4] In the directory examples/l3-machine-code/m0.

```
run_test_code debug
 'adds     r0, r0, i2     bcs      -#12    b      -#4
  adds     r0, r0, r2     bcs      -#12    b      -#4
  adds     r0, r0, r2     bcs      -#12'
 (SOME [0, 1, 0, 0, 1, 0, 0, 0])
 (Basic Breakpoint) [''instr_start 2 = 0x20001ffew : word32''];
```

The SMT solver then picks a state in which the loop runs the correct number of times. However, the chances of generating a sequence like this randomly are vanishingly small. One possible area for future work is to produce structural features like loops in conjunction with the instruction generation.

Generating instructions directly from the model. By writing our own instruction generator we duplicated some of the information contained in the model: the set and encodings of supported instructions. To apply the testing more widely it would be helpful to use the model directly. (Unsupported instructions are less of an issue because missing instructions do not affect the soundness of verification.)

L3 models feature a datatype for instructions, a decoding function and (optionally) an encoding function. An easy approach is to generate members of the datatype, then use the encoding function to produce binary code to test. However, we have few guarantees about these functions: the most we can expect is that decoding reverses encoding. The opposite may not be true.

For example, if we took this approach for the M0 model we would still not test the extra UNPREDICTABLE forms of the branch instructions, because they have the same representation in the datatype as the normal version, so the encoder will not produce them, but the decoder handles them.

We suggest two possibilities to consider: analysing the decoder function to guide generation of binary instructions; or generating the decoder and encoder functions from a single, more abstract, definition. An example of the latter approach would be a more principled version of our instruction format language.

There is another alternative which is suitable for some targets, including the M0: the Thumb instruction set is sufficiently dense that you can simply pick values at random, then check whether it is a valid instruction. The downside to this approach is that you cannot bias which instructions are chosen or the values used (such as the branch distance for **bl** instructions mentioned in Section 2).

The form of generated pre-states. The parts of the state most relevant to the execution are provided by the SMT-solver. These are certainly not randomly sampled, but can be pleasingly daemonic: for example, we have seen useful biases towards reusing locations and using the top and bottom of SRAM, which reveal self-modifying code (if allowed) and the timing anomaly we found. If we wished to generate a wider variety of pre-states we could investigate adding further constraints to force the solver to behave differently.

Potential extensions. More complete microprocessor models include system features such as interrupts and exceptions. We expect our model-driven approach would adapt well to these because we can generate tests where the event occurs on a particular instruction. For example, to produce a fault on a load instruction the SMT solver can be asked to ensure that the given address is invalid, and to interrupt at a given instruction the timing knowledge can be used to initialise a timer. Examining the behaviour of sequences of instructions would be vital in this context; even a relatively simple processor like the Cortex-M0 has complex interrupt handling features such as nesting and tail chaining.

7 Related Work

SMT solvers have already been used in dynamic test case generation, Bounimova et al. [3] have described deploying their SAGE fuzzer at scale to test Microsoft products. This derives new test cases by tracing the execution of existing cases, finding a set of constraints on the input that should alter the execution in an interesting way, then using Z3 to solve those constraints. These are then run against a runtime checker. Our testing is model-driven rather than trace-driven; and the constraint solving is for producing meaningful test cases rather than being the source of fresh test cases. They also perform much more engineering to scale up to mass testing on a large variety of products.

Brucker et al. [4] performed model-based test generation for Verisoft's VAMP architecture, using the HOL-TestGen tool for the Isabelle/HOL proof assistant. The tool takes theorem-like specifications for tests and produces 'abstract' test cases, plus test input data which fills in the details (selected randomly, or using Z3). In principle the whole pre-state could be generated by regarding it as an input, but they used an empty initial configuration because their representation of the model allows ill-formed states to be generated. Their work focused on test case generation and did not test against hardware.

Fox and Myreen [7] validated a previous ARMv7 model using single instruction randomised testing, successfully covering a large portion of the instruction set and revealing several bugs. As they did not have to solve complex constraints to construct the state they had more freedom to pick extreme values while searching for bugs.

A higher standard for models is a formal proof that they match a hardware design. There has been work in this area for decades; one particularly relevant example is Fox's verification of the ARM6 microarchitecture with respect to an ISA definition [5]. Proofs of processor designs can be difficult, and this is unusual for its high coverage of a commercial processor's instruction set. Similarly, Beyer et al. [2] have verified the VAMP gate-level design in the PVS system.

On a related note, Moore [11] promotes the usefulness of symbolic execution of executable processor models, and mentions the importance of testing even for low-level RTL models by recalling that testing an AMD processor model was crucial for persuading managers that the model was valid and worth investigating. This work involved executing existing test cases, whereas we have synthesised them by solving constraints revealed by symbolic execution.

8   Conclusion

We have gained confidence in our cycle-accurate Cortex-M0 model using this model-driven randomised testing. An off-the-shelf SMT solver handled the constraints involved in forming a valid pre-state well, and we used additional constraints to respect the model's limitations and validate our hypothesis about the only timing anomaly found. A key question for future work is whether we can make the testing easy to reuse with L3-generated models for other architectures.

Acknowledgements. Support for this work was provided by the EPSRC Programme Grant EP/K008528/1, Rigorous Engineering for Mainstream Systems (REMS). Our thanks go to Anthony Fox, Magnus Myreen, Peter Sewell and the other members of the REMS project for their assistance.

References

1. ARM: ARMv6-M Architecture Reference Manual, document DDI 0419C (2010), http://infocenter.arm.com/help/topic/com.arm.doc.ddi0419c/index.html
2. Beyer, S., Jacobi, C., Kröning, D., Leinenbach, D., Paul, W.J.: Putting it all together — formal verification of the VAMP. International Journal on Software Tools for Technology Transfer 8(4-5), 411–430 (2006)
3. Bounimova, E., Godefroid, P., Molnar, D.: Billions and billions of constraints: Whitebox fuzz testing in production. In: Proceedings of the 2013 International Conference on Software Engineering, ICSE 2013, pp. 122–131. IEEE (2013)
4. Brucker, A.D., Feliachi, A., Nemouchi, Y., Wolff, B.: Test program generation for a microprocessor. In: Veanes, M., Viganò, L. (eds.) TAP 2013. LNCS, vol. 7942, pp. 76–95. Springer, Heidelberg (2013)
5. Fox, A.: Formal specification and verification of ARM6. In: Basin, D., Wolff, B. (eds.) TPHOLs 2003. LNCS, vol. 2758, pp. 25–40. Springer, Heidelberg (2003)
6. Fox, A.: Directions in ISA specification. In: Beringer, L., Felty, A. (eds.) ITP 2012. LNCS, vol. 7406, pp. 338–344. Springer, Heidelberg (2012)
7. Fox, A., Myreen, M.O.: A trustworthy monadic formalization of the ARMv7 instruction set architecture. In: Kaufmann, M., Paulson, L.C. (eds.) ITP 2010. LNCS, vol. 6172, pp. 243–258. Springer, Heidelberg (2010)
8. HOL4, http://hol.sourceforge.net/
9. Myreen, M.O., Gordon, M.J.C., Slind, K.: Decompilation into logic - improved. In: Cabodi, G., Singh, S. (eds.) FMCAD, pp. 78–81. IEEE (2012)
10. Open on-chip debugger (2014), http://openocd.sourceforge.net/
11. Strother Moore, J.: Symbolic simulation: An ACL2 approach. In: Gopalakrishnan, G., Windley, P. (eds.) FMCAD 1998. LNCS, vol. 1522, pp. 334–350. Springer, Heidelberg (1998)
12. Weber, T.: SMT solvers: New oracles for the HOL theorem prover. International Journal on Software Tools for Technology Transfer (STTT) 13(5), 419–429 (2011)
13. Wilhelm, R., Engblom, J., Ermedahl, A., Holsti, N., Thesing, S., Whalley, D., Bernat, G., Ferdinand, C., Heckmann, R., Mitra, T., Mueller, F., Puaut, I., Puschner, P., Staschulat, J., Stenström, P.: The worst-case execution-time problem—overview of methods and survey of tools. ACM Trans. Embed. Comput. Syst. 7, 36:1–36:53 (2008)

Author Index